# Hands-On Object-Oriented Programming with C#

Build maintainable software with reusable code using C#

Raihan Taher

BIRMINGHAM - MUMBAI

# Hands-On Object-Oriented Programming with C#

Copyright © 2019 Packt Publishing

All rights reserved. No part of this book may be reproduced, stored in a retrieval system, or transmitted in any form or by any means, without the prior written permission of the publisher, except in the case of brief quotations embedded in critical articles or reviews.

Every effort has been made in the preparation of this book to ensure the accuracy of the information presented. However, the information contained in this book is sold without warranty, either express or implied. Neither the author, nor Packt Publishing or its dealers and distributors, will be held liable for any damages caused or alleged to have been caused directly or indirectly by this book.

Packt Publishing has endeavored to provide trademark information about all of the companies and products mentioned in this book by the appropriate use of capitals. However, Packt Publishing cannot guarantee the accuracy of this information.

**Commissioning Editor:** Aaron Lazar
**Acquisition Editor:** Sandeep Mishra
**Content Development Editor:** Anugraha Arunagiri
**Technical Editor:** Neha Pande
**Copy Editor:** Safis Editing
**Language Support Editors**: Mary McGowan, Storm Mann
**Project Coordinator:** Ulhas Kambali
**Proofreader:** Safis Editing
**Indexer:** Priyanka Dhadke
**Graphics:** Tania Dutta
**Production Coordinator:** Aparna Bhagat

First published: February 2019

Production reference: 2140519

Published by Packt Publishing Ltd.
Livery Place
35 Livery Street
Birmingham
B3 2PB, UK.

ISBN 978-1-78829-622-9

www.packtpub.com

mapt.io

Mapt is an online digital library that gives you full access to over 5,000 books and videos, as well as industry leading tools to help you plan your personal development and advance your career. For more information, please visit our website.

## Why subscribe?

- Spend less time learning and more time coding with practical eBooks and Videos from over 4,000 industry professionals
- Improve your learning with Skill Plans built especially for you
- Get a free eBook or video every month
- Mapt is fully searchable
- Copy and paste, print, and bookmark content

## Packt.com

Did you know that Packt offers eBook versions of every book published, with PDF and ePub files available? You can upgrade to the eBook version at www.packt.com and as a print book customer, you are entitled to a discount on the eBook copy. Get in touch with us at customercare@packtpub.com for more details.

At www.packt.com, you can also read a collection of free technical articles, sign up for a range of free newsletters, and receive exclusive discounts and offers on Packt books and eBooks.

# Contributors

## About the author

**Raihan Taher** is a young, skilled software developer who has gained extensive experience by being involved in a variety of projects throughout his career. His particular areas of interest are web development and software architecture. His ability to write clean code and observe best practices in software development are his major assets. Throughout his relatively short career, he has worked for a number of renowned multinational companies, including Accenture, Quintiq (Dassault Systèmes), and SEB Pension. His desire to share his knowledge has encouraged him to write technical blogs, create online video courses, write books, and conduct technical training sessions. His courses, blog posts, and books have already been well received by many new developers. As regards the future, his vision is to discover and establish best practices for software development and share those with fellow developers. His ability to write quality software is what makes him accomplished. Aside from this, he is an avid reader and is excited by the challenge of learning new things. He always pushes himself to learn and implement new technologies in his work. Keeping himself up to date with new technologies and implementing those in his work makes him an expert in the area of cutting-edge technologies. He also loves to travel and explore adventurous places with his wife.

## About the reviewer

**Gaurav Aroraa** completed his M.Phil in computer science. He is a Microsoft MVP, a lifetime member of the Computer Society of India (CSI), an advisory member of IndiaMentor, and is certified as a scrum trainer/coach, XEN for ITIL-F, and APMG for PRINCE-F and PRINCE-P. Gaurav is an open source developer, and the founder of Ovatic Systems Private Limited. Recently, he was conferred as icon of the year—excellence in mentoring technology start-ups for the year 2018-19 by Radio City, a Jagran initiative, for his extraordinary work during his 20-year career in industry in the field of technology mentoring. You can tweet Gaurav on his Twitter handle: `@g_arora`.

## Packt is searching for authors like you

If you're interested in becoming an author for Packt, please visit `authors.packtpub.com` and apply today. We have worked with thousands of developers and tech professionals, just like you, to help them share their insight with the global tech community. You can make a general application, apply for a specific hot topic that we are recruiting an author for, or submit your own idea.

# Table of Contents

**Preface**   1

**Chapter 1: Overview of C# as a Language**   7
  **Evolution of C#**   8
    Managed code   9
    Generics   9
    LINQ   9
    Dynamics   9
    Async/await   10
    Compiler as a service   10
    Exception filters   10
    C# 8 and beyond   10
  **Architecture of .NET**   11
    Common Language Runtime   12
    Common Type System   12
    .NET framework class libraries   12
    Just-in-time compiler   12
  **Fundamentals and syntax of C# language**   13
    Data types   13
    Nullable types   13
    Literals   14
      Boolean   14
      Integer   14
      Real   15
      Character   15
      String   15
    Programming syntax – conditions   16
      If-else construct   16
      Switch-case construct   16
      goto statements   17
    Programming syntax – loops   17
      The while construct   18
      The do-while construct   18
      The for construct   18
      The foreach construct   19
      Contextual – break and continue statements   19
        Break   19
        Continue   20
  **Writing your first C# program in a console application**   20
  **Visual Studio as an editor**   22
    Evolution of Visual Studio   23

*Table of Contents*

| | |
|---|---|
| Types of Visual Studio | 23 |
|     Visual Studio Community | 23 |
|     Visual Studio Professional | 23 |
|     Visual Studio Enterprise | 24 |
|     Visual Studio Code | 24 |
| Introduction to the Visual Studio IDE | 24 |
|     New Project | 24 |
|         Solution Explorer | 26 |
|         Main workspace area | 28 |
|         Output window | 30 |
|         The Command and Immediate windows | 30 |
|         Search option in IDE | 31 |
| **Writing your first program in Visual Studio** | **32** |
|     How to debug | 34 |
|     Debugging through code | 35 |
| **Summary** | **36** |
| **Chapter 2: Hello OOP - Classes and Objects** | **37** |
| **Classes in OOP** | **38** |
|     The general form of a class | 39 |
|     Writing a simple class | 40 |
| **Objects in OOP** | **41** |
|     How to create objects | 42 |
| **Variables in C#** | **42** |
| **Methods in a class** | **44** |
|     Creating a method | 44 |
|     Constructor of a class | 45 |
| **Characteristics of OOP** | **47** |
|     Inheritance | 47 |
|     Encapsulation | 48 |
|     Abstraction | 49 |
|     Polymorphism | 50 |
| **Summary** | **52** |
| **Chapter 3: Implementation of OOP in C#** | **53** |
| **Interfaces** | **53** |
| **The abstract class** | **55** |
| **The partial class** | **56** |
| **The sealed class** | **57** |
| **Tuples** | **58** |
| **Properties** | **59** |
| **Access specifiers for classes** | **60** |
|     Public | 60 |
|     Private | 61 |
|     Internal | 61 |
|     Protected | 62 |
|     Protected internal | 63 |

| | |
|---|---|
| **Summary** | 64 |
| **Chapter 4: Object Collaboration** | **65** |
|   **Examples of object collaboration** | 65 |
|   **Different types of object collaboration in C#** | 66 |
|     Case study | 67 |
|     Dependency | 68 |
|     Association | 72 |
|       Aggregation | 73 |
|       Composition | 75 |
|     Inheritance | 77 |
|   **Summary** | 79 |
| **Chapter 5: Exception Handling** | **81** |
|   **Why we need exception handling in programming** | 82 |
|     Exception handling in C# programming | 83 |
|   **Basics of exception handling** | 83 |
|   **Try and catch** | 84 |
|   **What happens if you don't handle exceptions?** | 84 |
|   **Multiple catch blocks** | 85 |
|   **Using the throw keyword** | 88 |
|   **What does the finally block do?** | 89 |
|   **Exception class** | 92 |
|     Some common exception classes | 93 |
|   **User-defined exceptions** | 94 |
|   **The exception filter** | 96 |
|   **Exception handling best practices** | 97 |
|   **Summary** | 98 |
| **Chapter 6: Events and Delegates** | **99** |
|   **What is a delegate?** | 99 |
|     How to create and use delegates | 100 |
|   **Method group conversion** | 102 |
|     Using the static and instance methods as delegates | 103 |
|   **Multicasting** | 104 |
|   **Covariance and contravariance** | 107 |
|   **Events** | 110 |
|     Multicasting events | 112 |
|     Event guidelines from .NET | 114 |
|   **Summary** | 116 |
| **Chapter 7: Generics in C#** | **117** |
|   **What are generics?** | 117 |
|   **Why do we need generics?** | 122 |
|   **Different constraints of generics** | 123 |

| | |
|---|---|
| Base class constraints | 124 |
| Interface constraints | 125 |
| Reference type and value type constraints | 126 |
| Multiple constraints | 126 |
| **Generic methods** | 126 |
| Type-inferencing | 128 |
| **Covariance and contravariance in generics** | 129 |
| Covariance | 129 |
| Contravariance | 130 |
| **Summary** | 132 |
| **Chapter 8: Modeling and Designing Software** | **133** |
| **The importance of design diagrams** | 134 |
| Different UML diagrams | 134 |
| **Class diagrams** | 135 |
| Inheritance | 136 |
| Association | 137 |
| Aggregation | 137 |
| Composition | 137 |
| Dependency | 138 |
| An example of a class diagram | 138 |
| **Use case diagrams** | 141 |
| The actor | 141 |
| The use case | 142 |
| The communication link | 142 |
| The system boundaries | 143 |
| An example of a use case diagram | 144 |
| **A sequence diagram** | 145 |
| An actor | 145 |
| A lifeline | 145 |
| An activation | 146 |
| A call message | 147 |
| A return message | 147 |
| A self message | 148 |
| A recursive message | 148 |
| A create message | 149 |
| A destroy message | 149 |
| A duration message | 150 |
| A note | 150 |
| An example of a sequence diagram | 150 |
| **Summary** | 152 |
| **Chapter 9: Visual Studio and Associated Tools** | **153** |
| **Visual Studio project types and templates** | 154 |
| **Visual Studio Editor and different windows** | 158 |
| Editor window | 158 |

| | |
|---|---|
| Solution Explorer | 163 |
| Output window | 165 |
| **Debugging windows** | **166** |
| Breakpoints window | 167 |
| Exception Settings | 168 |
| Output | 169 |
| Diagnostic Tools | 170 |
| Immediate window | 171 |
| Python debugger window | 171 |
| **Breakpoints, Call Stack Trace, and Watch** | **171** |
| Breakpoint | 172 |
| Call Stack Trace | 173 |
| Watch window | 174 |
| **Git in Visual Studio** | **175** |
| **Refactoring and code-optimization techniques** | **177** |
| Rename | 177 |
| Changing the method signature | 178 |
| Encapsulate Field | 179 |
| Extract Method | 180 |
| **Summary** | **181** |
| **Chapter 10: Exploring ADO.NET with Examples** | **183** |
| **The fundamentals of ADO.NET** | **184** |
| Data providers | 184 |
| Connection objects | 184 |
| The Command object | 185 |
| The DataReader object | 190 |
| DataAdapter | 191 |
| **Connecting to various databases** | **192** |
| SQL Server | 192 |
| The Oracle database | 193 |
| **Working with DataReaders and DataAdapters** | **193** |
| DataReaders | 194 |
| DataAdapters | 195 |
| **Working with stored procedures** | **196** |
| **Working with the Entity Framework** | **197** |
| What is an entity in the Entity Framework? | 197 |
| Different types of Entity properties | 198 |
| Scalar properties | 198 |
| Navigation properties | 199 |
| The code-first approach | 199 |
| The database-first approach | 200 |
| Using the Entity Framework | 200 |
| **Transactions in SQL** | **202** |
| Atomic | 203 |
| Consistent | 203 |

*Table of Contents*

    Isolated     203
    Durable     203
  **Summary**     204

## Chapter 11: New Features in C# 8     205
  **Environment Setup**     206
  **Nullable reference types**     206
  **Async streams**     208
  **Ranges and indices**     210
  **Default implementation of interface members**     212
  **Switch expressions**     213
  **Target-typed new expressions**     215
  **Summary**     215

## Chapter 12: Understanding Design Patterns and Principles     217
  **Design principles**     218
    The single responsibility principle     218
    The open-closed principle     219
    The Liskov substitution principle     219
    The interface segregation principle     219
    The dependency inversion principle     219
  **Creational design patterns**     220
    The abstract factory pattern     221
    The builder pattern     221
    The factory method pattern     222
    The prototype pattern     222
    The singleton pattern     223
  **Structural design patterns**     223
    The adapter pattern     224
    The decorator pattern     224
    The facade pattern     224
    The proxy pattern     225
  **Behavioral design patterns**     225
    The command pattern     226
    The observer pattern     226
    The strategy pattern     227
  **The MVC pattern**     228
  **Summary**     229

## Chapter 13: Git - The Version Control System     231
  **What is version control?**     231
  **How Git works**     232
    Modified     233
    Staged     233
    Committed     233

| | |
|---|---|
| **Installing Git on Windows** | 234 |
| **The basics of Git** | 236 |
| Git config | 236 |
| Git init | 237 |
| Git clone | 237 |
| Git status | 238 |
| Git add | 238 |
| Git commit | 240 |
| Git log | 241 |
| Git remote | 242 |
| Git push | 243 |
| Git pull | 244 |
| Git fetch | 244 |
| **Branching in Git** | 245 |
| Creating a branch | 247 |
| Viewing available branches | 248 |
| Changing branches | 248 |
| Deleting a branch | 249 |
| Merging in Git | 249 |
| **Summary** | 250 |
| **Chapter 14: Prepare Yourself - Interviews and the Future** | 251 |
| **Interview questions** | 252 |
| What are the fundamental principles of object-oriented programming? | 252 |
| What is inheritance? | 252 |
| What is encapsulation? | 252 |
| What is abstraction? | 253 |
| What is polymorphism? | 253 |
| What is an interface? | 253 |
| What is an abstract class? | 253 |
| What is a sealed class? | 253 |
| What is a partial class? | 254 |
| What are the differences between interfaces and abstract classes? | 254 |
| What is the difference between method-overloading and method-overriding? | 254 |
| What are access modifiers? | 255 |
| What is boxing and unboxing? | 255 |
| What are the differences between a struct and a class? | 255 |
| What is an extension method in C# and how do we use it? | 256 |
| What is managed and unmanaged code? | 256 |
| What is a virtual method in C#? | 256 |
| What do you understand by value types and reference types in C#.NET? | 256 |
| What are design principles? | 257 |
| What is the single responsibility principle? | 257 |
| What is the Open/Closed principle? | 257 |
| What is the Liskov substitution principle? | 257 |

| | |
|---|---|
| What is the interface segregation principle? | 258 |
| What is the dependency inversion principle? | 258 |
| **Interview and career tips** | **258** |
| Improving your communication skills | 258 |
| Keep practicing | 259 |
| **Things to learn next** | **260** |
| **Building the habit of reading** | **260** |
| **Summary** | **261** |

## Other Books You May Enjoy 263

## Index 267

# Preface

**Object-oriented programming (OOP)** is a programming paradigm organized around objects rather than actions, and data rather than logic. With the newest release of C#, there are a number of new additions that improve OOP. This book aims to teach OOP in C# in an engaging and interactive way. After going through the book, you will have an understanding of the four pillars of OOP, which are encapsulation, inheritance, abstraction, and polymorphism, and be able to leverage the latest features of C# 8.0, such as Nullable Reference Types and Asynchronous Streams. You will then explore various design patterns, principles, and best practices in OOP.

## Who this book is for

This book is intended for people who are new to OOP. It assumes that you already have basic C# skills. No knowledge of OOP in any other language is expected.

## What this book covers

Chapter 1, *Overview of C# as a Language*, covers a basic overview of the C# programming language to enable the beginner to understand the language constructs. The chapter will also explain why .NET exists as a framework and how to utilize the .NET framework in programs. The chapter will conclude by introducing Visual Studio as an editor for developing C# projects.

Chapter 2, *Hello OOP - Classes and Objects*, explains the most basic concepts of object-oriented programming. We start by explaining what a class is and how to write a class.

Chapter 3, *Implementation of OOP in C#*, covers the concepts that make C# an OOP language. This chapter covers some very important topics of the C# language and how to utilize those in real-life programming.

Chapter 4, *Object Collaboration*, covers object collaboration, what it is, how objects relate to one another in a program, and how many types of relationships exist between objects. We will also discuss dependency Collaboration, Association, and Inheritance.

*Preface*

Chapter 5, *Exception Handling*, covers how to handle exceptions in your code while executing it. We will explore the different types of exceptions and how to use the try/catch block to eliminate problems in your code.

Chapter 6, *Events and Delegates*, covers events and delegates. In this chapter, we will cover what an event is, what a delegate is, how an event is connected to a delegate, and their respective uses.

Chapter 7, *Generics in C#*, introduces a very interesting and important topic – generics. We will learn what generics are and why they are so powerful.

Chapter 8, *Modeling and Designing Software*, covers the different **Unified Modeling Language** (**UML**) diagrams used in software design. We will talk in detail about the most popular ones, including the class diagram, the use case diagram, and the sequence diagram.

Chapter 9, *Visual Studio and Associated Tools*, covers the best editor for C# programming. Visual Studio is a very rich IDE. It has some awesome features that make the life of a developer super productive. In this chapter, we will introduce the different projects and windows available in Visual Studio.

Chapter 10, *Exploring ADO.NET with Examples*, covers the ADO.NET classes, along with the fundamentals of various data adapters, stored procedures, and object relationship models through the Entity framework. We will also discuss transactions in ADO.NET.

Chapter 11, *New Features in C# 8*, covers new features of the C# language, which is improving day by day as C# language engineers incorporate additional features into the language. In 2019, Microsoft announced that C# 8.0 will be released, and outlined the new features that will come with this version. This chapter will discuss the new features that are going to be introduced in C# 8.0. We will talk about nullable reference types, async streams, ranges, default implementations of interface members, and several other topics.

Chapter 12, *Understanding Design Patterns and Principles*, contains information about design principles and some very popular and important design patterns.

Chapter 13, *Git – The Version Control System*, discusses the most popular version control system available today – Git. It is essential for all developers to learn Git.

Chapter 14, *Prepare Yourself, Interview, and The Future*, includes some of the most common interview questions and answers to those questions, so that you are prepared for your next interview. This chapter is mainly to give you an idea about potential interview questions.

# To get the most out of this book

The reader should have some prior knowledge of .NET Core and .NET Standard, along with a basic knowledge of C#, Visual Studio 2017 (as an IDE), version control, relational databases, and basic software design.

## Download the example code files

You can download the example code files for this book from your account at www.packt.com. If you purchased this book elsewhere, you can visit www.packt.com/support and register to have the files emailed directly to you.

You can download the code files by following these steps:

1. Log in or register at www.packt.com.
2. Select the **SUPPORT** tab.
3. Click on **Code Downloads & Errata**.
4. Enter the name of the book in the **Search** box and follow the onscreen instructions.

Once the file is downloaded, please make sure that you unzip or extract the folder using the latest version of:

- WinRAR/7-Zip for Windows
- Zipeg/iZip/UnRarX for Mac
- 7-Zip/PeaZip for Linux

The code bundle for the book is also hosted on GitHub at https://github.com/PacktPublishing/Hands-On-Object-Oriented-Programming-with-CSharp. In case there's an update to the code, it will be updated on the existing GitHub repository.

We also have other code bundles from our rich catalog of books and videos available at https://github.com/PacktPublishing/. Check them out!

## Download the color images

We also provide a PDF file that has color images of the screenshots/diagrams used in this book. You can download it here: https://www.packtpub.com/sites/default/files/downloads/9781788296229_ColorImages.pdf.

# Conventions used

There are a number of text conventions used throughout this book.

`CodeInText`: Indicates code words in text, database table names, folder names, filenames, file extensions, pathnames, dummy URLs, user input, and Twitter handles. Here is an example: "relationship between the `Tweet` and `Message` objects."

A block of code is set as follows:

```
class Customer
{
    public string firstName;
    public string lastName;
    public string phoneNumber;
    public string emailAddress;

    public string GetFullName()
    {
        return firstName + " " + lastName;
    }
}
```

When we wish to draw your attention to a particular part of a code block, the relevant lines or items are set in bold:

```
class class-name {
    // property 1
    // property 2
    // ...

    // method 1
    // method 2
    // ...
}
```

Any command-line input or output is written as follows:

```
git config --global user.name = "john"
git config --global user.email = "john@example.com"
```

**Bold**: Indicates a new term, an important word, or words that you see on screen. For example, words in menus or dialog boxes appear in the text like this. Here is an example: "Go to **Tools** | **Extensions and Updates**."

 Warnings or important notes appear like this.

 Tips and tricks appear like this.

# Get in touch

Feedback from our readers is always welcome.

**General feedback**: If you have questions about any aspect of this book, mention the book title in the subject of your message and email us at customercare@packtpub.com.

**Errata**: Although we have taken every care to ensure the accuracy of our content, mistakes do happen. If you have found a mistake in this book, we would be grateful if you would report this to us. Please visit www.packt.com/submit-errata, selecting your book, clicking on the Errata Submission Form link, and entering the details.

**Piracy**: If you come across any illegal copies of our works in any form on the internet, we would be grateful if you would provide us with the location address or website name. Please contact us at copyright@packt.com with a link to the material.

**If you are interested in becoming an author**: If there is a topic that you have expertise in, and you are interested in either writing or contributing to a book, please visit authors.packtpub.com.

# Reviews

Please leave a review. Once you have read and used this book, why not leave a review on the site that you purchased it from? Potential readers can then see and use your unbiased opinion to make purchase decisions, we at Packt can understand what you think about our products, and our authors can see your feedback on their book. Thank you!

For more information about Packt, please visit packt.com.

# Overview of C# as a Language

With the introduction of modern-day programming practices, it is evident that developers are looking for more advanced constructs to help them to deliver the best software in the most effective way. Languages that evolve on top of frameworks are built to enhance the capabilities of the developers in a way that allows them to quickly build their code with less complexity so that the code is maintainable, yet readable.

There are many high-level object, oriented programming languages available on the market, but among them I would say one of the most promising is C#. The C# language is not new in the programming world and has existed for over a decade, but with the dynamic progress of the language itself creating so many newer constructs, it has already left some of the most widely accepted language competition behind. C# is an object-oriented, type-safe, general-purpose language that is built on top of the .NET framework that was developed by Microsoft and approved by the **European Computer Manufacturers Association (ECMA)** and the **International Standards Organization (ISO)**. It is built to run on the Common Language Infrastructure and can interact with any other languages that are built based on the same architecture. Inspired by C++, the language is rich in delivering the best of breed applications without handling too many complexities in code.

In this chapter, we will cover the following topics:

- Evolution of C#
- Architecture of C#
- Fundamentals and syntax of the C# language
- Visual Studio as an editor
- Writing your first program in Visual Studio

*Overview of C# as a Language*

# Evolution of C#

C# has been one of the most dynamic languages in recent times. This language is open source and mostly driven by a group of software engineers, who recently came up with lots of major changes to enhance the language and provide features to handle the complexities in the languages that exist. Some of the major enhancements that have been put forward for the language include **Generics**, LINQ, Dynamics, and the async/await pattern:

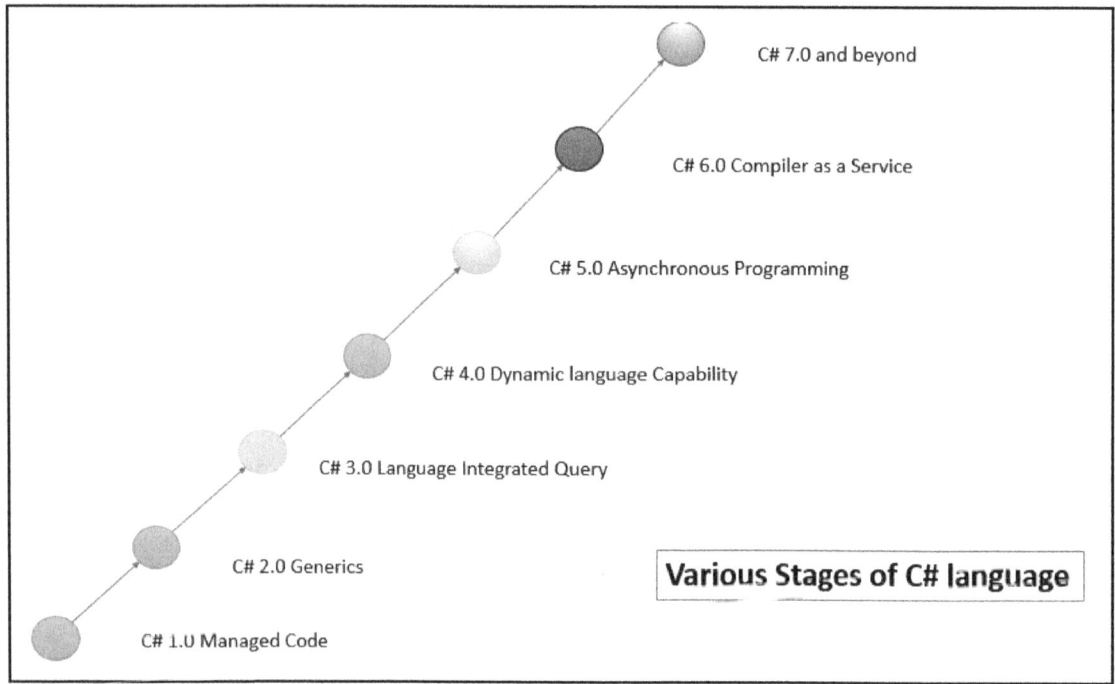

In the preceding diagram, we can see how the language has evolved from its inception with managed code in C# 1.0, to async programming constructs that were introduced in C# 5.0, to modern-day C# 8. Before going further, let's look at some of the highlights of C# in its different stages of evolution.

# Managed code

The phrase managed code came into being after Microsoft declared the .NET framework. Any code running in a managed environment is handled by **Common Language Runtime (CLR)**, which keeps

# Generics

Generics is a concept that was introduced with C# 2.0 and allows template type definition and type parameters. Generics allow the programmer to define types with open-ended type parameters that dramatically changed the way that programmers write code. The type-safety with dynamic typed generic templates improves readability, reusability, and code performance.

# LINQ

The third installment of the C# language introduced **Language Integrated Query (LINQ)**, a new construct of queries that can be run over object structures. LINQ is very new to the programming world and gives us a glimpse of functional programming on top of object-oriented general programming structure. LINQ also introduced a bunch of new interfaces in the form of the `IQueryable` interface, which introduced a number of libraries that can interact with the external world using LINQ. LINQ was boosted with the introduction of Lambda expressions and expression trees.

# Dynamics

The fourth instalment also provides a completely new construct. It introduces the dynamic language structure. The dynamic programming capability helps the developer to defer the programming calls to runtime. There is a specific syntactic sugar that was introduced in the language that compiles the dynamic code on the same runtime. The version also puts forward a number of new interfaces and classes that enhance its language capabilities.

## Async/await

With any language, threading or asynchronous programming is a pain. When dealing with asynchrony, the programmers have to come across many complexities that reduce the readability and maintainability of the code. With the async/await feature in the C# language, programming in an asynchronous way is as simple as synchronous programming. The programming has been simplified, with all of the complexities handled by the compiler and the framework internally.

## Compiler as a service

Microsoft has been working on how some parts of the source code of the compiler can be opened up to the world. Consequently, as a programmer, you are capable of querying the compiler on some of its internal work principles. C# 6.0 introduced a number of libraries that enable the developer to get an insight into the compiler, the binder, the syntax tree of the program, and so on. Although the features were developed for a long time as the Roslyn project, Microsoft have finally released it to the external world.

## Exception filters

C# 6.0 is adorned with a lot of smaller features. Some of the features give the developers an opportunity to implement complex logic with simple code, while some of them enhance the overall capabilities of the language. Exception filters are newly introduced with this version and give a program the capability to filter out certain exception types. The exception filters, being a CLR construct, have been hidden in the language throughout its lifetime, but were finally introduced with C# 6.0.

## C# 8 and beyond

With C# being the most dynamic language in the market, it is constantly improving. With the newer features, such as nullable reference types, async streams, ranges and indices, interface members, and many other features that came with the latest version of C#, they have enhanced the basic features and helped programmers to take advantage of these new constructs, hence making their lives easier.

Note that, during the language's evolution, the .NET framework was also made open source. You can find the source code of the .NET framework at the following link: `https://referencesource.microsoft.com/`.

# Architecture of .NET

Even though it is a decade old, the .NET framework is still well-built and makes sure to make it tiered, moduler, and hierarchical. Each tier provides specific functionalities to the user—some in terms of security and some in terms of language capabilities. The tiers produce a layer of abstraction to the end users and hide most of the complexities of the native operating system as much as possible. The .NET framework is partitioned into modules, with each of them having their own distinct responsibilities. The higher tiers request specific capabilities from the lower tiers and hence it is hierarchical.

Let's look at a diagram of the .NET architecture:

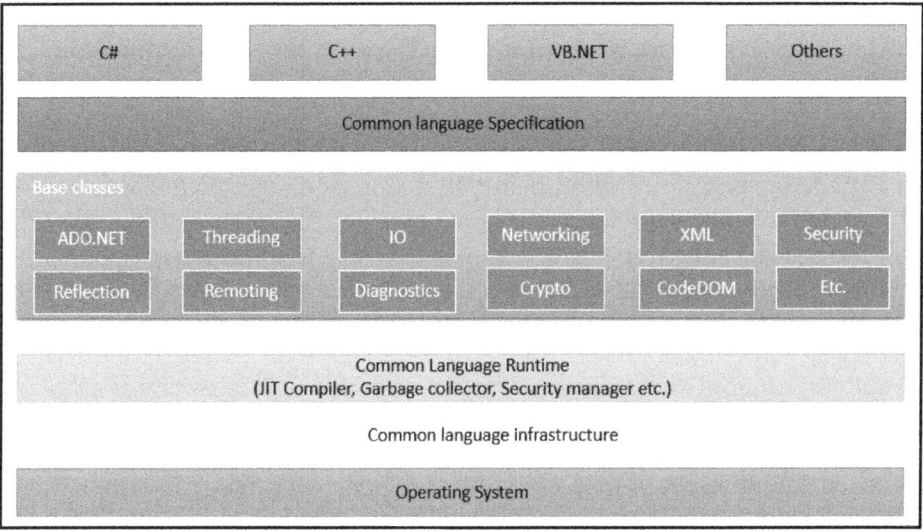

The preceding diagram depicts how the .NET framework architecture is laid out. On its lowest level, it is the operating system that interacts with the kernel APIs that are present in the operating system. The Common Language Infrastructure connects with the CLR, which provides services that monitor each code execution and managed memory, handles exceptions, and ensures that the application behaves as intended. Another important goal of the infrastructure is language inter-operability. The common language runtime is yet again abstracted with the .NET class libraries. This layer holds the binaries that the language is built on, and all of the compilers built on top of the libraries provide the same compiled code so that the CLR can understand the code and interact easily with one another.

Before going further, let's quickly look at some of the key aspects on which languages are built on the .NET framework.

# Common Language Runtime

The CLR provides an interfacing between the underlying unmanaged infrastructure with the managed environment. This provides all of the basic functionalities of the managed environment in the form of garbage collection, security, and interoperability. The CLR is formed with the just-in-time compiler, which compiles the assembly code that's produced with the specific compilers to the native calls. CLR is the most important portion of the .NET architecture.

# Common Type System

As there is a layer of abstraction between the language and the framework, it is evident that each of the language literals are mapped to specific CLR types. For instance, the integer of VB.NET is the same as the int of C#, as both of them point to the same type, System.Int32. It is always preferred to use language types since the compiler takes care of the mapping of types. The CTS system is built as a hierarchy of types with System.Object at its apex. The **Common Type System (CTS)** is divided into two kinds, one of which is value types, which are primitives that are derived from System.ValueTypes, while anything other than that is a reference type. The value types are treated differently to the reference types. This is because while allocation of memory value types are created on a thread stack during execution, reference types are always created on the heap.

# .NET framework class libraries

The framework class library lies in-between the language and the CLR, and therefore any type that's present in the framework is exposed to the language you code. The .NET framework is formed with a good number of classes and structures, exposing never-ending functionalities that you, as a programmer, can benefit from. The class libraries are stored in the form of binaries that can be referenced directly from your program code.

# Just-in-time compiler

.NET languages are compiled twice. During the first form of compilation, the high-level language is converted into a **Microsoft Intermediate Language (MSIL)**, which can be understood by the CLR, while the MSIL is again compiled during runtime when the program is executed. The JIT works inside the program runtime and periodically compiles the code that is expected to be required during execution.

# Fundamentals and syntax of C# language

Being a high-level language, C# is adorned with a lot of newer and updated syntax, which helps the programmer to write code efficiently. As we mentioned earlier, the type system that's supported by the language is divided into two types:

- Value types
- Reference types

The value types are generally primitive types that are stored in the stack during local execution for faster allocation and deallocation of memory. The value types are mostly used during the development of code and, consequently, this forms the major spectrum of the code altogether.

## Data types

The basic data types of C# are divided into the following categories:

- Boolean type: `bool`
- Character type: `char`
- Integer types: `sbyte`, `byte`, `short`, `ushort`, `int`, `uint`, `long`, and `ulong`
- Floating-point types: `float` and `double`
- Decimal precision: `decimal`
- String: `string`
- Object type: `object`

These are primitive data types. These data types are embedded in the C# programming language.

## Nullable types

The primitive types or value types are not nullable in C#. Consequently, there is always a requirement for the developer to make the type nullable, as a developer might need to identify whether the value is provided explicitly or not. The newest version of .NET provides nullable types:

```
Nullable<int> a = null;
int? b = a; //same as above
```

*Overview of C# as a Language*

Both lines in the preceding example define the nullable variable, while the second line is just a shortcut of the first declaration. When the value is null, the `HasValue` property will return `false`. This will ensure that you can detect whether the variable is explicitly specified as a value or not.

# Literals

Literals are also an important part of any program. C# language gives the developer different kinds of options that allow the programmer to specify literals in code. Let's take a look at the different types of literals that are supported.

## Boolean

Boolean literals are defined in the form of `true` or `false`. No other values except `true` and `false` can be assigned in the Boolean type:

```
bool result = true;
```

The default value of a Boolean type is `false`.

## Integer

An integer is a number that can have a plus (+) or minus (-) sign as a prefix, but this is optional. If no sign is given, it is considered as positive. You can define numeric literals in int, long, or hexadecimal form:

```
int numberInDec = -16;
int numberInHex = -0x10;
long numberinLong = 200L;
```

You can see that the first literal, -16, is a literal that's been specified in an integer variable, while the same value is assigned to an integer using a hexadecimal literal. The long variable is assigned a value with an `L` suffix.

## Real

Real values are sequences of digits with a positive or negative sign, like integers. This also makes it possible to specify fraction values:

```
float realNumber = 12.5f;
realNumber = 1.25e+1f;
double realdNumber = 12.5;
```

As you can see, the literal in the last line, `12.5`, is `double` by default, hence it needed to be assigned to a double variable, while the first two lines specify the literal in float types. You can also specify `d` or `D` as a suffix to define a `double`, like `f` or `F` for `float` and `m` for decimal.

## Character

Character literals need to be kept inside a single quote. The value of the literal can be as follows:

- A character, for example, `c`
- A character code, for example, `\u0063`
- An escape character, for example, `\\` (the forward slash is an escape character)

## String

A string is a sequence of characters. In C#, a string is represented by double quotation marks. There are different ways a string can be created in C#. Let's look at the different ways of creating a string in C#:

```
string s = "hello world";
string s1 = "hello \n\r world"; //prints the string with escape sequence
string s2 = @"hello \n\r world"; //prints the string without escape sequence
string s3 = $"S1 : {s1}, S2: {s2}"; // Replaces the {s1} and {s2} with values
```

The `@` character can be placed as a prefix before a string to take the string as it is, without worrying about any escape characters. It is called a verbatim string. The `$` character is used as a prefix for string interpolation. In case your string literal is preceded with the `$` sign, the variables are automatically replaced with values if they're placed within `{ }` brackets.

[ 15 ]

# Programming syntax – conditions

Conditions are one of the most common building blocks of any program. A program cannot have single dimensions; comparison, jumps, and breaks are the most common forms of practice in C#. There are three types of conditions available:

- `if...else`
- `switch-case`
- `goto` (lumps without condition)

## If-else construct

The most commonly used conditional statement is the if-else construct. The building block of the if-else structure contains an `if` keyword, followed by a Boolean expression and a set of curly brackets to specify the steps to execute. Optionally, there could be an `else` keyword, followed by curly brackets for the code to execute when the `if` block is `false`:

```
int a = 5;
if (a == 5)
{
    // As a is 5, do something
}
else
{
    // As a is not 5, do something
}
```

The if-else construct can also have an else-if statement to specify multiple criteria for execution.

## Switch-case construct

Switch-case, on the other hand, is almost similar to the `if` statement; in this statement, the cases will determine the execution step. In the case of `switch`, this always falls in a discrete set of values, and hence, those values can be set up:

```
int a = 5;
switch (a)
{
  case 4:
      // Do something;
      break;
  case 5:
```

```
        // Do something;
        break;
  default:
        // Do something;
        break;
}
```

The switch case automatically picks the correct case statement, depending on the value, and executes the steps defined inside the block. A case need to be concluded with a break statement.

## goto statements

Even though they are less popular and it is not advisable to use them, `goto` statements are used for unconditional jumps in the language and they are widely used by the language itself. As a developer, you can use a `goto` statement to jump to any location of your program with the context you have:

```
... code block
goto lbl1;
...
...
lbl1: expression body
```

The `goto` statement directly jumps to the location specified without any condition or criteria.

## Programming syntax – loops

For a repetitive task during execution, loops play a vital role. Loops allow the programmer to define a criteria in which the loop will end or until the loop should execute, depending on the type of loop. There are four types of loops:

- While
- Do-while
- For
- Foreach

## The while construct

A loop is used in the programming world to make a sequence of execution steps repeat itself until the condition is met. The `while` loop is one of the building blocks of the C# programming architecture and is used to loop through the body mentioned in curly brackets until the condition mentioned in the `while` criteria is `true`:

```
while (condition)
{
  loop body;
}
```

The condition mentioned in the loop should evaluate to `true` to execute the loop for the next iteration.

## The do-while construct

The `do...while` construct checks the condition after executing the step once. Even though the `do...while` loop is similar to the `while` loop, the only difference between a `do...while` loop and a `while` loop is that a `do...while` loop will execute the body at least once, even if the criteria is `false`:

```
do
{
  loop body;
}
while (condition);
```

## The for construct

The most popular loop in the language is the `for` loop, which handles complications by maintaining the number of executions of the loop efficiently within the block itself:

```
for (initialization; condition; update)
{
  /* loop body */
}
```

The `for` loop has a few sections in the criteria. Each of these is separated by a semicolon (;). The first portion defines the index variable, which is executed once before executing the loop. The second portion is the condition that is executed in every iteration of the `for` loop. If the condition becomes `false`, the `for` loop doesn't continue its execution and stops. The third portion is also executed after every execution of the loop body and it manipulates the variable that was used in the `for` loop initialization and condition.

## The foreach construct

The `foreach` loops are new to the language and are used to iterate over a sequence of objects. Even though this is purely syntactic sugar in the language, the `foreach` loop is widely used when dealing with collections. The `foreach` loop inherently uses an `IEnumerable<object>` interface and should only be used for objects implementing this:

```
foreach (type variable in collection)
{
    //statements;
}
```

## Contextual – break and continue statements

If you are working with loops, it is very important to understand two more contextual keywords that make it possible to interact with loops.

### Break

This allows the developer to break the loop and take the context out of the loop, even though the criteria is still valid. The programming contextual keyword, `break`, is used as a bypass to break the loop in which it is getting executed. The `break` statement is valid inside loops and switch statements.

## Continue

This is used to invoke the next iteration. The contextual keyword allows the developer to continue to the next step without executing any further code in the block.

Now, let's look at how we can use both of these contextual statements in our program:

```
var x = 0;
while(x<=10)
{
   x++;
   if(x == 2)continue;
   Console.WriteLine(x);
   if(x == 5) break;
   Console.WriteLine("End of loop body");
}
Console.WriteLine($"End of loop, X : {x}");
```

The preceding code will skip execution of the body for the iteration value, 2, because of the `continue` statement. The loop will execute until the value of x is 5 because of the `break` statement.

# Writing your first C# program in a console application

As you are now aware of the fundamentals and basics of the C# language, literals, loops, conditions, and so on, I think it is time to see a C# code example. So, let's start this section by writing a simple console application, compiling it, and running it using the C# compiler.

Open any notepad application that you have in your computer and type in the following code:

```
using System;

public Program
{
    static void Main(string[] args)
    {
        int num, sum = 0, r;
        Console.WriteLine("Enter a Number : ");
        num = int.Parse(Console.ReadLine());
        while (num != 0)
        {
```

```
            r = num % 10;
            num = num / 10;
            sum = sum + r;
        }
        Console.WriteLine("Sum of Digits of the Number : " + sum);
        Console.ReadLine();
    }
}
```

The preceding code is a classic example of calculating the sum of all of the digits of a number. It takes a number as input using the `Console.ReadLine()` function, parses it, and stores it into a variable, `num`, loops through while the number is 0, and takes modulus by `10` to get the reminder of the division, which is then summed up to produce the result.

You can see there is a `using` statement at the top of the code block, which ensures that `Console.ReadLine()` and `Console.WriteLine()` can be called. `System` is a namespace from the code, which enables the program to call the classes defined inside it without specifying the full namespace path of the class.

Let's save the class as `program.cs`. Now, open the console and move it to the location where you have saved the code.

To compile the code, we can use the following command:

```
csc Program.cs
```

The compilation will produce something like this:

```
Setting environment for using Microsoft Visual Studio 2017 x86 tools.
C:\Program Files Microsoft Visual Studio 14.0\VC>D:
D:\>cd csharp
D:\csharp>csc Program.cs
Microsoft Visual C# 2017 Compiler version 4.6.30729.4926 for Microsoft .NET Framework version 4.6.1 Copyright Microsoft Corporation. All rights reserved.
D:\csharp>
```

The compilation will produce `program.exe`. If you run this, it will take the number as input and produce the result:

```
Setting environment for using Microsoft Visual Studio 2017 x86 tools.
C:\Program Files Microsoft Visual Studio 14.0\VC>D:
D:\>cd csharp
D:\csharp>csc Program.cs
Microsoft Visual C# 2017 Compiler version 4.6.30729.4926 for Microsoft .NET Framework version 4.6.1 Copyright Microsoft Corporation. All rights reserved.
D:\csharp>Program.exe
Enter a Number :
123
Sum of Digits of the Number : 6
```

You can see that the code is being executed in the console window.

If we dissect how the code is being executed further, we can see that the .NET framework provides the `csc` compiler, an executable that is capable of compiling my C# code into a managed executable. The compiler produces an executable with MSIL as its content, and then, when the executable is being executed, the .NET framework invokes an executable and uses JIT to compile it further so that it can interact with the input/output devices.

The `csc` compiler provides various command-line hooks, which can be used further to add **dynamic link library (dll)** references to the program, target the output as dll, and much more. You can find the full functional document at the following link: https://docs.microsoft.com/en-us/dotnet/csharp/language-reference/compiler-options/listed-alphabetically.

## Visual Studio as an editor

Microsoft has created a number of improvement toolsets that help in creating, debugging, and running programs. One of these tools is called **Visual Studio** (**VS**). Microsoft VS is a Development Environment that works with Microsoft languages. It is a tool that developers can rely on so that they can work easily with Microsoft technologies. VS has been around for quite some time, but the new VS has been totally redesigned and was released as VS 2019 to support .NET languages.

# Evolution of Visual Studio

As time passed, Microsoft released newer versions of VS with more advantages and enhancements. Being a plugin host that hosts a number of services as plug-in, VS has evolved with a lot of tools and extensions. It has been the core part of every developer's activity. VS has been used by a large number of people who are not a part of the developer community, because they have found this IDE beneficial for editing and managing documents.

# Types of Visual Studio

Microsoft has introduced different types or editions of VS. The difference between these editions are features and pricing. Among the editions, one is free, while others you have to buy. Consequently, knowing which edition provides which features and which edition is better for which type of work will make it easier for a developer to choose the edition right.

Let's look at a comparison between all versions of VS.

## Visual Studio Community

VS Community edition is the free edition. This edition doesn't have some advanced features that are available in the others, but this Community edition is perfectly fine for building small/mid-sized projects. This is especially useful for a person who wants to explore the C# programming language, since they can download this edition for free and start building applications.

## Visual Studio Professional

This version of VS is for your own development, with important debugging tools and all of the commonly used developer tools. So, you can use the IDE as your primary orientation and then you can go ahead!

## Visual Studio Enterprise

VS Enterprise edition is for enterprises that require commercial levels of usage of the IDE. It supports special tools for testing, debugging, and so on. It also discovers common coding errors, generates test data, and much more.

## Visual Studio Code

VS Code is a small, open source tool that is not a full IDE, but a simple code editor that has been developed by Microsoft. This editor is very lightweight and platform-independent. VS Code doesn't come with most of the features that the VS IDE has, but has sufficient features for developing and debugging an application.

For this book, we are going to use VS Community in most of our cases, but you can install any version that you wish. You can download the Community edition free of cost at the following link: https://www.visualstudio.com/downloads/.

## Introduction to the Visual Studio IDE

After you first install VS, the VS installer will give you a few options regarding workloads, which means the type of applications you are going to develop using this IDE. For this book, we will only be creating C# console applications, so you can choose that option if you want. Now, let's start the VS IDE. After loading the IDE, it'll show you a start page with multiple options. Choose the option to create a new project.

## New Project

After you choose new project, the **New Project** dialog box will appear. In this dialog box, a number of options will be available based on the packages that are currently installed with the IDE, as shown in the following screenshot:

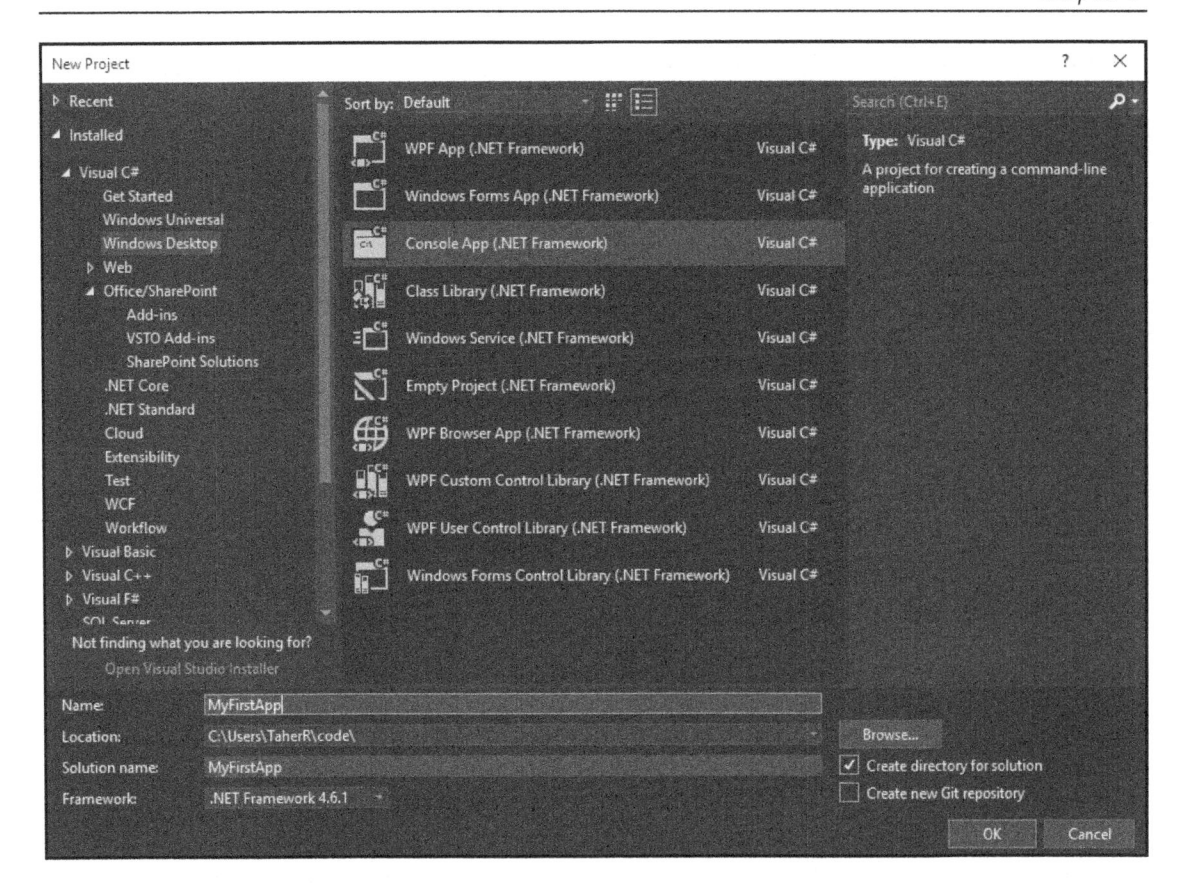

In the preceding screenshot, the left-hand side groups are the types of templates that you can choose from. Here, I have chosen Windows Desktop and, from the middle window, I have selected Console App (.NET framework) to create my application. The bottom of the screen allows you to name the project and choose the location to store the project files. There are two checkboxes available, one of which says **Create directory for solution** when selected (by default, this remains selected). This creates a directory below the chosen path and places the files inside it, otherwise it will create files just inside the folder.

Use **Search Installed Template** to search for any template by its name at the right corner of the dialog box if you do not find your template. Since more than one framework can exist in one PC, the **New Project** dialog will allow you to choose a framework; you need to use this while deploying the application. It shows **.NET framework 4.6.1** by default as the framework for the project, but you can change to any framework by selecting one from the drop-down menu.

Finally, click **OK** to create the project with the default files:

```
using System;
using System.Collections.Generic;
using System.Linq;
using System.Text;
using System.Threading.Tasks;

namespace MyFirstApp
{
    0 references
    class Program
    {
        0 references
        static void Main(string[] args)
        {
        }
    }
}
```

The preceding screenshot shows what a basic IDE looks like after the project is created. We can also see each section of IDE. The main IDE is composed of many tool windows. You can see some tool windows on all sides of the screen. The **Task List** window is at the bottom of the screen. The main IDE workspace is in the middle and forms the working area of the IDE. The workspace can be zoomed into by using the **Zoom** control in the corner of the screen. The IDE search box at the top of the screen gives you insight into finding options inside the IDE more elegantly and easily. We will now divide the whole IDE into those parts and explore the IDE.

## Solution Explorer

The folders and files are hierarchically depicted in the Solution Explorer. Solution Explorer is the main window and lists the entire solution that is loaded to the IDE. This gives you a view of projects and files that have a solution for easy navigation in the form of a tree. The outer node of the Solution Explorer is itself a solution, then the projects, and then the files and folders. The Solution Explorer supports loading folders inside the solution and storing documents in the first level, too. The project that is set as startup is marked in bold.

There are many buttons present at the top of the Solution Explorer called toolbar buttons. Based on the file that's selected in the tree, the toolbar buttons will be enabled or disabled. Let's look at each of them individually:

- **Collapse All button:** This button allows you to collapse all of the nodes below the node that's currently selected. While working with a big solution, it is often necessary to collapse a portion of the tree completely. You can use this feature without collapsing each node manually.
- **Properties:** As a shortcut to the Properties window, you can select this button to open the Properties window and load the metadata associated with the currently selected node.
- **Show all files:** A solution is generally mapped to a Folder structure on a directory in the filesystem. The files that are included in the solution are only shown on the Solution tree. Showing all files allows you to toggle between viewing all files in the directory and only the files that have been added to the solution.
- **Refresh:** This refreshes the state of files in the current solution. The Refresh button also checks every file from the filesystem and shows its status accordingly (if any).
- **View Class Diagram:** The class diagram is the logical tree of namespaces and classes rather than the files in the filesystem. When you select this option, VS launches the class diagram with all of the details of its properties, methods, and so on. The class diagram is useful for viewing all of the classes and their associations individually.
- **View Code:** When you select a code file, the View Code button appears, which loads the code file associated with the current selection. For instance, when you select a Windows Form, it will show its code behind where the code needs to be written.
- **View Designer:** Sometimes, based on the file type that is selected in the tree, the View Designer button appears. This button launches the Designer associated with the currently selected file type.
- **Add New Folder:** As I have already stated, a solution can also contain folders. You can add folders directly to the solution by using the **Add New Folder** button.
- **Create New Solution:** Sometimes, when working with large projects, you might need to create a subset of the entire solution and list only the items that you are currently working on. This button will create a separate Solution Explorer that is in sync with the original Solution Explorer, but projects a specific portion of the solution tree.

*Overview of C# as a Language*

The solution tree in VS also loads the class structure of the project in the way it is organized in the filesystem. If you see a collapsed folder, you can expand it to see what is inside it. If you expand a .cs file, all of the members of that class are listed. If you just want to see how the classes are organized, you can use the class view window, but by using the Solution Explorer, you can see the classes, as well as the other elements inside its own hierarchy. You can open the Class View by choosing **View** | **ClassView** or pressing *Ctrl + W and C*, so that you can view only a portion of the class and its members:

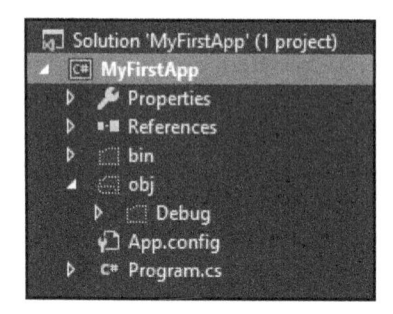

Some files are shown in the solution as blank files (in our case, folders such as `bin` and `obj`). This means that these files exist in the filesystem but are not included in the solution file.

Each file shows additional information on the right-hand side of the tree node in the solution. This button gives extra information that's associated with the file. For instance, if you click on the button corresponding to a .cs file, it will open a menu with `Contains`. This will get the associated class view for that particular file in the solution. The menu can be pretty long, depending on the items that cannot be shown in the generalized toolbar buttons. When the solution loads additional information, there are forward and backward buttons, which can be used to navigate between views on the solution.

## Main workspace area

The main workspace area is where you will actually write your code or apply different settings to your application. This section will open different kinds of files that you have in your project. This is the area which, as a developer, you will spend most of your time coding. You can open multiple files in this window. Different files will be shown in different tabs and you can switch from one tab to another just by clicking on the tab. If you need to, you can also pin tabs. You can make the tabs float if you think you need them that way, or you can also make it full-screen size so that you can focus on the code you are working on.

*Chapter 1*

So, when you double-click on files in the Solution Explorer or choose **Open** from the context menu of the file, that file is opened in a tab in the main editor area. This way, you can open multiple files in separate tabs in the editor window and switch between them when needed. Each tab header contains a few fixed sets of items:

```xml
<?xml version="1.0" encoding="utf-8" ?>
<configuration>
    <startup>
        <supportedRuntime version="v4.0" sku=".NETFramework,Version=v4.6.1" />
    </startup>
</configuration>
```

In the preceding screenshot, you can see that the tab header contains the name of the file (`Program.cs`) that links to the tab; it shows a * when the item needs to be saved, and it has a Toggle pinner button (just like all other IDE tool windows), which makes the tab sticky on the left side, and a close button. The title section also sometimes indicates some additional status, for example, when the file is locked, it shows a lock icon, and when the object is loaded from metadata, it shows that in square brackets, as in the preceding screenshot. In this section, as we keep on opening files, it goes in a stack of tab pages, one after another, until it reaches the end. After the whole area is occupied, it finally creates a menu on the rightmost corner of the workspace title to hold a list of all of the files that cannot be shown on the screen. From this menu, you can choose which file you need to open. *Ctrl + Tab* can also be used to toggle between the tabs that are already loaded in the workspace.

Below the title of the tab and before the main workable area are two drop-down menus. One has been loaded with the class that is opened in the IDE, and the right one loads all of the members that are created on the file. These drop-downs menu aid in easier navigation in the file by listing all of the classes that are loaded in the current file on the left, while on the right there is another that contextually lists all of the members that are there in the class. These two drop-downs menu are smart enough to update the drop-down values automatically whenever any new code is added to the editor.

The main workspace area is bounded by two scrollbars, which handle the overflow of the document. However, after the vertical scrollbar, there is a special button to split the window, as shown in the following screenshot:

The horizontal scrollbar, on the other hand, holds another drop-down menu that shows the current zoom percentage of the Editor. VS now allows you to scale your editor to your preferred zoom level. The shortcut for the Zoom feature is *Ctrl* + scroll mouse wheel.

## Output window

The output window is placed on the bottom of the IDE (in general) and it opens up at various times when you either compile, connect to various services, start debugging, or do something that requires the IDE to show some code. The **Output** window is used by the IDE to display log and trace messages:

The **Output** window is docked on the bottom of the page, which lists various types of output. From the drop-down menu at the top, you can select which output you want to see in the output window. You will also have the option to clear the log if you want to display only the newer logs.

## The Command and Immediate windows

The Command window is very similar to Command Prompt of the Windows operating system. You can execute commands using this tool. In the VS command line, you can execute commands on the project you are working on in. Commands are very handy and increase your productivity as you don't have to drag your mouse around to execute something. You can run a command to make this happen easily.

To open a Command window in VS, you can click on the **View** menu and then **Windows**. After this, select **Command Window**. Alternatively, you can use the keyboard shortcut, *Ctrl + Alt + A*, to open it. When you are in the Command window, you will see a > placed in front of every input. This is called a prompt. In the prompt, when you start typing, it will show an Intellisense menu for you. Start typing `Build.Compile`, at which point the project will be compiled for you as well. You can also use `Debug.Start` to start debugging the application. You can debug your application easily using commands. I will list some of the important commands that are used most often when debugging using the Command window:

- `?`: Tells you the value of a variable (you can also use `Debug.Print` to do the same)
- `??`: Sends the variable to the watch window
- `locals`: Shows the locals window
- `autos`: Shows the autos window
- `GotoLn`: Sets the cursor to a specific line
- `Bp`: Puts a breakpoint in the current line

Similar to the Command window, an Intermediate window lets you test code without having to run it. An Intermediate window is used to evaluate, execute a statement, or even print variable values. To open the Immediate window, go to **Debug | Windows** and select **Immediate**.

## Search option in IDE

On the very top-right corner of the screen, you will find a new Search box. This is called the IDE search box. VS IDE is vast. There are thousands of options available inside of it that you can configure. Sometimes, it is hard to find a specific option that you want. The IDE search feature helps you find this option easier:

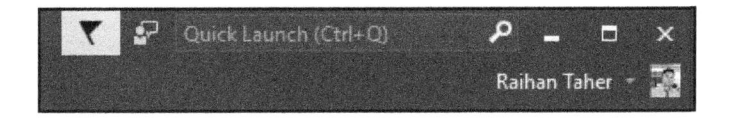

The search option will list all of the entries related to VS IDE options, and you can easily find any feature you are looking for here.

# Writing your first program in Visual Studio

VS is the IDE where developers mostly code while working with the C# language. As you already have a basic idea of how VS works, let's write our first program in VS. Let's create a console application, name the solution `MyFirstApp`, and press **OK**. The default solution template will be automatically added, which includes one `Program.cs` with the `Main` program, and a number of other files.

Let's build a program that generates an ATM machine. There will be a menu that has three options:

- Withdraw
- Deposit
- Balance check

The withdrawal will be performed on the balance (initially $1,000) and a deposit will add an amount to the current balance. Now, let's see what the program looks like:

```csharp
class Program
{
    static void Main(string[] args)
    {
        int balance, depositAmt, withdrawAmt;
        int choice = 0, pin = 0;
        Console.WriteLine("Enter your ledger balance");
        balance = int.Parse(Console.ReadLine());
        Console.WriteLine("Enter Your Pin Number ");
        pin = int.Parse(Console.ReadLine());

        if(pin != 1234)
        {
            Console.WriteLine("Invalid PIN");
            Console.ReadKey(false);
            return;
        }

        while (choice != 4)
        {
            Console.WriteLine("********Welcome to PACKT Payment Bank**************\n");
            Console.WriteLine("1. Check Balance\n");
            Console.WriteLine("2. Withdraw Cash\n");
            Console.WriteLine("3. Deposit Cash\n");
            Console.WriteLine("4. Quit\n");
Console.WriteLine("*************************************************\n\n");
            Console.WriteLine("Enter your choice: ");
```

```csharp
                choice = int.Parse(Console.ReadLine());

            switch (choice)
            {
                case 1:
                    Console.WriteLine("\n Your balance $ : {0} ", balance);
                    break;
                case 2:
                    Console.WriteLine("\n Enter the amount you want to withdraw : ");
                    withdrawAmt = int.Parse(Console.ReadLine());
                    if (withdrawAmt % 100 != 0)
                    {
                        Console.WriteLine("\n Denominations present are 100, 500 and 2000. Your amount cannot be processed");
                    }
                    else if (withdrawAmt > balance)
                    {
                        Console.WriteLine("\n Sorry, insufficient balance.");
                    }
                    else
                    {
                        balance = balance - withdrawAmt;
                        Console.WriteLine("\n\n Your transaction is processed.");
                        Console.WriteLine("\n Current Balance is {0}", balance);
                    }
                    break;
                case 3:
                    Console.WriteLine("\n Enter amount you want to deposit");
                    depositAmt = int.Parse(Console.ReadLine());
                    balance = balance + depositAmt;
                    Console.WriteLine("Your ledger balance is {0}", balance);
                    break;
                case 4:
                    Console.WriteLine("\n Thank you for using the PACKT ATM.");
                    break;
            }
        }
        Console.ReadLine();
    }
}
```

*Overview of C# as a Language*

Now, let's illustrate the program. The program requests a PIN number before opening the ATM machine. The PIN is not checked and can be anything. Once the program starts up, it creates a menu in the front of the console with all of the desired options.

You can see that the entire code is written inside a `while` loop, as it ensures that the program is kept alive for multiple executions. During execution, you can choose any of the options that are available and perform the action associated with it.

To execute the program, just click on the **Run** button on the toolbar of the IDE:

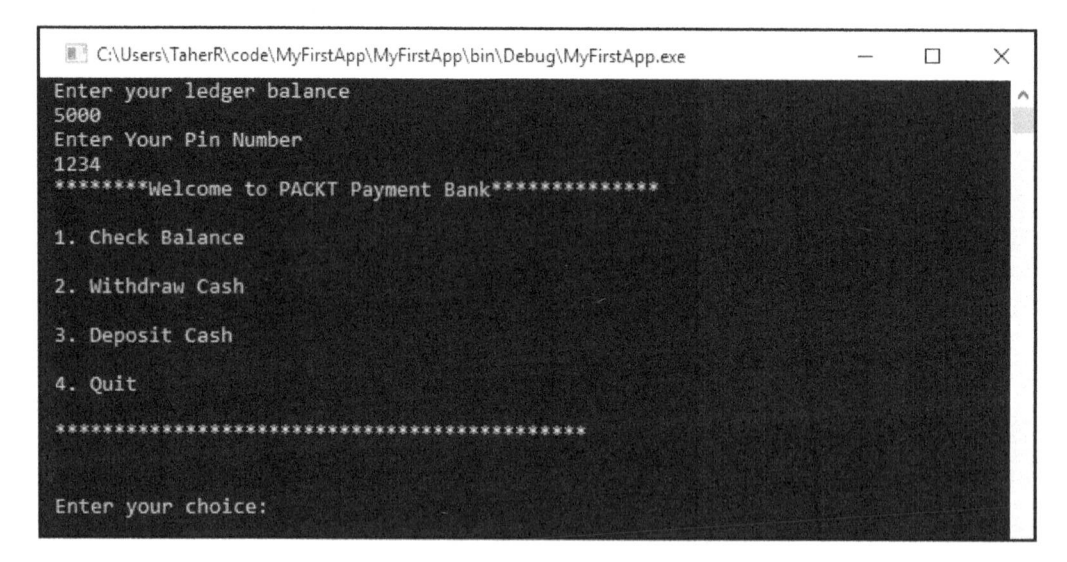

```
C:\Users\TaherR\code\MyFirstApp\MyFirstApp\bin\Debug\MyFirstApp.exe
Enter your ledger balance
5000
Enter Your Pin Number
1234
********Welcome to PACKT Payment Bank***************

1. Check Balance

2. Withdraw Cash

3. Deposit Cash

4. Quit

**************************************************

Enter your choice:
```

If the program does not run automatically, you can look at the Error List window to figure out the actual issue. If you made a mistake in the code, VS will show you the appropriate error message and you can double-click on this to navigate to the actual location.

# How to debug

If you have heard about VS, you must have heard about the debugging capabilities of the IDE. You can start the program in debug mode by pressing *F10*. The program will start in debug mode with the context in the first line. Let's execute a few of the lines. This will look as follows:

The highlighted line in the code editor workspace depicts the line where the current execution has halted. The line is also marked with an arrow on the very left of the code editor. You can continue pressing *F10* or *F11* (step into) buttons to execute these lines. You must inspect the Locals window to find out about all of the values of the local variables during their execution.

## Debugging through code

For really advanced users, the .NET class library opens up some of the interesting debugger APIs that you can invoke from your source code to call a debugger manually.

From the very beginning of a program, there is a `DEBUG` preprocessor variable, which determines whether the project was built in debug mode.

You can write the code in the following way:

```
#IF DEBUG
/// The code runs only in debug mode
#ENDIF
```

The preprocessor directives are actually evaluated during compile time. This means that the code inside `IF DEBUG` will only be compiled in the assembly when the project is built in debug mode.

There are other options such as `Debug.Assert`, `Debug.Fail`, and `Debug.Print`. All of these only work during debug mode. In release mode, these APIs won't be compiled.

You can also call the debugger attached to the process if there is any such process available, using the `Debugger.Break()` method, which will break in the debugger at the current line. You can check the debugger. `IsAttached` is used to find out whether the debugger is attached to the current process.

When you start debugging your code, VS launches the actual process as well as one in `.vshost` in its filename. VS enhances the experience of debugging by enabling Partial Trust's debugging and improving the *F5* experience by using the `.vshost` file. These files work in the background to attach the actual process with a predefined app domain for debugging to make a flawless debugging experience.

`.vshost` files are solely used by the IDE and shouldn't be shipped in an actual project.

VS needs Terminal Services to run these debuggers as it communicates with the process even when it is in the same machine. It does this by using a Terminal Service to maintain a seamless experience with both normal and remote debugging of a process.

# Summary

In this chapter, we looked at the basics of the C# language and introduced the VS Editor. We also tried to write our first program using the command line and VS.

In the next chapter, we will continue this discussion by looking at OOP concepts and techniques, which will allow us to write more classes.

# 2
# Hello OOP - Classes and Objects

**Object-oriented programming** (**OOP**) is something special. If you search the internet for books on OOP, you'll find hundreds of books on this topic. But still this topic will never become stale as it is the most efficient and most commonly used programming methodology in the industry. With the increase in the demand for software developers, there has also been an increase in the demand for good learning content. Our approach in this book is to describe the concepts of OOP in the simplest way. Understanding the basics of OOP is a must for developers who want to work with C#, as C# is a fully OOP language. In this chapter, we will try to understand what OOP actually is and the most basic concepts of OOP that are essential to begin our programming journey. Before anything else, let's first start by analyzing the meaning of the term **object-oriented programming**.

The first word is **object**. According to the dictionary, an object is something that can be seen, felt, or touched; something that has physical existence in the real world. If an item is virtual, this means that it doesn't have any physical existence and is not considered an object. The second word is **oriented**, which indicates a direction or something to aim for. For example, when we say that we are oriented toward the building, we mean that we are facing towards it. The third word is **programming**. I believe I don't have to explain what programming is, but in case you are totally unaware of what programming is and are reading this book to learn, let me explain briefly what programming is. Programming is just giving instructions to the computer. As the computer doesn't speak our language, we humans have to give instructions to the computer in a language that the computer understands. We humans call these instructions **computer programs**, as we are guiding or instructing a computer to do a particular thing.

Now that we know the definitions of those three keywords, if we put all these words together, we can understand the meaning of the phrase *object-oriented programming*. OOP means that we write our computer programs by keeping objects at the center of our thinking. OOP is neither a tool nor a programming language—it is just a concept. Some programming languages are designed to follow this concept. C# is one of the most popular object-oriented languages. There are other object-oriented languages, such as Java, C++, and so on.

In OOP, we try to think about our software components as small objects, and create relationships between them to solve a problem. You may have came across this approach with other programming concepts in the programming world, such as procedural programming, functional programming, and other kinds of programming. One of the most popular computer programming languages of all time—the C programming language—is a procedural programming language. F# is an example of a functional programming language.

In this chapter, we will cover the following topics of OOP:

- Classes in OOP
- The general form of a class
- What is an object?
- Methods in a class
- Characteristics of OOP

## Classes in OOP

In OOP, you derive objects from classes. In this section, we'll take a closer look at what a class actually is.

Classes are one of the most important concepts in OOP. You can say they are the building blocks of OOP. A class can be described as the blueprint of an object.

A class is like a template or blueprint that tells us what properties and behaviors an instance of this class will have. In most circumstances, a class itself can't actually do anything—it is just used to create objects. Let's look at an example to demonstrate what I am saying. Let's say we have a `Human` class. Here, when we say `Human`, we don't mean any particular person, but we are referring to a human being in general. A human that has two hands, two legs, and a mouth, and which can also walk, talk, eat, and think. These properties and their behaviors are applicable to most human beings. I know that this is not the case for disabled people, but for now, we will assume our generic human is able—bodied, keeping our example simple. So when we see the aforementioned properties and behaviors in an object, we can easily categorize that object as a human object or person. This classification is called a class in OOP.

Let's take a closer look at the properties and behaviors of a `Human` class. There are hundreds of properties that you can list for a human, but for the sake of simplicity, we can say that the following are the properties of a human being:

- Height
- Weight
- Age

We can do the same for behavioral properties. There are hundreds of particular behaviors that a person can perform, but here we will only consider the following:

- Walk
- Talk
- Eat

## The general form of a class

To create a class in C#, you have to follow a particular syntax. The general form of this is as follows:

```
class class-name {
    // this is class body
}
```

The `class` phrase is a **reserved keyword** in C#, and it is used to tell the compiler that we want to create a class. To create a class, place the `class` keyword and then the name of the class after a space. The name of the class can be anything that starts with a character or an underscore. We can also include numbers in the class name, but not the first character of a class name. After the chosen name of the class, you have to put an opening curly brace, which denotes the start of the class body. You can add content in the class, such as properties and methods, and then finish the class with a closing curly brace, as follows:

```
class class-name {
  // property 1
  // property 2
  // ...

  // method 1
  // method 2
  // ...
}
```

There are other keywords that can be used with classes to add more functionality, such as access modifiers, virtual methods, partial methods, and so on. Don't worry about these keywords or their uses, as we will discuss these later in this book.

## Writing a simple class

Now let's create our first class. Let's imagine that we are developing some software for a bank. Our application should keep track of the bank's customers and their bank accounts, and perform some basic actions on those bank accounts. As we are going to design our application using C#, we have to think of our application in an object-oriented way. Some objects that we will need for this application could be a customer object, a bank account object, and other objects. So, to make blueprints of these objects, we have to create a `Customer` class and a `BankAccount` class, as well as the other classes that we will need. Let's first create the `Customer` class using the following code:

```
class Customer
{
    public string firstName;
    public string lastName;
    public string phoneNumber;
    public string emailAddress;

    public string GetFullName()
    {
```

```
            return firstName + " " + lastName;
    }
}
```

We started with the `class` keyword and then the name of the class, which is `Customer`. After that, we added the class body inside curly braces, `{}`. The variables that the class has are `firstName`, `lastName`, `phoneNumber`, and `emailAddress`. The class also has a method called `GetFullName()`, which uses the `firstName` and the `lastName` fields to prepare the full name and return it.

Now let's create a `BankAccount` class using the following code:

```
class BankAccount {
    public string bankAccountNumber;
    public string bankAccountOwnerName;
    public double amount;
    public datetime openningDate;

    public string Credit(){
        // Amount credited
    }

    public string Debit(){
        // Amount debited
    }
}
```

Here, we can see that we have followed a similar approach to create a class. We have used the `class` keyword and then the name of the `BankAccount` class. After the name, we started the class body with an opening curly brace and entered fields such as `bankAccountNumber`, `bankAccountOwnerName`, `amount`, and `openningDate`, followed by two methods, `Credit` and `Debit`. By placing a closing curly brace, we end the class body.

For now, don't get worried about keywords such as **public**; we will learn about these keywords later in the book when we talk about access specifiers.

# Objects in OOP

We now know what a **class** is. Now let's look at what **object** refers to in OOP.

An object is an instance of a class. In other words, an object is an implementation of a class. For example, in our banking application, we have a `Customer` class, but that doesn't mean that we actually have a customer in our application. To create a customer, we have to create an object of the `Customer` class. Let's say that we have a customer called Mr. Jack Jones. For this customer, we have to create an object of the `Customer` class, where the name of the person is Jack Jones.

As Mr. Jones is our customer, this means that he also has an account in our bank. To create a bank account for Mr. Jones, we have to create an object of the `BankAccount` class.

## How to create objects

In C#, to create an object of a class, you have to use the `new` keyword. Let's look at an example of an object:

```
Customer customer1 = new Customer();
```

Here, we started by writing `Customer`, which is the name of the class. This represents the type of the object. After that, we gave the name of the object, which in this case is `customer1`. You can give any name to that object. For example, if the customer is Mr. Jones, we could name the object `jackJones`. After the object name, we then inserted an equals sign (=), which means that we are assigning a value to the `customer1` object. After that, we entered a keyword called `new`, which is a special keyword that tells the compiler to create a new object of the class that is given next to it. Here, we gave `Customer` again with `()` next to it. When we place `Customer()`, we are actually calling the constructor of that class. We will talk about constructors in subsequent chapters.

We can create `jackJones` by using the following code:

```
Customer jackJones = new Customer();
```

## Variables in C#

In the previous code, you might have noticed that we created a few variables. A **variable** is something that varies, which means it is not constant. In programming, when we create a variable, the computer actually allocates a space in memory for it so that a value of the variable can be stored there.

Let's assign some values to the variables of the objects that we created in the previous section. We will first work with the `customer1` object, as shown in the following code:

```
using System;

namespace Chapter2
{
    public class Code_2_2
    {
        static void Main(string[] args)
        {
            Customer customer1 = new Customer();
            customer1.firstName = "Molly";
            customer1.lastName = "Dolly";
            customer1.phoneNumber = "98745632";
            customer1.emailAddress = "mollydolly@email.com";

            Console.WriteLine("First name is " + customer1.firstName);
            Console.ReadKey();
        }
    }

    public class Customer
    {
        public string firstName;
        public string lastName;
        public string phoneNumber;
        public string emailAddress;

        public string GetFullName()
        {
            return firstName + " " + lastName;
        }
    }
}
```

Here, we are assigning values to the `customer1` object. The code instructs the computer to create a space in the memory and store the value in it. Later, whenever you access the variable, the computer will go to the memory location and find out the value of the variable. Now, if we write a statement that will print the value of the `firstName` variable with the additional string before it, it will look as follows:

```
Console.WriteLine("First name is " + customer1.firstName);
```

The output of this code will be as follows:

```
First name is Molly
```

## Methods in a class

Let's talk about another important topic—namely methods. A **method** is a piece of code that is written in the code file and can be reused. A method can hold many lines of code, which will be executed when it is called. Let's take a look at the general form of a method:

```
access-modifier return-type method-name(parameter-list) {
    // method body
}
```

We can see that the first thing in the method declaration is an `access-modifier`. This will set the access permission of the method. Then, we have the `return-type` of the method, which will hold the type that the method will return, such as `string`, `int`, `double`, or another type. After that, we have the `method-name` and then brackets, `()`, which indicate that it is a method. In the brackets, we have the `parameter-list`. This can either be empty or can contain one or more parameters. Finally, we have curly brackets, `{}`, which hold the method body. The code that the method will execute goes inside here.

Any code following this structure will be considered a method by the C# compiler.

## Creating a method

Now that we know what a method is, let's take a look at an example, as shown in the following code:

```
public string GetFullName(string firstName, string lastName){
    return firstName + lastName;
}
```

This code will create a method called `GetFullName`. This method takes two parameters, `firstName` and `lastName`, which are placed inside the parentheses. We can also see that we have to specify the types of those parameters. In this particular example, both the parameter types are `string`.

Now, take a look at the method body, which is the section between the curly brackets, `{}`. We can see that the code returns `firstName + lastName`, which means that it is concatenating the two parameters, `firstName` and `lastName`, and returning the `string`. As we are planning to return a `string` from this method, we set the return type of the method to `string`. Another thing to notice is that the access type is set to `public` for this method, which means that any other class can access it.

## Constructor of a class

In every class, there is a special type of method, called a **constructor**. You can create a constructor in a class and program it. If you don't create one yourself, the compiler will create a very simple constructor and use that instead. Let's take a look at what the constructor is and what it does.

A constructor is a method that gets triggered when an object of a class is created. A constructor is mainly used to set the prerequisites of the class. For example, if you are creating an object of the `Human` class, that human object must have a `date of birth`. Without a date of birth, no human would exist. You can set this requirement in the constructor. You can also configure the constructor to set the `date of birth` as today if no date of birth is given. This depends on the needs of your application. Another example could be a `bank account` object, for which you have to provide the bank account holder. No bank account can exist without an owner, so you can set this requirement in the constructor.

Let's take a look at the general form of a constructor, as shown in the following code:

```
access-modifier class-name(parameter-list) {
    // constructor body
}
```

Here, we can see that there is a difference between a constructor and a normal method, namely that a constructor doesn't have a return type. This is because a constructor can't return anything; it's for initialization, not for any other type of action. Normally, the type of access is `public` for constructors, because otherwise no object can be instantiated. If you specifically want to prevent objects of a class from being instantiated, you can set the constructor as `private`. Let's look at an example of a constructor, as shown in the following code:

```
class BankAccount {
    public string owner;

    public BankAccount(){
        owner = "Some person";
    }
}
```

# Hello OOP - Classes and Objects

In this example, we can see that we have a class called `BankAccount` and that it has a variable called `owner`. As we know, no bank account can exist without an owner, so we need to assign a value to the `owner` when an object is created. In order to create a `constructor`, we just make the access type of the constructor `public`, as we want objects to get instantiated. We can also take the name of the owner of the bank account as a parameter in the constructor and use it to assign the variable, as shown in the following code:

```
class BankAccount {
    public string owner;
    public BankAccount(string theOwner){
        owner = theOwner;
    }
}
```

If you put parameters in the constructor, then, when initializing the object, the parameters need to be passed, as shown in the following code:

```
BankAccount account = new BankAccount("Some Person");
```

Another interesting thing is that you can have multiple constructors in a class. You might have one constructor that takes one argument and another that doesn't take any arguments. Depending on the way in which you are initializing the object, the respective constructor will be called. Let's look at the following example:

```
class BankAccount {
    public string owner;
    public BankAccount(){
        owner = "Some person";
    }
    public BankAccount(string theOwner){
        owner = theOwner;
    }
}
```

In the preceding example, we can see that we have two constructors for the `BankAccount` class. If you pass a parameter when you create a `BankAccount` object, it will call the second constructor, which will set the value and create the object. If you don't pass a parameter while creating the object, the first constructor will be called. If you don't have either one of these constructors, this method of object creation won't be available.

If you don't create a class, then the compiler creates an empty constructor for that class, as follows:

```
class BankAccount {
    public string owner;
    public BankAccount()
    {
    }
}
```

## Characteristics of OOP

OOP is one of the most important programming methodologies nowadays. The whole concept depends on four main ideas, which are known as the **pillars of OOP**. These four pillars are as follows:

- Inheritance
- Encapsulation
- Polymorphism
- Abstraction

## Inheritance

The word **inheritance** means receiving or deriving something from something else. In real life, we might talk about a child inheriting a house from his or her parents. In that case, the child has the same power over the house that his parents had. This concept of inheritance is one of the pillars of OOP. In programming, when one class is derived from another class, this is called inheritance. This means that the derived class will have the same properties as the parent class. In programming terminology, the class from which another class is derived is called the **parent class**, while the classes that inherit from these are called **child classes**.

Let's look at an example:

```
public class Fruit {
    public string Name { get; set; }
    public string Color { get; set; }
}

public class Apple : Fruit {
    public int NumberOfSeeds { get; set; }
```

}

In the preceding example, we used inheritance. We have a parent class, called `Fruit`. This class holds the common properties that every fruit has: a `Name` and a `Color`. We can use this `Fruit` class for all fruits.

If we create a new class, called `Apple`, this class can inherit the `Fruit` class because we know that an apple is a fruit. The properties of the `Fruit` class are also properties of the `Apple` class. If the `Apple` inherits the `Fruit` class, we don't need to write the same properties for the `Apple` class because it inherits these from the `Fruit` class.

# Encapsulation

**Encapsulation** means hiding or covering. In C#, encapsulation is achieved by **access modifiers**. The access modifiers that are available in C# are the following:

- Public
- Private
- Protected
- Internal
- Internal protected

Encapsulation is when you want to control other classes' access to a certain class. Let's say you have a `BankAccount` class. For security reasons, it isn't a good idea to make that class accessible to all classes. It's better to make it `Private` or use another kind of access specifier.

You can also limit access to the properties and variables of a class. For example, you might need to keep the `BankAccount` class `public` for some reason, but make the `AccountBalance` property `private` so that no other class can access this property except the `BankAccount` class. You can do this as follows:

```
public class BankAccount {
    private double AccountBalance { get; set; }
}
```

Like variables and properties, you can also use access specifiers for methods. You can write `private` methods that are not needed by other classes, or that you don't want to expose to other classes. Let's look at the following example:

```
public class BankAccount{
    private double AccountBalance { get; set; }
    private double TaxRate { get; set; }
    public double GetAccountBalance() {
        double balanceAfterTax = GetBalanceAfterTax();
        return balanceAfterTax;
    }

    private double GetBalanceAfterTax(){
        return AccountBalance * TaxRate;
    }
}
```

In the preceding example, the `GetBalanceAfterTax` method is a method that will not be needed by other classes. We only want to provide the `AccountBalance` after tax, so we can make this method private.

Encapsulation is a very important part of OOP as it gives us control over code.

# Abstraction

If something is abstract, it means that it doesn't have an instance in reality but does exist as an idea or concept. In programming, we use this technique to organize our thoughts. This is one of the pillars of OOP. In C#, we have `abstract` classes, which implement the concept of abstraction. **Abstract classes** are classes that don't have any instances, classes that implement the `abstract` class will implement the properties and methods of that `abstract` class. Let's look at an example of an `abstract` class, as shown in the following code:

```
public abstract class Vehicle {
    public abstract int GetNumberOfTyres();
}

public class Bicycle : Vehicle {
    public string Company { get; set; }
    public string Model { get; set; }
    public int NumberOfTyres { get; set; }

    public override int GetNumberOfTyres() {
        return NumberOfTyres;
```

*Hello OOP - Classes and Objects*

```
    }
}

public class Car : Vehicle {
    public string Company { get; set; }
    public string Model { get; set; }
    public int FrontTyres { get; set; }
    public int BackTyres { get; set; }

    public override int GetNumberOfTyres() {
        return FrontTyres + BackTyres;
    }
}
```

In the preceding example, we have an abstract class called `Vehicle`. It has one abstract method, called `GetNumberOfTyres()`. As it is an abstract method, this has to be overridden by the classes that implement the abstract class. Our `Bicycle` and `Car` classes implement the `Vehicle` abstract class, so they also override the abstract method `GetNumberOfTyres()`. If you take a look at the implementation of these methods in the two classes, you will see that the implementation is different, which is due to abstraction.

## Polymorphism

The word **polymorph** means many forms. To understand the concept of **polymorphism** properly, let's work with an example. Let's think about a person, such as Bill Gates. We all know that Bill Gates is a great software developer, businessman, philanthropist, and also a great human being. He is one individual, but he has different roles and performs different tasks. This is polymorphism. When Bill Gates was developing software, he was playing the role of a software developer. He was thinking about the code he was writing. Later, when he became the CEO of Microsoft, he started managing people and thinking about growing the business. He's the same person, but with different roles and different responsibilities.

In C#, there are two kind of polymorphism: **static polymorphism** and **dynamic polymorphism**. Static polymorphism is a kind of polymorphism where the role of a method is determined at compilation time, whereas, in dynamic polymorphism, the role of a method is determined at runtime. Examples of static polymorphism include **method overloading** and **operator overloading**. Let's take a look at an example of method overloading:

```
public class Calculator {
    public int AddNumbers(int firstNum, int secondNum){
        return firstNum + secondNum;
```

```
    }
    public double AddNumbers(double firstNum, double secondNum){
        return firstNum + secondNum;
    }
}
```

Here, we can see that we have two methods with the same name, `AddNumbers`. Normally, we can't have two methods that have the same name; however, as the parameters of those methods are different, methods are allowed to have the same name by the compiler. Writing a method with the same name as another method, but with different parameters, is called method overloading. This is a kind of polymorphism.

Like method overloading, **operator overloading** is also a static polymorphism. Let's look at an example of operator overloading to demonstrate this:

```
public class MyCalc
{
    public int a;
    public int b;
    public MyCalc(int a, int b)
    {
        this.a = a;
        this.b = b;
    }

    public static MyCalc operator +(MyCalc a, MyCalc b)
    {
        return new MyCalc(a.a * 3 ,b.b * 3);
    }
}
```

In the preceding example, we can see that the plus sign (+) is overloaded with another kind of calculation. So if you sum up two `MyCalc` objects, you will get an overloaded result instead of the normal sum, and this overloading happens at compile time, so it is static polymorphism.

**Dynamic polymorphism** refers to the use of the abstract class. When you write an abstract class, no instance can be created from that abstract class. When any other class uses or implements that abstract class, the class also has to implement the abstract methods of that abstract class. As different classes can implement the abstract class and can have different implementations of abstract methods, polymorphic behavior is achieved. In this case, we have methods with the same name but different implementations.

# Summary

This chapter covers classes and objects, the most important building blocks of OOP. These are the two things that we should learn before jumping into any other topics in OOP. It is important to make sure that these concepts are clear in our minds before moving on to other ideas. In this chapter, we learned about what a class is and why it's needed in OOP. We also looked at how to create a class in C# and how to define an object. After that, we looked at the relationship between classes and objects and how to instantiate a class and use it. We also talked about variables and methods in a class. Lastly, we covered the four pillars of OOP. In the next chapter, we will learn more about inheritance and class hierarchy.

# Implementation of OOP in C# 3

In the previous chapter, we looked at classes, objects, and the four principles of OOP. In this chapter, we will learn about some C# language features that make the language an OOP language. Without knowing these concepts, writing object-oriented code with C# programming could be difficult, or will prevent you from using it to its full potential. In `Chapter 2`, *Hello OOP - Classes and Objects,* we learned that abstraction, inheritance, encapsulation, and polymorphism are the four basic principles of OOP, but we haven't yet learned how the C# language can be used to fulfill these principles. We are going to discuss this topic in this chapter.

In this chapter, we will cover the following topics:

- Interfaces
- The abstract class
- The partial class
- The scaled class
- Tuples
- Properties
- Access specifiers for classes

## Interfaces

A class is a blueprint, which means it contains the members and methods that the instantiated objects will have. An **interface** can also be categorized as a blueprint, but unlike a class, an interface doesn't have any method implementation. Interfaces are more like a guideline for classes that implement the interface.

The main features of interfaces in C# are as follows:

- Interfaces can't have a method body; they can only have the method signature.
- Interfaces can have methods, properties, events, and indexes.
- An interface can't be instantiated, so no object of an interface can be created.
- One class can extend multiple interfaces.

One of the major uses of an interface is dependency injection. By using interfaces, you can reduce the dependencies in a system. Let's look at an example of an interface:

```
interface IBankAccount {
    void Debit(double amount);
    void Credit(double amount);
}
class BankAccount : IBankAccount {
    public void Debit(double amount){
        Console.WriteLine($"${amount} has been debited from your account!");
    }
    public void Credit(double amount){
        Console.WriteLine($"${amount} has been credited to your account!");
    }
}
```

In the preceding example, we can see that we have one interface, called `IBankAccount`, that has two members: `Debit` and `Credit`. Both of these methods have no implementations in the interface. In the interface, the method signatures are more like guidelines or requirements for the classes that will implement this interface. If any class implements this interface, then the class has to implement the method body. This is a great use of the OOP concept of inheritance. The class will have to give an implementation of the methods that are mentioned in the interface. If the class doesn't implement any of the methods of the interface, the compiler will throw an error that the class has not implemented all the methods of the interface. By language design, if an interface is implemented by a class, all the members of the interface must be taken care of in the class. Consequently, in the preceding code, the `BankAccount` class has implemented the `IBankAccount` interface and this is why the two methods, `Debit` and `Credit`, have to be implemented.

# The abstract class

An **abstract class** is a special kind of class that comes with the C# programming language. This class has similar functionalities to an interface. For example, an abstract class can have methods without implementation and with implementation. Consequently, when a class implements an abstract class, the class has to override the **abstract methods** of the abstract class. One of the main characteristics of an abstract class is that it can't be instantiated. An abstract class can only be used for inheritance. It might or might not have abstract methods and assessors. Sealed and abstract modifiers can't be placed in the same class, as they have completely separate meanings.

Let's take a look at an example of an abstract class:

```
abstract class Animal {
    public string name;
    public int ageInMonths;
    public abstract void Move();
    public void Eat(){
        Console.WriteLine("Eating");
    }
}
class Dog : Animal {
    public override void Move() {
        Console.WriteLine("Moving");
    }
}
```

In the preceding example, we saw that the Dog class is implementing the Animal class, and as the Animal class has an abstract method called Move(), the Dog class must override it.

If we try to instantiate the abstract class, the compiler will throw an error, as follows:

```
using System;
namespace AnimalProject {
    abstract class Animal {
        public string name;
        public int ageInMonths;
        public abstract void Move();
        public void Eat(){
            Console.WriteLine("Eating");
        }
    }
    static void Main(){
        Animal animal = new Animal(); // Not possible as the Animal class is abstract class
```

        }
}

# The partial class

You can split a class, a struct, or an interface into smaller portions that can be placed in different code files. If you want to do this, you have to use the keyword **partial**. Even though the code is in separate code files, when complied, they will be treated as one class altogether. There are many benefits of partial classes. One benefit is that different developers can work on different code files at a time. Another benefit is that if you are using autogenerated code and you want to extend some functionality of that autogenerated code, you can use a partial class in a separate file. Consequently, you are not directly touching the autogenerated code, but adding new functionality in the class.

The partial class has a few requirements, one of which is that all classes must have the keyword `partial` in their signatures. All the partial classes also have to have the same name, but the file names can be different. The partial classes also have to have the same accessibility, such as public, private, and so on.

The following is an example of a partial class:

```
// File name: Animal.cs
using System;
namespace AnimalProject {
    public partial class Animal {
        public string name;
        public int ageInMonths;
        public void Eat(){
            Console.WriteLine("Eating");
        }
    }
}
// File name: AnimalMoving.cs
using System;
namespace AnimalProject {
    public partial class Animal {
        public void Move(){
            Console.WriteLine("Moving");
        }
    }
}
```

As shown in the preceding code, you can create many partial classes of a class. This will increase the readability of your code, and your code organization will be more structured.

## The sealed class

One of the principles of OOP is inheritance, but sometimes you may need to restrict inheritance in your code for the sake of your application's architecture. C# provides a keyword called `sealed`. If this keyword is placed before a class's signature, the class is considered a **sealed class**. If a class is sealed, that particular class can't be inherited by other classes. If any class tries to inherit a sealed class, the compiler will throw an error. Structs can also be sealed, and in that case, no class can inherit that struct.

Let's look at an example of a sealed class:

```
sealed class Animal {
    public string name;
    public int ageInMonths;
    public void Move(){
        Console.WriteLine("Moving");
    }
    public void Eat(){
        Console.WriteLine("Eating");
    }
}
public static void Main(){
    Animal dog = new Animal();
    dog.name = "Doggy";
    dog.ageInMonths = 1;
    dog.Move();
    dog.Eat();
}
```

In the preceding example, we can see how we can create a sealed class. Just using the `sealed` keyword before the `class` keyword makes the class a sealed class. In the preceding example, we created an `Animal` sealed class, and in the `main` method, we instantiated the class and used it. This is now working fine. However, if we try to create a `Dog` class that will inherit the `Animal` class, as in the following code, then the compiler will throw an error, saying that the sealed `Animal` class can't be inherited:

```
class Dog : Animal {
    public char gender;
}
```

*Implementation of OOP in C#*

Here is a screenshot of what the compiler will show:

> ⊗ CS0509  'Dog': cannot derive from sealed type 'Animal'

# Tuples

A **tuple** is a data structure that holds a set of data. Tuples are mainly helpful when you want to group data and use it. Normally, a C# method can only return one value. By using a tuple, it is possible to return multiple values from a method. The `Tuple` class is available under the `System.Tuple` namespace. A tuple can be created using the `Tuple<>` constructor or by an abstract method named `Create` that comes with the `Tuple` class.

You can fix any data type in a tuple and access it using `Item1`, `Item2`, and so on. Let's look at an example to get a better idea of this:

```
var person = new Tuple<string, int, string>("Martin Dew", 42, "Software Developer"); // name, age, occupation
or
var person = new Tuple.Create("Martin Dew", 42, "Software Developer");
```

Let's take a look at how to return a tuple from a method by using the following code:

```
public static Tuple<string, int, string> GetPerson() {
    var person = new Tuple<string, int, string>("Martin Dew", 42, "Software Developer");
    return person;
}
static void Main() {
    var developer = GetPerson();
    Console.WriteLine("The person is {0}. He is {1} years old. He is a {2}", developer.Item1, developer.Item2, developer.Item3 );
}
```

# Properties

For security reasons, all the fields of a class shouldn't be exposed to the outside world. Consequently, exposing private fields is done by properties in C#, which are members of that class. Underneath the properties are special methods that are called **accessors**. A property contains two accessors: `get` and `set`. The `get` accessor gets values from the field while the `set` accessor sets values to the field. There is a special keyword for a property, named `value`. This represents the value of a field.

By using access modifiers, properties can have different access levels. A property can be `public`, `private`, `read only`, `open for read and write`, and `write only`. If only the `set` accessor is implemented, this means that the `only write` permission is given. If both `set` and `get` accessors are implemented, this means that both `read` and `write` permissions are open for that property.

C# provides a smart way of writing `setter` and `getter` methods. If you create a property in C#, you don't have to manually write `setter` and `getter` methods for a particular field. Consequently, the common practice in C# is to create properties in a class, rather than creating fields and `setter` and `getter` methods for those fields.

Let's take a look at how to create property in C#, as shown in the following code:

```
class Animal {
    public string Name {set; get;}
    public int Age {set; get;}
}
```

The `Animal` class has two properties: `Name` and `Age`. Both the properties have `Public` access modifiers as well as `setter` and `getter` methods. This means that both properties are open for `read` and `write` operations. The convention is that properties should be in camel case.

If you want to modify your `set` and `get` methods, you can do so in the following way:

```
class Animal {
    public string Name {
        set {
            name = value;
        }
        get {
            return name;
        }
    }
}
```

```
    public int Age {set; get;}
}
```

In the preceding example, we are not using the shortcut of creating `setters` and `getters` for the `Name` property. We have extensively written what the `set` and `get` methods should do. If you look closely, you will see the `name` field in lowercase. This means that when you create a property in camel case, a field with the same name is created internally, but in Pascal case. The `value` is a special keyword that actually represents the value of that property.

Properties are working behind the scenes in the background, which makes the code much cleaner and easier to use. It's very much recommended that you use properties instead of local fields.

# Access specifiers for classes

**Access specifiers**, or **access modifiers**, are some reserved keywords that determine the accessibility of a class, method, property, or other entity. The object-oriented principle of encapsulation is achieved by using these access specifiers in C#. In total, there are five access specifiers. Let's take a look at what these are and what the differences are between them.

# Public

The **public** access specifier means that there is no limitation to access the entity being modified. If a class or member is set as `public`, it can be accessed by other classes or programs in the same assembly, other assemblies, and even other programs that are installed in the operating system that the program is running in. Normally, the starting point of an application or main method is set as `public`, meaning that it can be accessed by others. To make a class `public`, you just need to put a `public` keyword before the keyword class, as shown in the following code:

```
public class Animal {
}
```

The preceding `Animal` class can be accessed by any other class, and as the member `Name` is also public, it can also be accessed from any location.

## Private

The **private** specifier is the most secure access specifier available in the C# programming language. By setting a class or member of a class as `private`, you are determining that the class or the member won't be allowed to be accessed by other classes. The scope of a `private` member is within the class. For example, if you create a `private` field, that field can't be accessed outside the class. That `private` field can only be used internally in that class.

Let's look at an example of a class with a `private` field:

```
public class Animal {
    private string name;
    public string GetName() {
        return name;
    }
}
```

Here, as the `GetName()` method and the `private` field `name` are in the same class, the method can access the field. However, if another method outside of the `Animal` class tries to access the `name` field, it won't be able to.

For example, in the following code, the `Main` method is trying to set the `private` field name, which is not permissible:

```
using System;
namespace AnimalProject {
    static void Main(){
        Animal animal = new Animal();
        animal.name = "Dog"; // Not possible, as the name field is private
        animal.GetName(); // Possible, as the GetName method is public
    }
}
```

## Internal

If you set `internal` as an access specifier, this means that the entity is only accessible within the same assembly. All the classes in the assembly can access this class or member. When you build a project in .NET, it creates an assembly file, either `dll` or `exe`. There could be many assemblies in one solution, and internal members are only accessible by the classes on those particular assemblies.

Let's look at an example of this, as shown in the following code:

```
using System;
namespage AnimalProject {
    static void Main(){
        Dog dog = new Dog();
        dog.GetName();
    }
    internal class Dog {
        internal string GetName(){
            return "doggy";
        }
    }
}
```

# Protected

**Protected** members are accessible by the class itself, as well as the child classes that inherit the class. Other than that, no other class can access a protected member. The protected access modifier is very useful when inheritance takes place.

Let's learn how to use this by looking at the following code:

```
using System;
namespage AnimalProject {
    static void Main(){
        Animal animal = new Animal();
        Dog dog = new Dog();
        animal.GetName(); // Not possible as Main is not a child of Animal
        dog.GetDogName();
    }
    class Animal {
        protected string GetName(){
            return "doggy";
        }
    }
    class Dog : Animal {
        public string GetDogName() {
            return base.GetName();
        }
    }
}
```

## Protected internal

A **protected internal** is a combination of a protected access modifier and an internal access modifier. A member whose access modifier is `protected internal` can be accessed by all classes in the same assembly, as well as by any class that inherits it, regardless of the assembly. For example, say that you have a class named `Animal` in an assembly called `Assembly1.dll`. In the `Animal` class, there is a protected internal method called `GetName`. Any other class in `Assembly1.dll` can access the `GetName` method. Now, suppose there is another assembly named `Assembly2.dll`. In `Assembly2.dll`, there is a class named `Dog` that extends the `Animal` class. As `GetName` is a protected internal, even though the `Dog` class is in a separate assembly, it can still access the `GetName` method.

Let's look at the following example to get a clearer understanding of this:

```
//Assembly1.dll
using System;
namespace AnimalProject {
    public class Animal {
        protected internal string GetName(){
            return "Nice Animal";
        }
    }
}
//Assembly2.dll
using System;
namespace AnimalProject2 {
    public class Dog : Animal {
        public string GetDogName(){
            return base.GetName(); // This will work
        }
    }
    public class Cat {
        Animal animal = new Animal();
        public string GetCatName(){
            return animal.GetName(); // This is not possible, as GetName is protected internal
        }
    }
}
```

# Summary

In this chapter, we looked at class hierarchies and some other features that make the C# programming language an OOP language. Knowing these concepts is essential for a C# developer. By knowing class hierarchies, you can design your system so that it is decoupled and flexible. You need to know how to use inheritance in your application to get the best of OOP. The interface, abstract class, sealed class, and partial class will give you good control of your application. When working in a team, defining the class hierarchies properly will help you to maintain code quality and security.

Knowing about tuples and properties will improve your code cleanness and make your life much easier when developing the application. Access specifiers are implementations of the OOP concept of encapsulation. It is important to be familiar with these concepts. You need to know which piece of code should be available publicly, which should be private, and which should be protected. If you misuse these access specifiers, you might end up in a situation where your application will have security holes and code repetition.

In the next chapter, we will discuss the important and interesting topic of object collaboration.

# 4
# Object Collaboration

As we saw in earlier chapters, OOP is all about objects, which are the main focus of this programming methodology. When we design our software using this methodology, we will keep the concepts of OOP in mind. We will also try to break our software components into smaller objects and create proper relationships between the objects so that all of them can work together to give us our desired output. This relationship between objects is called **object collaboration**.

In this chapter, we will cover the following topics:

- What is object collaboration?
- Different types of collaboration
- What is dependency collaboration?
- What is association?
- What is inheritance?

## Examples of object collaboration

Object collaboration is one of the most important topics in OOP. If the objects don't collaborate with each other in a program, nothing can be achieved. For example, if we think about a simple web application, we can see how the relationship between different objects plays an important role in constructing the application. Twitter, for example, has many objects that are related to each other in order to make the application work. The `User` object consists of the username, password, first name, last name, picture, and other user-related information belonging to Twitter users. There could be another object called `Tweet` that consists of a message, date and time, the username of the user who posted the tweet, and some other properties. There may also be another object called `Message` that holds the content of the message, who it was from, who it was sent to, and the date and time. This is the simplest breakdown possible for a big application like Twitter; it almost certainly contains many other objects. But for now, let's just think about these three objects and try to find a relationship between them.

First, we will look at the `User` object. This is one of the most important objects in Twitter, as it holds the user information. Everything in Twitter is either made or performed *by* a user or *for* a user, so we can assume that there should be some other objects that will need to have a relationship with this `User` object. Now let's try to see whether the `Tweet` object has any relationship with the `User` object or not. A tweet is a message that should be available for all users to see if the `Tweet` object is public. If it is private, only that user's followers will see it. As we can see, a `Tweet` object has a very strong relationship with a `User` object. So, with the OOP approach, we can say that the `User` object has a collaboration with the `Tweet` object in the Twitter application.

If we also try to analyze the relationship between `User` and `Message` objects, we will see that the `Message` object also has a very strong relationship with the `User` object. A message is sent by a user to another user; therefore, without a user, the `Message` object has no proper implementation.

But is there any relationship between the `Tweet` and `Message` objects? From what has been said, we can say that there is no relationship between these two objects. It's not necessary for every object to be related to all other objects, but an object usually has a relationship with at least one other object. Now let's see what different types of object collaborations are available in C#.

# Different types of object collaboration in C#

There are many ways an object can collaborate with other objects in programming. However, in this chapter, we will only talk about the three most important collaboration rules.

We will first try to explain each of these types, looking at some examples to help us to understand them. If you can't relate these concepts to your work, it might be a little hard for you to understand the importance of object collaboration, but trust me, these concepts are very important on your path to becoming a good software developer.

All these concepts and terms will come in handy when you have discussions about software design with other people, or even when you design your own software. As a consequence, my suggestion would be to focus on understanding the concepts and relate them to your work in order to reap the benefits of this information.

*Chapter 4*

Now, let's look at the three collaboration types that we are going to be talking about in this chapter, as shown in the following list:

- Dependency
- Association
- Inheritance

Let's think of an imaginary application and try to relate these collaboration concepts to the objects of this application. Learning is easier and more interesting when you can relate concepts to the real world, so this is the approach we will take in the following sections.

# Case study

Since the main goal of this chapter is to learn about the concepts involved in object collaboration rather than design a fully fledged, super-duper application, we will design our objects in a simple and minimal manner.

For our example, we are going to develop some restaurant management software. This could be for a luxury restaurant, or a small cafe where people come to drink coffee and relax. In our case, we are thinking of a restaurant with mid-range pricing. To begin building this application, let's think about what classes and objects we need. We will be needing a `Food` class, a `Chef` class, a `Waiter` class, and maybe a `Beverage` class.

When you are done reading this chapter, don't jump straight into the next chapter. Instead, spend some time thinking about some of the objects that aren't mentioned in this chapter and try to analyze the relationships between the objects you have thought about. This will help you to develop your knowledge of the concept of object collaboration. Remember: software development is not a typing job, it requires heavy brain work. Consequently, the more you think about the concepts, the better at software developing you will become.

Now, let's see what objects I came up with when I did some thinking about the objects that should be included in our imaginary restaurant application:

- `Food`
- `Beef Burger`
- `Pasta`

*Object Collaboration*

- `Beverage`
- `Cola`
- `Coffee`
- `Order`
- `OrderItem`
- `Staff`
- `Chef`
- `Waiter`
- `FoodRepository`
- `BeverageRepository`
- `StaffRepository`

Some of these objects might not make much sense to you right now. For example, the `FoodRepository`, `BeverageRepository`, and `StaffRepository` objects are not actually business objects, but are helper objects that help different modules to interact with each other in the application. The `FoodRepository` object, for example, will be used to save and retrieve `Food` objects from the database and the UI. Similarly, the `BeverageRepository` object will deal with beverages. We also have a class called `Food` that is a general type of class, as well as more specific food objects such as `Beef Burger` and `Pasta`. These objects are subcategories of the `Food` object. As software developers, we have identified the objects that are needed to develop this software. Now, it's time to use these objects in a way that solves the problem that the software will be used for; however, before we start writing code, we need to understand and figure out how the objects can relate to each other so that the application is the best that it can be. Let's start with the dependency relationship.

# Dependency

When an object uses another unrelated object to carry out a task, the relationship between them is called a **dependency**. In the software world, we also refer to this relationship as **uses a relation**. Now, let's see if any kind of dependency relationship exists between the objects that we have thought about for our restaurant application.

If we analyze our `FoodRepository` object, which will be saving and retrieving `Food` objects from the database and passing them to the UI, we can say that the `FoodRepository` object has to use the `Food` object. This means that the relationship between the `Food` and `FoodRepository` object is a type of dependency relationship. If we think about the flow in the frontend when a new `Food` objects is created, that object will be passed to the `FoodRepository`. The `FoodRepository` will then serialize the `Food` object to database data in order to save it in the database. If the `FoodRepository` doesn't use the `Food` object, then how would it know what to serialize and store in the database? Here, the `FoodRepository` must have a dependency relationship with the `Food` object. Let's look at the code for this:

```
public class Food {
 public int? FoodId {get;set;}
 public string Name {get;set;}
 public decimal Price {get;set;}
}

public class FoodRepository {
 public int SaveFood(Food food){
 int result = SaveFoodInDatabase(food);
 return result;
 }

 public Food GetFood(int foodId){
 Food result = new Food();
 result = GetFoodFromDatabaseById(foodId);
 return result;
 }
}
```

In the preceding code, we can see that the `FoodRepository` class has two methods. One method is `SaveFood` and the other is `GetFood`.

The `SaveFood` method involves taking one `Food` object and saving it in the database. After saving the food item in the database, it returns the newly created `foodId` back to the `FoodRepository`. The `FoodRepository` then passes the newly created `FoodId` to the UI to inform the user that the food item creation was successful. On the other hand, the other `GetFood` method takes an ID as parameter from the UI and checks whether or not the ID is a valid input. If it is, the `FoodRepository` passes the `FoodId` to the `databasehandler` object, which searches the food in the database and maps it back as a `Food` object. After this, the `Food` object is returned to the view.

*Object Collaboration*

Here, we can see that the `FoodRepository` object needs to use the `Food` object to do its work. This type of relationship is called a **dependency relationship**. We can also use the *uses a* phrase to identify this relationship. The `FoodRepository` uses a `Food` object to save food in the database.

Like `FoodRepository`, the `BeverageRepository` does the same thing for a `Beverage` object: it saves and retrieves beverage objects in the database and UI. Now let's see what the `BeverageRepository` looks like as code:

```
public class Beverage {
    public int? BeverageId {get;set;}
    public string Name { get;set;}
    public decimal Price {get;set;}
}

public class BeverageRepository {
    public int SaveBeverage(Beverage beverage){
        int result = SaveBeverageInDatabase(beverage);
        return result;
    }

    public Beverage GetBeverage(int beverageId) {
        Beverage result = new Beverage();
        result = GetBeverageFromDatabaseById(beverageId);
        return result;
    }
}
```

If you look at the preceding code, you will see that the `BeverageRepository` has two methods: `SaveBeverage` and `GetBeverage`. Both of these methods use the `Beverage` object. This means that the `BeverageRepository` has a dependency relationship with a `Beverage` object.

Now let's take a look at the two classes we have created so far, as shown in the following code:

```
public class FoodRepository {
    public int SaveFood(Food food){
        int result = SaveFoodInDatabase(food);
        return result;
    }

    public Food GetFood(int foodId){
        Food result = new Food();
        result = GetFoodFromDatabaseById(foodId);
        return result;
```

```
        }
    }

    public class BeverageRepository {
        public int SaveBeverage(Beverage beverage){
            int result = SaveBeverageInDatabase(beverage);
            return result;
        }

        public Beverage GetBeverage(int beverageId){
            Beverage result = new Beverage();
            result = GetBeverageFromDatabaseById(beverageId);
            return result;
        }
    }
```

One object can be related to multiple objects using a dependency relationship. In OOP, this type of relationship is very common.

Let's look at another example of dependency relationships. A relationship between a `Programmer` and a `Computer` could be a dependency relationship. How? Well, we know that a `Programmer` is most likely a human and a `Computer` is a machine. A `Programmer` uses a `Computer` to write computer programs, but the `Computer` is not a property of the `Programmer`. A `Programmer` *uses a* computer, and this doesn't have to be one specific computer—it can be any computer. So can we say that a relationship between a `Programmer` and a `Computer` is a type of dependency relationship? Yes, we surely can. Let's see how we can represent this in code:

```
    public class Programmer {
        public string Name { get; set; }
        public string Age { get; set; }
        public List<ProgrammingLanguages> ProgrammingLanguages { get; set; }
        public ProgrammerType Type { get; set; } // Backend/Frontend/Full
    Stack/Web/Mobbile etc

        public bool WorkOnAProject(Project project, Computer computer){
            // use the provided computer to do the project
            // here we can see that the programmer is using a computer
        }
    }

    public class Computer {
        public int Id { get; set; }
        public string ModelNumber { get; set; }
        public Company Manufacturer { get; set; }
        public Ram Ram { get; set; }
```

*Object Collaboration*

```
        public MotherBoard MotherBoard { get; set; }
        public CPU CPU { get; set; }
}
```

In the preceding example, we can clearly see how a `Programmer` and a `Computer` have a dependency relationship, however, this is not always the case: it depends on how you design your objects. If you have designed your `Programmer` class in such a way that each programmer has to have a dedicated computer, you could have used `Computer` as a property in the `Programmer` class, and then the relationship between the programmer and the computer would have changed. Consequently, the relationship depends on how the objects are designed.

My main goal in this section was to clarify the dependency relationship. I hope the nature of dependency relationships is now clear to you.

Now let's see how the dependency relationship is drawn in a **Unified Modeling Language (UML)** diagram, as shown in the following diagram:

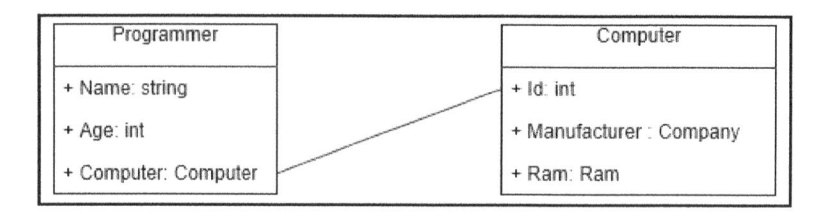

| Programmer | Computer |
|---|---|
| + Name: string | + Id: int |
| + Age: int | + Manufacturer : Company |
| + Computer: Computer | + Ram: Ram |

A solid line is used to represent a dependency relationship.

## Association

Another type of relationship is the association relationship. This type of relationship is unlike the dependency relationship. In this type of relationship, one object knows another object and is associated with it. This relationship is achieved by having one object as a property of another object. In the software community, this relationship type is also referred to as a *has a* relationship. For example, a car has an engine. If you think of any objects that you can relate to each other using the phrase *has a*, then that relationship is an association relationship. In our car example, the engine is a part of the car. Without an engine, the car can't carry out any functions. While the engine itself is a separate object, it is part of the car, and therefore there is an association between the car and the engine.

This association relationship can be divided into the following two categories:

- Aggregation
- Composition

Let's see what these two types of relationship are and how they differ from each other.

# Aggregation

When one object has another object in it as a property and this other object is independent, this is called an **aggregation relationship**. Let's take the example in the previous section and try to see whether this was an aggregation relationship or not.

The previous example looked at the relationship between a car and an engine. We all know that a car must have an engine, and that is why an engine is the property of a car, as shown in the following code:

```
public class Car {
    public Engine Engine { get; set; }
    // Other properties and methods
}
```

Now the question is, what is this type of relationship? The deciding factor is that an engine is a separate object that functions independently of a car. When the manufacturer creates an engine, they don't make it when they are creating the other parts of the car: they can create it separately. Even without a car, an engine can be tested or even used for another purpose. Consequently, we can say that the type of relationship that the car has with the engine is an *aggregation relationship*.

Now let's look at the example of our restaurant management software. If we analyze the relationship between the Food and Chef objects, it is clear that no food can exist without a chef. Someone has to cook, bake, and prepare the food, the food cannot do this itself. Consequently, we can say that the food has a chef. This means that the Food object should have a property named Chef, which will hold the Chef object of that Food. Let's look at the code for this relationship:

```
public class Food {
    public int? FoodId {get;set;}
    public string Name { get; set; }
    public string Price { get; set; }
    public Chef Chef { get; set; }
}
```

[ 73 ]

## Object Collaboration

If we think about the `Beverage` object, every beverage must have a company or maker. For example, commercial beverages are made by companies such as Pepsi Co., Coca Cola Company, and so on. The beverages that these companies produce are their legal property. Beverages can also be made locally, in which case the company name would be the name of the local shop. However, the main idea here is that a beverage must have a manufacturer company. Let's see how the `Beverage` class would look in code:

```
public class Beverage {
    public int? BeverageId {get;set;}
    public string Name { get; set; }
    public string Price { get; set; }
    public Manufacturer Manufacturer { get; set; }
}
```

In both of these examples, the `Chef` and `Manufacturer` objects are objects that are used as the property of `Food` and `Beverage` respectively. We also know that a `Chef` or a `Manufacturer` company is independent. Consequently, the relationship between `Food` and `Chef` is an aggregation relationship. This is also the case for `Beverage` and `Manufacturer`.

To make things clearer, let's look at another example of aggregation. Our computer that we use for programming or for any other task is made up of different components. We have a motherboard, RAM, CPU, graphics card, screen, keyboard, mouse, and many other things. Some components have an aggregation relationship with the computer. For example, the motherboard, RAM, and CPU are internal components that are needed to build a computer. All of these components can exist independently of the computer, and consequently, all of these have aggregation relationships with the computer. Let's look at how the `Computer` class is related to the `MotherBoard` class in the following code:

```
public class Computer {
    public int Id { get; set; }
    public string ModelNumber { get; set; }
    public Company Manufacturer { get; set; }
    public Ram Ram { get; set; }
    public MotherBoard MotherBoard { get; set; }
    public CPU CPU { get; set; }
}

public class Ram {
    // Ram properties and methods
}

public class CPU {
    // CPU properties and methods
}
```

```
public class MotherBoard {
    // MotherBoard properties and methods
}
```

Now, let's see how the aggregation relationship is drawn in a UML diagram. If we try to display the preceding computer class aggregation relationship with the RAM, CPU, and motherboard, then it would look something like the following:

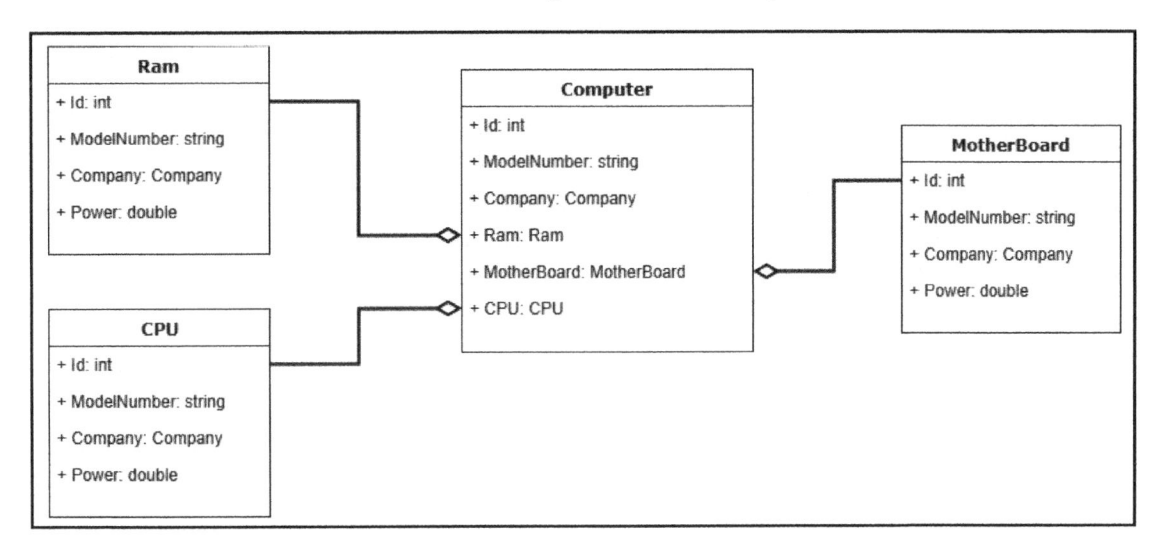

A solid line and a diamond are used to represent an aggregation relationship. The diamond is placed at the side of the class that holds the property, as shown in the following diagram:

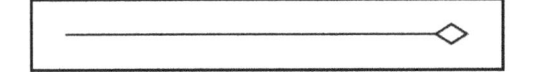

## Composition

A composition relationship is a type of association relationship. This means that one object will have another object as its property, but where it differs from aggregation is that, in composition, the object that is used as a property can't exist independently; it must have the help of another object in order to be functional. If we think about the `Chef` and `Manufacturer` classes, the existence of these classes is not fully dependent on the `Food` and `Beverage` classes. Instead, these classes can exist independently, and therefore have an aggregation relationship.

*Object Collaboration*

However, if we think about the relationship between the `Order` and `OrderItem` objects, we can see that the `OrderItem` object has no meaning without `Order`. Let's look at the following code of the `Order` class:

```
public class Order {
    public int OrderId { get; set; }
    public List<OrderItem> OrderItems { get; set; }
    public DateTime OrderTime { get; set; }
    public Customer Customer { get; set; }
}
```

Here, we can see that the `Order` object has a list of `OrderItems` in it. These `OrderItems` are the `Food` items that the customer has ordered. A customer can order one dish or multiple dishes, which is why the `OrderItems` is a list type. So now it's time to justify our thinking. Does an `OrderItem` really have a composition relationship with `Order`? Are we making any mistakes here? Are we thinking about an aggregation relationship as a composition relationship?

To identify which type of association relationship it is, we have to ask ourselves some questions. Can `OrderItem` exist without `Order`? If not, then why not? It's a separate object! However, if you think a little more deeply, you will realize that no `OrderItem` can exist without an `Order`, as a customer has to order an item, and without an `Order` object, the `OrderItem` object is not trackable. The `OrderItem` item cannot be served to any customer as there is no data for which customer the `OrderItem` is for. Consequently, we can say that the `OrderItem` has a composition relationship with the `Order` object.

Let's look at another example of composition. In our schooling system, we have students, teachers, subjects, and grades, right? Now, I would say that the relationship between a `Subject` object and a `Grade` object is a composition relationship. Let me justify my answer. Take a look at the following code of these two classes:

```
public class Subject {
    public int Id { get; set; }
    public string Name { get; set; }
    public Grade Grade { get; set; }
}

public class Grade {
    public int Id { get; set; }
    public double Mark { get; set; }
    public char GradeSymbol { get; set; } // A, B, C, D, F etc
}
```

Here, we can see that the `Grade` object holds the mark that a student has scored on a test for a particular subject. It also holds the `GradeSymbol`, such as A, B, or F, depending on the marking rules of that school. We can see in the `Subject` class that there is a property called `Grade`. This holds the grade for that particular `Subject` object. If we just think about `Grade` individually rather than in association with the `Subject` class, we will get a bit confused and wonder what subject the grade is for.

Consequently, the relationship between `Grade` and `Subject` is a composition relationship.

Let's look at how we can show a composition relationship in a UML diagram using the preceding example of `Subject` and `Grade`:

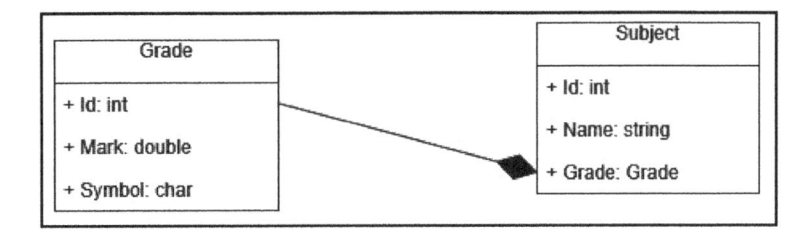

| Grade | | Subject |
|---|---|---|
| + Id: int | | + Id: int |
| + Mark: double | | + Name: string |
| + Symbol: char | | + Grade: Grade |

A solid line and a black diamond are used to represent a composition relationship. The diamond is placed at the side of the class that holds the property:

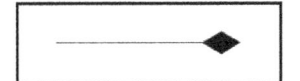

## Inheritance

This is one of the four pillars of OOP. **Inheritance** is when one object inherits or reuses another object's properties or methods. The class that gets inherited is called the **base class** and the class that inherits the base class is normally called the **derived class**. The inheritance relationship can be treated as an *is a relationship*. For example, pasta is a `Food`. The `Pasta` object has a unique ID in the database, which has other properties such as name, price, and chef. So, as `Pasta` satisfies all the attributes of the `Food` class, it can inherit the `Food` class and use the properties of the `Food` class. Let's look at the code:

```
public class Pasta : Food {
    public string Type { get; set; }
    public Sauce Sauce { get; set; }
    public string[] Spices { get; set; }
}
```

*Object Collaboration*

The case is the same for beverages. For example, `Coffee` is a type of beverage that has all the attributes that the `Beverage` object has. A coffee has a name and price, and it might have sugar, milk, and coffee beans. Let's write the `Coffee` class and see how it looks:

```
public class Coffee : Beverage {
    public int Sugar { get; set; }
    public int Milk { get; set; }
    public string LocationOfCoffeeBean { get; set; }
}
```

So here, we can say that `Coffee` is inheriting the `Beverage` class. Here, `Coffee` is the derived class and `Beverage` is the base class.

In an earlier example, we used the `Programmer` object. In that case, do you think that the `Programmer` class can actually inherit the `Human` class? Yes, for sure. A programmer is nobody other than a human in this example. If we look at the properties of a `Programmer` and the properties of a `Human`, we will find that there are some common properties, such as the name, age, and so on. Consequently, we can modify the code of the `Programmer` class to resemble the following:

```
public class Programmer : Human {
 // Name, Age properties can be inherited from Human
 public List<ProgrammingLanguages> ProgrammingLanguages { get; set; }
 public ProgrammerType Type { get; set; } // Backend/Frontend/Full Stack/Web/Mobbile etc

 public bool WorkOnAProject(Project project, Computer computer){
 // use the provided computer to do the project
 // here we can see that the programmer is using a computer
 }
}
```

Now, let's see how we can draw a UML diagram for our `Programmer` class:

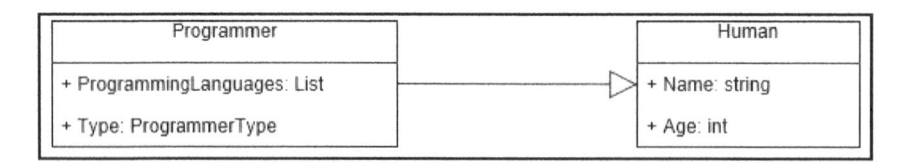

| Programmer | | Human |
|---|---|---|
| + ProgrammingLanguages: List | ──────▷ | + Name: string |
| + Type: ProgrammerType | | + Age: int |

Inheritance is represented by a solid line with a triangle sign attached to it. This triangle points in the direction of the super class:

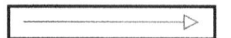

───────▷

# Summary

The object collaboration types that we looked at in this chapter are the most commonly used types in C#. When designing an application or architecting some software, object collaboration is very important. It will define how flexible the software is, how many new functions can be added, and how easy it will be to maintain the code. Object collaboration is very important.

In the next chapter, we will talk about exception handling. This is another very important part of programming.

# 5
# Exception Handling

Let's begin this chapter by looking at two words: exception and handling. In English, the word **exception** refers to something unusual that doesn't usually happen. In programming, the word exception has a similar meaning, but is related to software code. By their nature, computer programs should do only those things that we instruct them to do, and it is considered abnormal when a computer won't or can't follow our instructions. If the computer program fails to follow our instructions, it is classified as an exception in the software world.

**Error** is another word that is heavily used in programming. It is important for us to understand that an error and an exception are not the same thing. An error refers to an incident where the software couldn't even run. More specifically, an error means that the code that is written contains something wrong, and that is why the compiler couldn't compile/build the code. On the other hand, an exception is something that happens at runtime. The easiest way to distinguish between these two concepts is—if the code doesn't compile/build, then there is an error in your code. If the code compiles/builds, but when you run it you get some unusual behavior, then it's an exception.

**Exception handling** means handling/controlling/supervising exceptions that occur while we are running the program. The topics that we are going to explore in this chapter are as follows:

- Why we need exception handling in programming
- Exception handling in C# programming
- The basics of exception handling
- `try` and `catch`
- What happens if you don't handle exceptions
- Multiple `catch` blocks
- What the `throw` keyword is used for

- What the `finally` block does
- Exception classes
- Some common exception classes
- Exception-handling best practices

# Why we need exception handling in programming

Imagine that you have written some code. The code should do what you have instructed it to, right? But for some reason, the software is unable to execute the commands you have given. Maybe the software is facing some issues that make it impossible to run.

For example, let's say that you have instructed the software to read a file, collect data, and store it in a database. However, the software is unable to find the file at the location where the file is supposed to be. There could be many reasons why the file isn't found there: the file may have been deleted by someone or may have been moved to another location. Now, what will your software do? It's not smart enough to handle this situation automatically. If the software is not clear about its work, it will throw an exception. It is our duty as a software developer to tell the software what to do in these kind of situations.

The software will let us know that it is stuck and can't resolve the situation by passing a message. But what should it say to us? *"Help! Help!"* won't be an appropriate message, and this kind of message won't make the developer's life any easier. We need more information about the situation so that we can guide the computer to work accordingly. For that reason, the .NET framework has created some very common exceptions that occur very often in programming. If the problem that the software is facing has a predefined exception, it will throw that. For example, say that there is a program that is trying to divide a number by zero. Mathematically, this is not possible, but the computer has to do it because you have instructed it to do so. Now the computer is in big trouble; it's confused and helpless. It tries to divide the number by zero as you instructed, but then the compiler will stop it and say *"Ask for help, Mr. Program!"*, which means, *"Throw a* `DivideByZeroException` *to your master for help"*. The program will then throw a `DivideByZeroException` and expect some code that the programmer has written to handle it. This is how we will actually know what exceptions we need to handle in the program. This is why we need exceptions in programming.

# Exception handling in C# programming

The .NET framework and C# programming language have developed some powerful ways to handle exceptions. `System.Exceptions` is a class in .NET under the system namespace and has some functionality that will help you to manage exceptions that occur during runtime and prevent your program from crashing. If you don't handle exceptions properly in your code, your software will crash. This is why exception handling is very important in software development.

Now, you might be wondering how you can handle exceptions in your code. An exception is something unexpected. How can you know which exception will occur in your code and cause the program to crash? This is a very good question, and I am sure this question was also asked when language developers were designing the language. That is why they came up with a solution for .NET that has created a very beautiful mechanism to handle exceptions.

# Basics of exception handling

Exception handling in C# is mainly achieved by four keywords: `try`, `catch`, `throw`, and `finally`. Later, we will talk about these keywords in detail. However, just to give you a basic idea of what is meant by those keywords, let's briefly discuss them:

- `try`: When you are not sure of the expected behavior of a piece of code or if there is a possibility of an exception, you should put that code in a `try` block. The `try` block will throw an exception if any exception happens inside the code for that block. If no exception occurs, the `try` block will act like a normal code block. The `try` block is actually designed to throw exceptions, which is its main task.
- `catch`: The `catch` block is executed when an exception is caught. Exceptions thrown by the `try` block will be handled by the following `catch` block. There could be multiple `catch` blocks for a `try` block. Each `catch` block can be dedicated to a particular exception. Consequently, we should write different `catch` blocks for different types of exception.
- `throw`: This is used when you manually want to throw an exception. There could be situations in which you want to do this to control a specific kind of situation.
- `finally`: This is a block of code that will be compulsorily executed. It doesn't matter whether the `try` block threw an exception or not—the `finally` block will be executed. This is mainly used to code some tasks that are essential to handle in any case.

# Try and catch

The `try` and `catch` keywords are the two most important keywords for exception handling in C#. If you write a `try` block without a `catch` block, then it won't make any sense because, if a `try` block throws an exception and there is no `catch` block to handle it, then what is the benefit? The exception will still be unhandled. The `catch` block actually depends on a `try` block. A `catch` block can't exist if there is no `try` block associated with it. Let's look at how we can write a `try-catch` block:

```
try
{
  int a = 5 / 0;
}
catch(DivideByZeroException ex)
{
  Console.WriteLine("You have divided by zero");
}
```

We can also have more `catch` blocks for a `try` block. Let's look at an example of this:

```
try
{
  int a = 5 / 0;
}
catch(DivideByZeroException ex)
{
  Console.WriteLine("You have divided by zero");
}
catch(Exception ex)
{
  Console.WriteLine("Normal exception");
}
```

# What happens if you don't handle exceptions?

Are exceptions really important? Are they worth the time spent handling them when you have tons of complexities in the logic? Yes, they are super important. Let's explore what will happen if you don't take care of exceptions. When an exception is triggered, if no code handles it, the exception goes to the system runtime.

Furthermore, when the system runtime faces an exception, it just terminates the program. So, now you understand why you should handle exceptions. If you fail to do this, your application might break down in the middle of running. I am sure you personally don't like programs that crash while you are using them, so we have to be careful about writing exception-free software. Let's look at an example of what happens during system runtime if the exception is not handled:

```
Using system;

class LearnException {
    public static void Main()
    {
        int[] a = {1,2,3,4};
        for (int i=0; i<10; i++)
        {
            Console.WriteLine(a[i]);
        }
    }
}
```

If we run this code, then the first four times that it is run, it will perform perfectly and print some numbers from one to four. But after that, it will throw an exception of `IndexOutOfRangeException` and the system runtime will terminate the program.

## Multiple catch blocks

It's normal to get different types of exceptions in one `try` block. But how can you handle them? You should not use a general exception to do this. If you throw a general exception instead of throwing a specific exception, you might miss some important information about the exception. For this reason, the C# language introduced multiple `catch` blocks for a `try` block. You can specify one `catch` block that will be called for one type of exception, and you can create other `catch` blocks just after one-by-one with different exception types. When a specific exception is thrown, only that particular `catch` block will be executed if it has a dedicated `catch` block for that kind of exception. Let's look at an example:

```
using System;

class ManyCatchBlocks
{
    public static void Main()
    {
        try
        {
```

*Exception Handling*

```
            var a = 5;
            var b = 0;
            Console.WriteLine("Here we will divide 5 by 0");
            var c = a/b;
        }
        catch(IndexOutOfRangeException ex)
        {
            Console.WriteLine("Index is out of range " + ex);
        }
        catch(DivideByZeroException ex)
        {
            Console.WriteLine("You have divided by zero, which is not correct!");
        }
    }
}
```

If you run the preceding code, you will see that only the second `catch` block is executed. If you open up the console window, you will see that the following line has been printed out:

```
You have divided by zero, which is not correct!
```

So, we can see that if you have multiple `catch` blocks, only the particular `catch` block that matches the type of exception that was thrown will be executed.

Now you might be thinking, *"You said we shouldn't use a general exception handler. But why is that? Yes, we might miss some information but my system isn't crashing! Isn't it better this way?"* Actually, the answer to this question is not straightforward. It may vary from system to system, but let me tell you why you want the system to crash sometimes. Suppose you have a system where you deal with very complex and sensitive data. When an exception happens in such a system, it might be very risky to allow the customer to use the software. The customer could do some serious damage to the data, as the exception was not handled properly. But yes, if you think your system will be fine if you allow the user to continue, even if they got an unknown exception, you can use a general `catch` block. Now let me show you how you can do this. If you want a `catch` block to catch any kind of exception, regardless of the exception type, then your `catch` block should accept the `Exception` class as a parameter, as shown in the following code:

```
using System;

namespace ExceptionCode
{
  class Program
  {
    static void Main(string[] args)
    {
```

```csharp
      try
      {
        var a = 0;
        var b = 5;
        var c = b / a;
      }
      catch (IndexOutOfRangeException ex)
      {
        Console.WriteLine("Index out of range " + ex);
      }
      catch (Exception ex)
      {
        Console.WriteLine("I will catch you exception! You can't hide from me!" + ex);
      }

      Console.WriteLine("Hello");
      Console.ReadKey();
    }
  }
}
```

Alternatively, you can also pass a `no` parameter to the `catch` block. This will also catch every kind of exception and execute the code in the body. An example of this is given in the following code:

```csharp
using System;

namespace ExceptionCode
{
  class Program
  {
    static void Main(string[] args)
    {
      try
      {
        var a = 0;
        var b = 5;
        var c = b / a;
      }
      catch (IndexOutOfRangeException ex)
      {
        Console.WriteLine("Index out of range " + ex);
      }
      catch
      {
        Console.WriteLine("I will catch you exception! You can't hide from me!");
```

```
            }
        Console.WriteLine("Hello");
        Console.ReadKey();
        }
    }
}
```

However, keep in mind that this has to be the last `catch` block, otherwise, there will be a runtime error.

## Using the throw keyword

Sometimes, in your own program, you have to create exceptions by yourself. No, not to take revenge on the user, but for the sake of your application. Sometimes, there are situations where you need to throw an exception to bypass a difficulty, to log something, or just redirect the flow of the software. Don't worry: by doing this you are not becoming the bad guy; you are actually the hero who is saving the program from trouble. But how can you create an exception? To do that, C# has a keyword called `throw`. This keyword will help you to create an instance of a type of exception and throw it. Let me show you an example of the `throw` keyword:

```
using System;

namespace ExceptionCode
{
 class Program
  {
  public static void Main(string[] args)
  {
  try
  {
  Console.WriteLine("You are the boss!");
  throw new DivideByZeroException();
  }
  catch (IndexOutOfRangeException ex)
  {
  Console.WriteLine("Index out of range " + ex);
  }
  catch (DivideByZeroException ex)
  {
  Console.WriteLine("Divide by zero " + ex);
  }
  catch
  {
```

```
        Console.WriteLine("I will catch you exception! You can't hide from me!");
    }

    Console.WriteLine("See, i told you!");
    Console.ReadKey();
    }
  }
}
```

The output is as follows:

```
You are the boss!
Divide by zero System.DivideByZeroException: Attempted to divide by zero.
   at ExceptionCode.Program.Main(String[] args) in C:\Users\TaherR\code\hello\ExceptionCode\ExceptionCode\Program.cs:line 12
See, i told you!
```

You can see that, if you run the preceding code, you will get the `DivideByZeroException` catch block executed.

So, if you want to throw an exception (because you want the upper-layer catch block to handle it, for example), you simply throw a new instance of an exception. This could be any kind of exception, including a system exception or a self-created exception. Just keep in mind that there is a catch block that will handle it.

# What does the finally block do?

When we say "finally", we mean something that we were waiting for or something that is going to conclude the process. This is almost the same in exception handling. A finally block is a block of code that will be executed no matter what happens in the try or catch block. It doesn't matter what types of exception were thrown or whether or not they were handled, the finally block will be executed. Now you may ask, *"Why do we need this finally block? If there is any exception in our program, we will handle it with the catch block! Can't we write the code inside the catch block instead of the finally block?"*

Yes, you can, but what happens if an exception was thrown but the catch block wasn't triggered? This would mean that the code inside the catch block will not get executed. For this reason, the finally block is important. It doesn't matter whether or not there was any exception; the finally block will run. Let me show you an example of the finally block:

```
using System;

namespace ExceptionCode
{
```

## Exception Handling

```
class Program
{
static void Main(string[] args)
{
try
{
int a = 0;
int b = 5;
int c = b / a;
}
catch (IndexOutOfRangeException ex)
{
Console.WriteLine("Index out of range " + ex);
}
catch (DivideByZeroException ex)
{
Console.WriteLine("Divide by zero " + ex);
}
catch
{
Console.WriteLine("I will catch you exception! You can't hide from me!");
}
finally
{
Console.WriteLine("I am the finally block i will run by hook or by crook!");
}
Console.ReadLine();
}
}
}
```

The output is as follows:

```
Divide by zero System.DivideByZeroException: Attempted to divide by zero.
   at ExceptionCode.Program.Main(String[] args) in C:\Users\TaherR\code\hello\ExceptionCode\ExceptionCode\Program.cs:line 13
I am the finally block i will run by hook or by crook!
```

An important use case of the `finally` block could be when you open a database connection in the `try` block! You have to close this, otherwise, that connection will be open for the rest of the program and it will use a lot of resources. In addition, there are a limited number of connections a database can make, so if you open one and don't close it, that connection string is wasted. The best practice is to close the connection as soon as your work with it is complete.

The `finally` block plays the best role here. It doesn't matter what will happen in the `try` block, the `finally` block will close the connection, as shown in the following code:

```
using System;

namespace ExceptionCode
{
  class Program
  {
    static void Main(string[] args)
    {
      try
      {
        // Step 1: Established database connection

        // Step 2: Do some activity in database
      }
      catch (IndexOutOfRangeException ex)
      {
        // Handle IndexOutOfRangeExceptions here
      }
      catch (DivideByZeroException ex)
      {
        // Handle DivideByZeroException here
      }
      catch
      {
        // Handle All other exception here
      }
      finally
      {
        // Close the database connection
      }
    }
  }
}
```

Here, we are performing two main tasks in the `try` block. First, we open a database connection, and secondly, we perform some activity in the database. Now, if any exception happens while we do any of this, an exception will be thrown that will be handled by a `catch` block. At the very end, the `finally` block will close the database connection.

The `finally` block is not something that you must have to have to handle exceptions, but you should use it if you need it.

*Exception Handling*

# Exception class

An `exception` is simply a class in C#. This has a few properties and methods. The four most commonly used properties are as follows:

| Property | Description |
| --- | --- |
| `Message` | This contains what the exception is about. |
| `StackTrace` | This contains the method call-stack information. |
| `TargetSite` | This gives an object that contains the method where the exception happened. |
| `InnerException` | This gives the instance of the exception that caused the exception. |

Exception class properties and methods

One of the most popular methods in this class is `ToString()`. This method returns a string that contains information about the exception. The exception is easier to read and understand when it is represented in string format.

Let's look at an example of using these properties and methods:

```
using System;

namespace ExceptionCode
{
 class Program
 {
 static void Main(string[] args)
 {
 try
 {
 var a = 0;
 var b = 5;
 var c = b / a;
 }
 catch (DivideByZeroException ex)
 {
 Console.WriteLine("Message:");
 Console.WriteLine(ex.Message);
 Console.WriteLine("Stack Trace:");
 Console.WriteLine(ex.StackTrace);
 Console.WriteLine("String:");
 Console.WriteLine(ex.ToString());
 }

 Console.ReadKey();
 }
```

        }
    }

The output is as follows:

```
Message:
Attempted to divide by zero.
Stack Trace:
    at ExceptionCode.Program.Main(String[] args) in C:\Users\TaherR\code\hello\ExceptionCode\ExceptionCode\Program.cs:line 13
String:
System.DivideByZeroException: Attempted to divide by zero.
    at ExceptionCode.Program.Main(String[] args) in C:\Users\TaherR\code\hello\ExceptionCode\ExceptionCode\Program.cs:line 13
```

Here, we can see that the `message` property of the exception holds the information `Attempted to divide by zero`. In addition, the `ToString()` method gives a lot of information about the exception. These properties and methods will help you a lot when handling exceptions in your program.

## Some common exception classes

There are many exception classes available in .NET Framework. The .NET Framework team created these to make the developer's life easier. The .NET Framework provides specific information about the exceptions. The following are some of the most common exception classes:

| Exception Class | Description |
| --- | --- |
| `DivideByZeroException` | This exception is thrown when any number is divided by zero. |
| `IndexOutOfRangeException` | This exception is thrown when the application tries to use an index of an array that doesn't exist. |
| `InvalidCastException` | This exception is thrown when trying to perform invalid casting. |
| `NullReferenceException` | This exception is thrown when trying to use or access a null reference type. |

Different exception classes of .NET framework

Let's look at an example in which one of these exception classes is used. In this example, we are using the `IndexOutOfRange` exception class:

```
using System;

namespace ExceptionCode
{
  class Program
```

*Exception Handling*

```
{
static void Main(string[] args)
{
int[] a = new int[] {1,2,3};

try
{
Console.WriteLine(a[5]);
}
catch (IndexOutOfRangeException ex)
{
Console.WriteLine("Message:");
Console.WriteLine(ex.Message);
Console.WriteLine("Stack Trace:");
Console.WriteLine(ex.StackTrace);
Console.WriteLine("String:");
Console.WriteLine(ex.ToString());
}

Console.ReadKey();
}
}
}
```

The output is as follows:

```
Message:
Index was outside the bounds of the array.
Stack Trace:
   at ExceptionCode.Program.Main(String[] args) in C:\Users\TaherR\code\hello\ExceptionCode\ExceptionCode\Program.cs:lin
e 13
String:
System.IndexOutOfRangeException: Index was outside the bounds of the array.
   at ExceptionCode.Program.Main(String[] args) in C:\Users\TaherR\code\hello\ExceptionCode\ExceptionCode\Program.cs:lin
e 13
```

## User-defined exceptions

Sometimes, you'll encounter a situation where you might think that the predefined exceptions do not satisfy your condition. In this instance, you might wish there was a way to create your own exception classes and use them. Thankfully, in C#, there is actually a mechanism where you can create your own custom exceptions, and can write whatever message is appropriate for that kind of exception. Let's look at an example of how to create and use custom exceptions:

```
using System;
```

```
namespace ExceptionCode
{
  class HelloException : Exception
  {
  public HelloException() { }
  public HelloException(string message) : base(message) { }
  public HelloException(string message, Exception inner) : base(message,
inner) { }
  }

  class Program
  {
  static void Main(string[] args)
  {
  try
  {
  throw new HelloException("Hello is an exception!");
  }
  catch (HelloException ex)
  {
  Console.WriteLine("Exception Message:");
  Console.WriteLine(ex.Message);
  }

  Console.ReadKey();
  }
  }
}
```

The output is as follows:

```
Exception Message:
Hello is an exception!
```

So, we can see from the preceding example that you just have to create a class that will extend the `Exception` class. This class should have three constructors: one shouldn't take any parameter, one should take a string and pass it to the base, and one should take a string and an exception and pass it to the base.

Using a custom exception is like using any other built-in exception provided by .NET Framework.

# The exception filter

The exception filter feature isn't very old at the time of writing—it was introduced in C# 6. The main benefit of this is that you can catch more specific exceptions in a block. Let's look at an example:

```csharp
using System;

namespace ExceptionCode
{
 class Program
 {
 static void Main(string[] args)
 {

 int[] a = new int[] {1,2,3};

 try
 {
 Console.WriteLine(a[5]);
 }
 catch (IndexOutOfRangeException ex) when (ex.Message == "Test Message")
 {
 Console.WriteLine("Message:");
 Console.WriteLine("Test Message");
 }
 catch (IndexOutOfRangeException ex) when (ex.Message == "Index was outside the bounds of the array.")
 {
 Console.WriteLine("Message:");
 Console.WriteLine(ex.Message);
 Console.WriteLine("Stack Trace:");
 Console.WriteLine(ex.StackTrace);
 Console.WriteLine("String:");
 Console.WriteLine(ex.ToString());
 }

 Console.ReadKey();
 }
 }
}
```

The output is as follows:

```
Message:
Index was outside the bounds of the array.
Stack Trace:
    at ExceptionCode.Program.Main(String[] args) in C:\Users\TaherR\code\hello\ExceptionCode\ExceptionCode\Program.cs:line 14
String:
System.IndexOutOfRangeException: Index was outside the bounds of the array.
    at ExceptionCode.Program.Main(String[] args) in C:\Users\TaherR\code\hello\ExceptionCode\ExceptionCode\Program.cs:line 14
```

To filter out exceptions, you have to use the `when` keyword just next to the `catch` declaration line. So first, when any exception is thrown, it will check what type of exception it is and then check the condition provided after the `when` keyword. In our example, the exception type is `IndexOutOfRangeException` and the condition is `ex.Message == "Index was outside the bounds of the array."`. We can see that, when the code ran, only that particular `catch` block was executed, which fulfilled all the conditions.

# Exception handling best practices

As you can see, there are different ways in which you can handle exceptions: sometimes you can throw exceptions, sometimes you can use the `finally` block, and sometimes you can use multiple `catch` blocks. Consequently, there is a chance that you can get confused at the beginning if you don't have enough experience with exception handling. But thanks to the C# community, there are some best practices for exception handling. Let's have a look at some of them:

- Use a `finally` block to close/clean up dependent resources that could cause a problem in the future.
- Catch the specific exception and handle it properly. Use multiple `catch` blocks if needed.
- Create your own exceptions if needed and use them.
- Handle exceptions as soon as possible.
- Don't use a general exception handler if you can handle an exception using a specific handler.
- The exception messages should be very clear.

## Summary

We all dream of a perfect world where there are no errors or unexpected situations, but in reality, this is impossible. Software development is also not free from errors and exceptions. Software developers don't want their software to break down, but unexpected exceptions happen every now and then. Consequently, handling these exceptions is necessary for developing awesome software. In this chapter, we familiarized ourselves with what an exception is in software development. We have also learned how to handle exceptions, why we need to handle exceptions, how to create custom exceptions, and many other important topics. When implementing exception handling in your application, try to follow best practices so that you get an application that runs smoothly.

# 6
# Events and Delegates

Events and delegates may seem like complex programming topics, but actually, they are not. In this chapter, we will first learn about these concepts by analyzing the meaning of their respective names. Then we will relate the general meaning of these words to programming. We will look at a lot of example code in this chapter, which will help us understand the concepts with ease. Before we dive into this, let's look at the topics that we are going to cover in this chapter:

- How to create and use delegates
- Method group conversion
- Multicasting
- Covariance and contravariance
- Events and multicast events
- .NET event guidelines

## What is a delegate?

A **delegate** is a proxy, an alternative, or a representative of someone else. For example, we may read in the newspaper that a delegate from another country is coming to our country to meet a high official. This person is a delegate because they have come to our country to represent their own country. They could be a representative for the president, prime minister, or any other high official of that country. Let's imagine that the delegate is representing the president of a country. Maybe the president was unable to attend this meeting in person for some reason, and that is why a delegate was sent on their behalf. This delegate will do the same work that the president was supposed to do on the trip and make decisions on behalf of the president. The delegate is not a fixed individual; could be any qualified person that the president chooses.

*Events and Delegates*

The concept of a delegate is similar in software development. We can have a functionality where a method doesn't do the actual work that it was ask to do, but rather, it will call another method to execute that work. Furthermore, in programming, the method that doesn't do the actual work, but passes it to another method, is called a **delegate**. Consequently, a delegate will actually hold a reference of a method. When the delegate is called, the referenced method will actually be called and executed.

Now, you may ask, *"Why should I call a delegate if it is going to call another method? Why don't I just call the method directly?"* Well, we do this because if you directly call the method, you lose your flexibility by making your code coupled. You are hard coding the method name in your code so that, whenever that line of code will run, that method will be executed. However, with a delegate, you can decide which method to call at runtime instead of compile time.

## How to create and use delegates

To create a delegate, we need to use the `delegate` keyword. Let me show you how to declare a delegate in a general form:

```
delegate returnType delegateName(parameters)
```

Now let me show you some real example code:

```
using System;

namespace Delegate1
{
  delegate int MathFunc(int a, int b);

  class Program
  {
    static void Main(string[] args)
    {
      MathFunc mf = new MathFunc(add);

      Console.WriteLine("add");
      Console.WriteLine(mf(4, 5));

      mf = new MathFunc(sub);

      Console.WriteLine("sub");
      Console.WriteLine(mf(4, 5));

      Console.ReadKey();
    }
```

```
    public static int add(int a, int b)
    {
      return a + b;
    }

    public static int sub(int a, int b)
    {
      return (a > b) ? (a - b) : (b - a);
    }
  }
}
```

The output of the preceding code will be as follows:

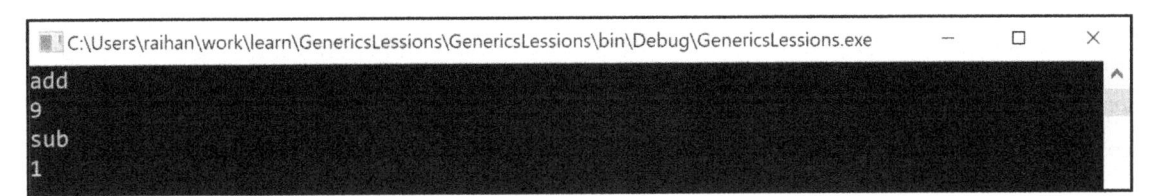

```
add
9
sub
1
```

Let's now discuss the preceding code. At the very top, inside the namespace, we can see the declaration of the delegate, as shown in the following code:

```
delegate int MathFunc(int a, int b);
```

We used the `delegate` keyword to let the compiler know that we are declaring a `delegate`. Then we set the return type to `int` and named the delegate `MathFunc`. We also passed two `int` type parameters in this delegate.

After that, the `program` class gets started, and in that class, we have two methods in addition to the main method. One is `add` and the other is `sub`. If you pay close attention to these methods, you will see that they have the same signature as the delegate. This is done deliberately, because a method can use a `delegate` when the method has the same signature as the `delegate`.

Now, if we look at the main method, we will find the following interesting code:

```
MathFunc mf = new MathFunc(add);
```

*Events and Delegates*

In this first line of the main method, we create an object of the delegate. While doing this, we pass the `add` method in the constructor. This is required, as you need to pass a method for which you want to use the delegate. Then we can see that, when we call the delegate `mf(4,5)`, it returns 9. This means that it is actually calling the `add` method. After that, we assign `sub` to the `delegate`. Upon calling the `mf(4,5)`, this time we get 1. This means that the `sub` method was called. In this way, a `delegate` can be used for many methods that have the same signature.

## Method group conversion

In the last example, we saw how we can create an object of a delegate and pass the method name in the constructor. Now we will look at another way of achieving the same thing, but in an easier way. This is called **method group conversion**. Here, you don't need to initialize the `delegate` object, but you can directly assign the method to it. Let me show you an example:

```
using System;

namespace Delegate1
{
 delegate int MathFunc(int a, int b);

 class Program
 {
 static void Main(string[] args)
 {
 MathFunc mf = add;

 Console.WriteLine("add");
 Console.WriteLine(mf(4, 5));

 mf = sub;

 Console.WriteLine("sub");
 Console.WriteLine(mf(4, 5));
 Console.ReadKey();
 }

 public static int add(int a, int b)
 {
 return a + b;
 }

 public static int sub(int a, int b)
```

```
        {
            return (a > b) ? (a - b) : (b - a);
        }
    }
}
```

Here, we can see that instead of passing the method name in the constructor, we directly assign the method to it. This is a quick way of assigning a delegate in C#.

# Using the static and instance methods as delegates

In the previous examples, we used static methods in our delegates. However, you can also use instance methods in delegates. Let's look at an example:

```
using System;

namespace Delegate1
{
    delegate int MathFunc(int a, int b);

    class Program
    {
        static void Main(string[] args)
        {
            MyMath mc = new MyMath();

            MathFunc mf = mc.add;

            Console.WriteLine("add");
            Console.WriteLine(mf(4, 5));

            mf = mc.sub;

            Console.WriteLine("sub");
            Console.WriteLine(mf(4, 5));

            Console.ReadKey();
        }
    }
    class MyMath
    {
        public int add(int a, int b)
        {
            return a + b;
```

*Events and Delegates*

```
    }

    public int sub(int a, int b)
    {
      return (a > b) ? (a - b) : (b - a);
    }
  }
}
```

In the preceding example, we can see that we have instance methods under the `MyMath` class. To use those methods in delegates, we first have to create an object of that class and simply assign the methods to a delegate using the object instance.

## Multicasting

**Multicasting** is an excellent feature of delegates. With multicasting, you can assign more than one method to a delegate. When that delegate is executed, it runs all the methods that were assigned one after another. Using the + or += operator, you can add methods to a delegate. There is also a way to remove added methods from the delegate. To do this, you have to use the - or -= operator. Let's look at an example to understand clearly what multicasting is:

```
using System;

namespace MyDelegate
{
  delegate void MathFunc(ref int a);

  class Program
  {
    static void Main(string[] args)
    {
      MathFunc mf;
      int number = 10;
      MathFunc myAdd = MyMath.add5;
      MathFunc mySub = MyMath.sub3;

      mf = myAdd;
      mf += mySub;

      mf(ref number);

      Console.WriteLine($"Final number: {number}");

      Console.ReadKey();
```

```
        }
    }

    class MyMath
    {
        public static void add5(ref int a)
        {
            a = a + 5;
            Console.WriteLine($"After adding 5 the answer is {a}");
        }

        public static void sub3(ref int a)
        {
            a = a - 3;
            Console.WriteLine($"After subtracting 3 the answer is {a}");
        }
    }
}
```

The preceding code will give the following output:

```
After adding 5 the answer is 15
After subtracting 3 the answer is 12
Final number: 12
```

Here, we can see how our delegate executed the two methods one after the other. We have to keep in mind that it works like a queue, so the first method you add will be the first method to get executed. Now let's see how we can remove a method from a delegate:

```
using System;

namespace MyDelegate
{
    delegate void MathFunc(ref int a);

    class Program
    {
        static void Main(string[] args)
        {
            MathFunc mf;
            MathFunc myAdd = MyMath.add5;
            MathFunc mySub = MyMath.sub3;
            MathFunc myMul = MyMath.mul10;
```

## Events and Delegates

```
        mf = myAdd;
        mf += mySub;
        int number = 10;

        mf(ref number);

        mf -= mySub;
        mf += myMul;
        number = 10;

        mf(ref number);

        Console.WriteLine($"Final number: {number}");

        Console.ReadKey();
      }
    }

    class MyMath
    {
      public static void add5(ref int a)
      {
        a = a + 5;
        Console.WriteLine($"After adding 5 the answer is {a}");
      }

      public static void sub3(ref int a)
      {
        a = a - 3;
        Console.WriteLine($"After subtracting 3 the answer is {a}");
      }

      public static void mul10(ref int a)
      {
        a = a * 10;
        Console.WriteLine($"After multiplying 10 the answer is {a}");
      }
    }
}
```

The preceding code will give us the following output:

```
After adding 5 the answer is 15
After subtracting 3 the answer is 12
After adding 5 the answer is 15
After multiplying 10 the answer is 150
Final number: 150
```

Here, we have firstly added two methods to the delegate. Then, we removed the `sub3` method and added the `mul10` method. After making all these changes when we executed the delegate, we saw that `5` was added to the number, then `10` was multiplied by the number. No subtraction took place.

## Covariance and contravariance

There are two important delegate features. What we have learned so far is that normally, to register a method in a delegate, the method has to match the signature of the delegate. This means that the return type and the parameters of the method and the delegate have to be the same. However, with the use of the concepts of covariance and contravariance, you can actually register methods to a delegate that don't have the same return types or parameters. The delegate will then be able to execute them when called.

**Covariance** is when you assign a method to a delegate that has a return type that is a derived type of the delegate's return type. For example, if class B is derived from class A, and if the delegate returns class A, then a method can be registered to the delegate that returns class B. Let's look at the example in the following code:

```
using System;

namespace EventsAndDelegates
{
 public delegate A DoSomething();

 public class A
 {
 public int value { get; set; }
 }

 public class B : A {}
```

[ 107 ]

```
public class Program
{
public static A WorkA()
{
A a = new A();
a.value = 1;
return a;
}

public static B WorkB()
{
B b = new B();
b.value = 2;
return b;
}

public static void Main(string[] args)
{
A someA = new A();

DoSomething something = WorkB;

someA = something();

Console.WriteLine("The value is " + someA.value);

Console.ReadLine();
}
}
}
```

The output of the preceding code will be as follows:

```
The value is 2
```

On the other hand, **contravariance** is when a method is passed to a delegate and the parameters of the method don't match the parameters of the delegate. Here, we have to keep in mind that the parameter type of the method has to be at least derived from the parameter type of the delegate. Let's look at an example of contravariance:

```
using System;

namespace EventsAndDelegates
```

The preceding code will give us the following output:

```
After adding 5 the answer is 15
After subtracting 3 the answer is 12
After adding 5 the answer is 15
After multiplying 10 the answer is 150
Final number: 150
```

Here, we have firstly added two methods to the delegate. Then, we removed the `sub3` method and added the `mul10` method. After making all these changes when we executed the delegate, we saw that 5 was added to the number, then 10 was multiplied by the number. No subtraction took place.

# Covariance and contravariance

There are two important delegate features. What we have learned so far is that normally, to register a method in a delegate, the method has to match the signature of the delegate. This means that the return type and the parameters of the method and the delegate have to be the same. However, with the use of the concepts of covariance and contravariance, you can actually register methods to a delegate that don't have the same return types or parameters. The delegate will then be able to execute them when called.

**Covariance** is when you assign a method to a delegate that has a return type that is a derived type of the delegate's return type. For example, if class B is derived from class A, and if the delegate returns class A, then a method can be registered to the delegate that returns class B. Let's look at the example in the following code:

```
using System;

namespace EventsAndDelegates
{
 public delegate A DoSomething();

 public class A
 {
 public int value { get; set; }
 }

 public class B : A {}
```

```
public class Program
{
public static A WorkA()
{
A a = new A();
a.value = 1;
return a;
}

public static B WorkB()
{
B b = new B();
b.value = 2;
return b;
}

public static void Main(string[] args)
{
A someA = new A();

DoSomething something = WorkB;

someA = something();

Console.WriteLine("The value is " + someA.value);

Console.ReadLine();
}
}
}
```

The output of the preceding code will be as follows:

```
The value is 2
```

On the other hand, **contravariance** is when a method is passed to a delegate and the parameters of the method don't match the parameters of the delegate. Here, we have to keep in mind that the parameter type of the method has to be at least derived from the parameter type of the delegate. Let's look at an example of contravariance:

```
using System;

namespace EventsAndDelegates
```

```
{
 public delegate int DoSomething(B b);

 public class A
 {
 public int value = 5;
 }

 public class B : A {}

 public class Program
 {
 public static int WorkA(A a)
 {
 Console.WriteLine("Method WorkA called: ");
 return a.value * 5;
 }

 public static int WorkB(B b)
 {
 Console.WriteLine("Method WorkB called: ");
 return b.value * 10;
 }

 public static void Main(string[] args)
 {
 B someB = new B();

 DoSomething something = WorkA;

 int result = something(someB);

 Console.WriteLine("The value is " + result);

 Console.ReadLine();
 }
 }
}
```

The preceding code will give the following output:

```
Method WorkA called:
The value is 25
```

Here, we can see that the delegate takes type B as a parameter. However, when the `WorkA` method had been registered as a method in the delegate, it didn't give any error or warning, even though the parameter that `WorkA` method takes is type A. The reason why it works is because type B is derived from type A.

# Events

You can think of an **event** as a kind of method that gets executed in some circumstances and notifies handlers or delegates about that incident. For example, when you sign up for an email newsletter, you get emails from the website about the latest articles, blog posts, or news that are posted. These emails could be daily, weekly, monthly, yearly, or according to some other specified period of time that you have chosen. These emails are not sent by a human being manually, but by an automatic system/software. This automatic email sender can be developed using events. Now, you might think, why do I need an event for this, can't I send an email to the subscriber by a normal method? Yes, you can. However, suppose that in the near future, you also want to introduce a feature where you will be notified on the mobile app. You'd have to change the code and add the functionality for that. A few days after that, if you want to further extend your system and send an SMS to specific subscribers, you have to change the code again. Not only that, but the code you write to achieve this will be very strongly coupled if you write it using normal methods. You can solve these kinds of problem using `event`. You can also create different event handlers and assign those event handlers to an event so that, whenever that event gets fired, it will notify all the registered handlers that will perform their work. Let's now look at an example to make this a little clearer:

```
using System;

namespace EventsAndDelegates
{
    public delegate void GetResult();

    public class ResultPublishEvent
    {
        public event GetResult PublishResult;

        public void PublishResultNow()
        {
            if (PublishResult != null)
            {
                Console.WriteLine("We are publishing the results now!");
                Console.WriteLine("");
                PublishResult();
```

```
      }
    }
  }

  public class EmailEventHandler
  {
    public void SendEmail()
    {
      Console.WriteLine("Results have been emailed successfully!");
    }
  }

  public class Program
  {
    public static void Main(string[] args)
    {
      ResultPublishEvent e = new ResultPublishEvent();

      EmailEventHandler email = new EmailEventHandler();

      e.PublishResult += email.SendEmail;
      e.PublishResultNow();

      Console.ReadLine();
    }
  }
}
```

The output of the preceding code is as follows:

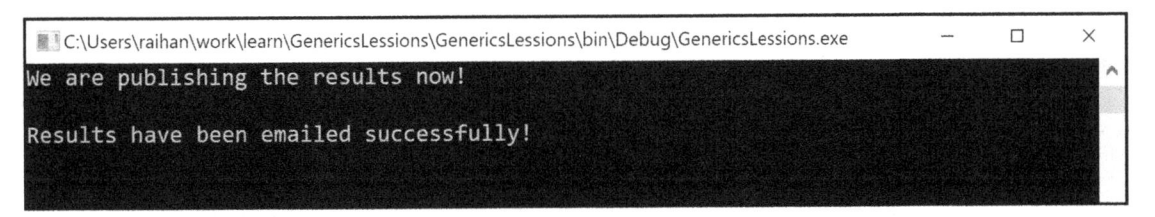

```
We are publishing the results now!

Results have been emailed successfully!
```

In the preceding code, we can see that, when the PublishResultNow() method gets called, it basically fires the PublishResult event. Furthermore, the SendMail() method that did subscribe to the event gets executed and prints Results have been emailed successfully! on the console.

# Multicasting events

You can multicast in an event in the same way that you can in a delegate. This means that you can register multiple event handlers (methods that have subscribed to the event) to an event and all of them will be executed one by one when the event gets fired. To multicast, you have to use the += sign to register event handlers to the event. You can also remove event handlers from the event by using the -= operator. When you apply multicast, the first event handler that was registered will get executed first, then the second, and so on. By multicasting, you can easily extend or reduce event handlers in your application without doing much work. Let's look at an example of multicasting:

```
using System;

namespace EventsAndDelegates
{
 public delegate void GetResult();

 public class ResultPublishEvent
 {
 public event GetResult PublishResult;

 public void PublishResultNow()
 {
 if (PublishResult != null)
 {
 Console.WriteLine("");
 Console.WriteLine("We are publishing the results now!");
 Console.WriteLine("");
 PublishResult();
 }
 }
 }

 public class EmailEventHandler
 {
 public void SendEmail()
 {
 Console.WriteLine("Results have been emailed successfully!");
 }
 }

 public class SmsEventHandler
 {
 public void SmsSender()
 {
 Console.WriteLine("Results have been messaged successfully!");
```

```
        }
    }

    public class Program
    {
        public static void Main(string[] args)
        {
            ResultPublishEvent e = new ResultPublishEvent();

            EmailEventHandler email = new EmailEventHandler();
            SmsEventHandler sms = new SmsEventHandler();

            e.PublishResult += email.SendEmail;
            e.PublishResult += sms.SmsSender;
            e.PublishResultNow();

            e.PublishResult -= sms.SmsSender;

            e.PublishResultNow();

            Console.ReadLine();
        }
    }
}
```

The following is the output of the preceding code:

```
C:\Users\raihan\work\learn\GenericsLessions\GenericsLessions\bin\Debug\GenericsLessions.exe

We are publishing the results now!

Results have been emailed successfully!
Results have been messaged successfully!

We are publishing the results now!

Results have been emailed successfully!
```

Now if we analyze the preceding code, we can see that we have created another class, SmsEventHandler, and this class has a method called SmsSender, which follows the same signature as our delegate GetResult, as shown in the following code:

```
public class SmsEventHandler
{
    public void SmsSender()
```

```
    {
      Console.WriteLine("Results have been messaged successfully!");
    }
}
```

Then, in the main method, we create an instance of this `SmsEventHandler` class and register the `SmsSender` method to the event, as shown in the following code:

```
e.PublishResult += sms.SmsSender;
```

After firing the event once, we remove the `SmsSender` event handler from the event using the `-=` operator, as follows:

```
e.PublishResult -= sms.SmsSender;
```

When we fire the event again, we can see in the output that only the email event handler was executed.

## Event guidelines from .NET

For better stability, .NET Framework has provided some guidelines for using events in C#. It's not that you absolutely must follow these guidelines, but following these guidelines will certainly make your program more productive. Now let's see what guidelines we need to follow.

An event should take the following two parameters:

- The reference to the object that generated the event
- The type of `EventArgs` that will hold other important information needed by the event handlers

The general form of the code should be as follows:

```
void eventHandler(object sender, EventArgs e)
{
}
```

Let's look at an example that follows these guidelines:

```
using System;

namespace EventsAndDelegates
{
  class MyEventArgs : EventArgs
  {
```

```
    public int number;
}

delegate void MyEventHandler(object sender, MyEventArgs e);

class MyEvent
{
  public static int counter = 0;

  public event MyEventHandler SomeEvent;

  public void GetSomeEvent()
  {
    MyEventArgs a = new MyEventArgs();

    if (SomeEvent != null)
    {
      a.number = counter++;
      SomeEvent(this, a);
    }
  }

}

class X
{
  public void Handler(object sender, MyEventArgs e)
  {
    Console.WriteLine("Event number: " + e.number);
    Console.WriteLine("Source Object: " + sender);
    Console.WriteLine();
  }
}

public class Program
{
  public static void Main(string[] args)
  {
    X x = new X();

    MyEvent myEvent = new MyEvent();

    myEvent.SomeEvent += x.Handler;

    myEvent.GetSomeEvent();
    myEvent.GetSomeEvent();

    Console.ReadLine();
```

```
        }
    }
}
```

The output of the preceding code is as follows:

```
Event number: 0
Source Object: EventsAndDelegates.MyEvent

Event number: 1
Source Object: EventsAndDelegates.MyEvent
```

If we analyze the preceding code, we will see that we have passed the counter value using the `EventArgs` parameter, and the reference of the object using the `object` parameter.

# Summary

In this chapter, we learned about delegates and events. These topics are very important in software development as they provide the functionality to automate code over a particular occasion. These concepts are both heavily used in the field of web development.

In the next chapter, we will look into generics and collections in C#. These are very interesting features of the C# programming language that you can use to write generic delegates in your programs.

# 7
# Generics in C#

Generics is a very important topic in the C# programming language. As far as I know, it would be hard to find any modern software written in C# that doesn't use generics.

The topics we will cover in this chapter are as follows:

- What are generics?
- Why do we need generics?
- Different constraints of generics
- Generic methods
- Covariance and Contravariance in generics

## What are generics?

In C#, generics are used to create classes, methods, structs and other components that are not specific, but general. This allows us to use the generic component for different reasons. For example, if you have a general-purpose soap, you can use that soap for any kind of washing. You can use it to wash your hands, to wash your clothes, or even to wash your dirty dishes. However, if you have a specific category of soap, such as laundry detergent, it can only be used for washing clothes and not for any other thing. Consequently, generics give us some extra power of re-usability in our code, which is good for an application as there would be less code which does similar work. Generics are not newly developed; they has been available since C# 2. So, with so many years of usage, generics have become commonly used by programmers.

# Generics in C#

Let's take a look at an example of a Generic class:

```csharp
using System;
using System.Collections.Generic;
using System.Linq;
using System.Text;
using System.Threading.Tasks;

namespace Chapter7
{
  class Price<T>
  {
    T ob;

    public Price(T o)
    {
      ob = o;
    }

    public void PrintType()
    {
      Console.WriteLine("The type is " + typeof(T));
    }

    public T GetPrice()
    {
      return ob;
    }
  }

  class Code_7_1
  {
    static void Main(string[] args)
    {
      Price<int> price = new Price<int>(55);

      price.PrintType();

      int a = price.GetPrice();

      Console.WriteLine("The price is " + a);

      Console.ReadKey();
    }
  }
}
```

The output of the preceding code is as follows:

```
C:\Users\raihan\work\learn\GenericsLessions\GenericsLessions\bin\Debug\GenericsLessions.exe
The type is System.Int32
The price is 55
```

If you are totally new to the syntax of generics, you might be surprised to see the angle brackets, <>, next to the Price class. You also might be wondering what the T inside <> is. This is the syntax of generics in C#. By putting <> next to the class name, we are telling the compiler that this is a generic class. Furthermore, the T inside <> is a type parameter. Yes, I know what you are asking: *"What is a type parameter?"* A **type parameter** is like any other parameter in C# programming, except it passes a type instead of a value or reference. Now, let's analyze the preceding code.

We created a generic Price class. To make it generic, we placed <T> next to the class name. Here, the T is a type parameter, but it's not something fixed that you have to use T with to represent the type parameter—you can use anything to represent it. However, it is traditional to use T for the type parameter. If there are more type parameters, V and E are used. There is another popular convention when using two or more parameters, which is to name the parameter something such as TValue and TKey, instead of just V and E, which is done for better readability. However, as you can see, we have prefixed T before the words Value and Key, which is done to distinguish between a type parameter and a general parameter.

In the Price<T> class, we first created a variable named ob, which is a type of T:

```
T ob;
```

When we run the preceding code, the type that we pass in the class will be the type of this object. Consequently, we can say that T is a placeholder, which will be replaced with some other concrete C# types (int, double, string, or any other complex type) in the runtime.

On the next lines, we created a constructor:

```
public Price(T o)
{
    ob = o;
}
```

*Generics in C#*

In the constructor, we passed a parameter of the T type and then assigned the value of the passed parameter, o, to the local variable, ob. We can do this assignment as the parameter passed in the constructor is also the T type.

Then, we created a second method:

```
public void PrintType()
{
    Console.WriteLine("The type is " + typeof(T));
}

public T GetPrice()
{
    return ob;
}
```

Here, the first method prints the type of T. This will be helpful for identifying the type when we run the program. Another method is to return the local variable, ob. Here is where we notice that we are returning T from the GetPrice method.

Now, if we focus on our main method, we will see that in the first line we are instantiating our generic class, Price, with int as a type parameter, and passing an integer value, 55, to the constructor:

```
Price<int> price = new Price<int>(55);
```

When we do this, the compiler treats every T in the Price class as int. Consequently, the local parameter, ob, will be of the int type. When we run the PrintType method, this should print **System.Int32** on the screen, and when we run the GetPrice method, it should return an Int type value.

Now, as the Price method is generic, we can use this Price method for string types as well. To do that, we have to set the type parameter as string. Let's add some more code into the preceding example, which will create a Price object that deals with strings:

```
using System;
using System.Collections.Generic;
using System.Linq;
using System.Text;
using System.Threading.Tasks;

namespace Chapter7
{
  class Price<T>
  {
    T ob;
```

[ 120 ]

```csharp
    public Price(T o)
    {
      ob = o;
    }

    public void PrintType()
    {
      Console.WriteLine("The type is " + typeof(T));
    }

    public T GetPrice()
    {
      return ob;
    }
  }

  class Code_7_2
  {
    static void Main(string[] args)
    {
      Price<int> price = new Price<int>(55);

      price.PrintType();

      int a = price.GetPrice();

      Console.WriteLine("the price is " + a);

      Price<string> priceStr = new Price<string>("Hello People");

      priceStr.PrintType();

      string b = priceStr.GetPrice();

      Console.WriteLine("the string is " + b);

      Console.ReadKey();
    }
  }
}
```

Generics in C#

The output of the preceding code is as follows:

```
C:\Users\raihan\work\learn\GenericsLessions\GenericsLessions\bin\Debug\GenericsLessions.exe
The type is System.Int32
the price is 55
The type is System.String
the string is Hello People
```

# Why do we need generics?

After seeing the previous example, you might wonder why we need generics when we can use the object type instead. The object type can be used for any type in C#, and the preceding example can be achieved through the use of an object type. Yes, the preceding example can be achieved through the use of the object type, but there won't be any type-safety. In contrast, generics ensure that the type-safety is there when the code gets executed.

If you are like me, you definitely want to know what type-safety is. **Type-safety** actually refers to keeping the type secure or unchangeable when executing any task in the program. This helps us reduce runtime errors.

Now, let's write the preceding program, using the object type instead of a generic, to see how generics can handle type-safety and object types can't:

```
using System;
using System.Collections.Generic;
using System.Linq;
using System.Text;
using System.Threading.Tasks;

namespace Chapter7
{
  class Price
  {
    object ob;

    public Price(object o)
    {
      ob = o;
    }
```

```
    public void PrintType()
    {
      Console.WriteLine("The type is " + ob.GetType());
    }

    public object GetPrice()
    {
      return ob;
    }
  }

  class Code_7_3
  {
    static void Main(string[] args)
    {
      Price price = new Price(55);

      price.PrintType();

      int a = (int)price.GetPrice();

      Console.WriteLine("the price is " + a);

      Console.ReadKey();
    }
  }
}
```

The output of the preceding code is as follows:

```
The type is System.Int32
the price is 55
```

# Different constraints of generics

There are different types of constraints available in C# generics:

- Base class constraints
- Interface constraints

*Generics in C#*

- Reference type and value type constraints
- Multiple constraints

The most common and popular types are base class constraints and interface constraints, so we will focus on them in the following sections.

## Base class constraints

The idea of this constraint is that only the classes that extend a base class can be used as generic type. For example, if you have a class named `Person` and you use this `Person` class as a base for the `Generic` constraint, only the `Person` class or any other class that inherits the `Person` class can be used as the type argument for that generic class. Let's look at an example:

```
using System;
using System.Collections.Generic;
using System.Linq;
using System.Text;
using System.Threading.Tasks;

namespace Chapter7
{
  public class Person
  {
    public void PrintName()
    {
      Console.WriteLine("My name is Raihan");
    }
  }

  public class Boy : Person
  {

  }

  public class Toy
  {

  }

  public class Human<T> where T : Person
  {
    T obj;

    public Human(T o)
```

```
    {
      obj = o;
    }

    public void MustPrint()
    {
      obj.PrintName();
    }
  }

  class Code_7_3
  {
    static void Main(string[] args)
    {
      Person person = new Person();
      Boy boy = new Boy();
      Toy toy = new Toy();

      Human<Person> personTypeHuman = new Human<Person>(person);
      personTypeHuman.MustPrint();

      Human<Boy> boyTypeHuman = new Human<Boy>(boy);
      boyTypeHuman.MustPrint();

      /* Not allowed
      Human<Toy> toyTypeHuman = new Human<Toy>(toy);
      toyTypeHuman.MustPrint();
      */

      Console.ReadKey();
    }
  }
}
```

## Interface constraints

Similar to the Base class constraint, we see the interface constraint when your generic class constraint is set as an Interface. Only those classes can be used in the generic method that implements that interface.

## Reference type and value type constraints

When you want to differentiate between your generic class and reference types and value types, you need to use this constraint. When you use a Reference type constraint, the generic class will only accept the Reference type objects. To achieve that, you have to extend your generic class with a `class` keyword:

```
... where T : class
```

Furthermore, when you want to use a value type, you need to write the following code:

```
... where T : struct
```

As we know, `class` is a reference type and `struct` is a value type. So, when you make a value type constraint, this means that the generic will only work for value types such as `int` or `double`. No reference type, such as string or any other custom class, will work.

## Multiple constraints

In C#, you can use multiple constraints in a generic class. When you do this, you need to take care of the sequence. There is actually no limit to how many constraints you can include; you can use as many you need.

## Generic methods

Like the `Generic` class, there can be generic methods, and a generic method does not necessarily have to be inside a generic class. A generic method can be inside a non-generic class as well. To create a generic method, you have to place the type parameter next to the method name and before the parenthesis. The general form is given here:

```
access-modifier return-type method-name<type-parameter>(params){ method-body }
```

Now, let's look at an example of a generic method:

```
using System;
using System.Collections.Generic;
using System.Linq;
using System.Text;
using System.Threading.Tasks;

namespace Chapter7
```

```
{
    class Hello
    {
        public static T Larger<T>(T a, T b) where T : IComparable<T>
        {
            return a.CompareTo(b) > 0 ? a : b;
        }
    }

    class Code_7_4
    {
        static void Main(string[] args)
        {
            int result = Hello.Larger<int>(3, 4);

            double doubleResult = Hello.Larger<double>(4.3, 5.6);

            Console.WriteLine("The Large value is " + result);
            Console.WriteLine("The Double Large value is " + doubleResult);

            Console.ReadKey();
        }
    }
}
```

The output of the preceding code is as follows:

```
C:\Users\raihan\work\learn\GenericsLessions\GenericsLessions\bin\Debug\GenericsLessions.exe
The Large value is 4
The Double Large value is 5.6
```

Here, we can see that our Hello class is not a Generic class. However, the Larger method is a generic method. This method takes two parameters and compares them, returning the larger value. This method has also implemented a constraint, which is IComparable<T>. In the main method, we have called this generic method several times, once with int values and once with double values. In the output, we can see that the method was successfully able to compare and return the larger value.

In this example, we have used only one type of parameter, but it is possible to have more than one parameter in a generic method. We have also created a static method in this example code, but a generic method can be non-static as well. Being static/non-static doesn't have anything to do with being a generic method.

*Generics in C#*

# Type-inferencing

Compilers are getting smarter. One such example is type-inferencing in a generic method. **Type-inferencing** means calling a generic method without specifying the type parameter, and letting the compiler identify which type to use. This means that in the previous example, we could not have specified the type parameter when calling the method.

Let's see some example code of type-inferencing:

```
using System;
using System.Collections.Generic;
using System.Linq;
using System.Text;
using System.Threading.Tasks;

namespace Chapter7
{
  class Hello
  {
    public static T Larger<T>(T a, T b) where T : IComparable<T>
    {
      return a.CompareTo(b) > 0 ? a : b;
    }
  }

  class Code_7_5
  {
    static void Main(string[] args)
    {
      int result = Hello.Larger(3, 4);

      double doubleResult = Hello.Larger(4.3, 5.6);

      Console.WriteLine("The Large value is " + result);
      Console.WriteLine("The Double Large value is " + doubleResult);

      Console.ReadKey();
    }
  }
}
```

The output of the preceding code is as follows:

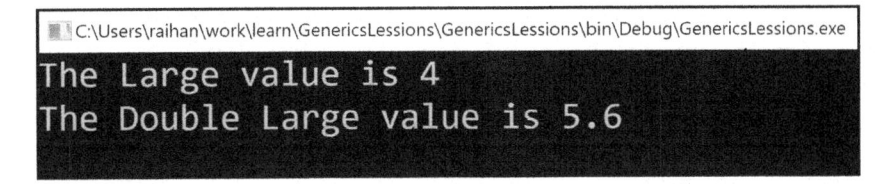

```
C:\Users\raihan\work\learn\GenericsLessions\GenericsLessions\bin\Debug\GenericsLessions.exe
The Large value is 4
The Double Large value is 5.6
```

In this code, we can see that we haven't specified the type parameter in the generic method. However, the code still compiles and shows the correct output. This is because the compiler used type inferences to figure out the type of arguments that were passed in the methods and executed the method as if the parameter type was already given to the compiler. Because of that, when you use a type inference, it's not allowed to provide different types of arguments in a generic method. If you need to pass different types of arguments, you should explicitly do that. You can also apply the constraints on a method that can be applied on the classes as well.

## Covariance and contravariance in generics

If you have studied delegates, I am sure you have heard about covariance and contravariance. These were mainly introduced for non-generic delegates. However, from C# 4, these are also available for generic interfaces and delegates. The concepts of covariance and contravariance in generics is almost the same as it is in delegates. Let's look into this with examples.

### Covariance

This means that the generic interface that has a `T` type parameter can return `T` or any class that is derived from `T`. To achieve this, the parameter should be used with the `out` keyword. Let's see the generic form:

```
access-modifier interface-name<out T>{}
```

# Contravariance

Contravariance is another feature that is implemented in generics. The word "Contravariance" might sound a little complex, but the concept behind it is very simple. Normally, when creating a generic method, the argument we pass to it is the same type as T. If you try to pass another type of argument, it will give you a compile-time error. However, when using contravariance, you can pass the base class, which the type parameter implements. In addition, to use contravariance, there is a special syntax we have to follow. Let's see the generic syntax:

```
access-modifier interface interface-name<in T>{}
```

If you analyze the preceding statement, you will see that there is a keyword used before T, which is in. This keyword tells the compiler that this is contravariance. If you don't include the in keyword, contravariance will not be applicable.

Now, let's look at some example code to make our understanding clearer:

```
using System;
using System.Collections.Generic;
using System.Linq;
using System.Text;
using System.Threading.Tasks;

namespace Chapter7
{
  public interface IFood<in T>
  {
    void PrintMyName(T obj);
  }

  class HealthyFood<T> : IFood<T>
  {
    public void PrintMyName(T obj)
    {
      Console.WriteLine("This is " + obj);
    }
  }

  class Vegetable
  {
    public override string ToString()
    {
      return "Vegetable";
    }
  }
```

```
class Potato : Vegetable
{
  public override string ToString()
  {
    return "Potato";
  }
}

class Code_7_6
{
  static void Main(string[] args)
  {
    IFood<Potato> mySelf = new HealthyFood<Potato>();
    IFood<Potato> mySelf2 = new HealthyFood<Vegetable>();

    mySelf2.PrintMyName(new Potato());

    Console.ReadKey();
  }
}
```

The output of the preceding code is as follows:

```
This is Potato
```

If we now analyze this code, we will see that we have created an Interface named `IFood`, which uses contravariance. This means that if this interface is implemented in a generic class, that class will allow the **base class** of the provided type parameter.

The `IFood` interface has a method signature:

```
void PrintMyName(T obj);
```

Here, T is used as a parameter in the method.

Now, a class named `HealthyFood` implements the interface, and the method that is implemented in the class only prints a string:

```
class HealthyFood<T> : IFood<T>
{
  public void PrintMyName(T obj)
  {
    Console.WriteLine("This is " + obj);
```

```
    }
}
```

Then, we created two classes: `Vegetable` and `Potato`. `Potato` extends `Vegetable`. Both classes override the `ToString()` method, and return `Potato` if the class is `Potato` or `Vegetable` if the class is `Vegetable`.

In the main method, we create an object of the `Potato` class and an object of the `Vegetable` class. Both of these are kept in the `IFood<Potato>` variable:

```
IFood<Potato> mySelf = new HealthyFood<Potato>();
IFood<Potato> mySelf2 = new HealthyFood<Vegetable>();
```

The interesting part here is that the `mySelf2` variable is of the `IFood<Potato>` type, but it holds an object of the `HealthyFood<Vegetable>` type. This is only possible because of contravariance.

Check out the following statement:

```
mySelf2.PrintMyName(new Potato());
```

When we execute it, we can see that the output is as follows:

```
This is Potato
```

If you remove the `in` keyword and try to run the program again, you will fail and the compiler will throw an error to say that this is not possible. It was only possible to run the code because of contravariance.

# Summary

Generics in C# is a very powerful feature that reduces code duplication, makes the program more structured, and provides extensibility. Some of the important data structures are created based on the concept of generics; for example, List (collection) is a generic type in C#. This is one of the most heavily used data structures in modern-day development.

In the next chapter, we are going to learn how to design and model our software using diagrams for better communication. When developing software, if the software design is not clearly communicated to the developers, there is a high likelihood that the software will not serve the purpose it was built for. Consequently, understanding important models and diagrams is very important.

# 8
# Modeling and Designing Software

As civil engineering emerged and large structures were created, the practice of modeling and designing became really important. The same happened with software development. Nowadays, software is everywhere: in your computer, mobile phone, TV, car, and so on. As the uses of software expanded, software development became increasingly complex and expensive, requiring both time and money.

Software modeling and design are important parts of the software development life cycle. If you have an idea and you are planning to start a software project, the first thing you should do is design and model the software, not just jump into writing the code. This will give you a high-level view of the software and the opportunity to architect it in such a way that it will be easy to extend and modify. If you don't carry out modeling beforehand, you might end up in a situation where you have to restructure your software architecture, which could be very expensive.

The topics that we will cover in this chapter are as follows:

- The importance of design diagrams
- Different **Unified Modeling Language (UML)** diagrams
- Class diagrams
- Use case diagrams
- Sequence diagrams

# The importance of design diagrams

The UML is a design language that is the standard language that is used for software modeling and design. It was first developed by Grady Booch, Ivar Jacobson, and James Rumbaugh at Rational Software between 1994–1995. In 1997, the **Object Management Group (OMG)** adopted it as the standard language for modeling. Later, in 2005, the **International Organization for Standardization (ISO)** approved UML as an ISO standard, and since then, it has been adopted by every software community.

UML diagrams allow developers to convey software design to other people. It is a language that has a set of rules that encourages easy communication. If you learn to read UML, you can understand any software model that is written in UML. Explaining a software model in plain English would be very difficult.

## Different UML diagrams

There are many types of UML diagrams, but we will only discuss the most important ones in this chapter. UML diagrams fall into the following two major categories:

- Structural diagrams
- Behavioral diagrams

The following list shows the diagrams that come under the category of structural diagrams:

- Class diagrams
- Component diagrams
- Composite structure diagrams
- Deployment diagrams
- Object diagrams
- Package diagrams
- Profile diagrams

Behavioral diagrams include the following:

- Activity diagrams
- Communication diagrams
- Interaction overview diagrams
- Sequence diagrams

- State diagrams
- Timing diagrams
- Use case diagrams

# Class diagrams

A class diagram is a structural diagram that is mainly used to provide the design of a piece of object-oriented software. This diagram demonstrates the structure of a software, the attributes and methods of a class, and the relationship between classes in the system. It can be used for development as well as for documentation; software developers frequently use this diagram to get a quick idea of the code and to help fellow developers understand the system. It is also occasionally used by employees involved in the business side of a company.

The following are the three main parts of a class diagram:

- The class name
- The attribute section
- The method section

A class diagram consists of different classes that are represented as boxes or rectangles. A rectangle is normally divided into the aforementioned sections. The first part holds the name of the class, the second portion holds the attributes, and the third section contains the methods.

Let's take a look at an example of a class diagram:

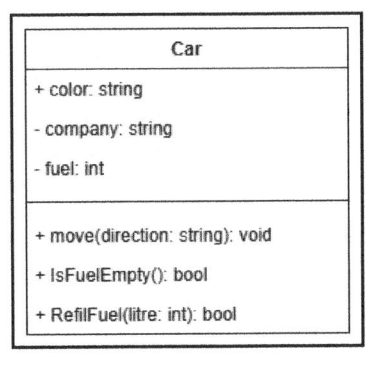

| Car |
|---|
| + color: string |
| - company: string |
| - fuel: int |
| + move(direction: string): void |
| + IsFuelEmpty(): bool |
| + RefilFuel(litre: int): bool |

*Modeling and Designing Software*

Here, we can see that we have a class called `Car`, as indicated by the top box. Below that, we have the attributes of that class. We can see that `color` is the name of an attribute, which has a + sign in front of it, indicating that it is a public variable. We can also see that there is a : (colon) next to the variable name, which is a separator. Whatever is given after the colon represents the type of the variable. In this case, we can see that the `color` variable is of the `string` type. The next attribute is `company`, which is also a variable of the `string` type. This has a – sign in front of it, which means that it is a private variable. The third attribute is `fuel`, and we can see that this is a private variable of the `integer` type.

If we look below the attributes, we will see the methods of the `Car` class. We can see that it has three methods: `move(direction: string)`, `IsFuelEmpty()`, and `RefilFuel(litre: int)`. Like the attributes, we can see that the methods have a : (colon). In this case, the type that is given after the colon is the return type of the method. The first method, `move`, doesn't return anything, so the type is void. In the `IsFuelEmpty()` method, the return type is Boolean, and this is also the case for the third method. Another thing to note here is the parameters of the methods, which are placed in parentheses after the method name. For example, the `move` method has a parameter called `direction`, which is a `string` type. The `RefilFuel(litre: int)` method has an `int` type parameter, which is `litre`.

In the preceding example, we saw how a class is represented in a class diagram. Normally, a system has multiple classes that are related to each other in some way. A class diagram demonstrates the relationships of the classes as well, which gives the viewer a full picture of the system's object relationships. In `Chapter 4`, *Object Collaboration*, we learned about the different relationships between classes and objects in object-oriented software. Let's now take a look at how we can represent these different object relationships using class diagrams.

# Inheritance

**Inheritance** is a relationship in which one class is like another class, in the same way that a BMW i8 Roadster is a kind of car. This type of relationship is shown using a line and a hollow arrow. The arrow points from the class to the super class, as shown in the following diagram:

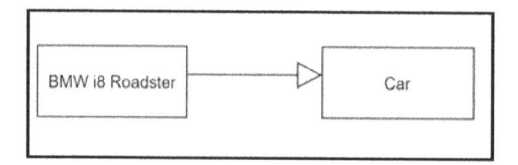

[ 136 ]

## Association

An association relationship is the most basic relationship between objects. When one object has some kind of logic or physical relationship with another object it is called **association relationship**. It is represented by a line and an arrow. If there is an arrow on both sides, this represents a bidirectional relationship. An example of an association could be the following:

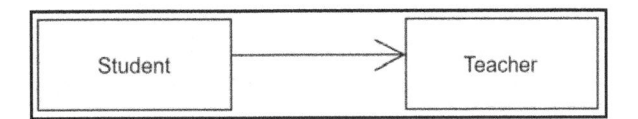

[Diagram: Student → Teacher]

## Aggregation

An **aggregation relationship** is a special type of association relationship. This relationship is usually known as a **has-a relationship**. When one class has another class/object in it, this is an aggregation relationship. This is represented using a line and a hollow diamond. For example, a car has a tire. A tire and a car have an aggregation relationship, as shown in the following diagram:

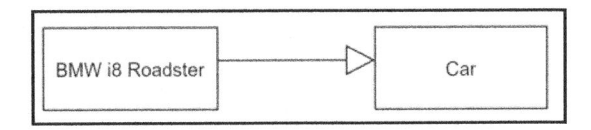

[Diagram: BMW i8 Roadster ─▷ Car]

## Composition

When one class has another class in it and the dependent class can't exist without the super class, this is a **composition relationship**. For example, a bank account can't exist without a bank, as shown in the following diagram:

[Diagram: Bank Account ─◆ Bank]

*Modeling and Designing Software*

# Dependency

When a class has a dependent class, but the class itself is not dependent on its own dependent class, the relationship between those classes is called a **dependency relationship**. In a dependency relationship, any change in the dependent class doesn't have any effect on the class it is dependent on. But the dependent class will be affected if the class that it is dependent on changes.

This relationship is represented by a dashed line with an arrow at the end. For example, let's imagine that we have a theme on our mobile phone. If we change the theme, the phone's icons will change, so the icons have a dependency on the theme. This relationship is shown in the following diagram:

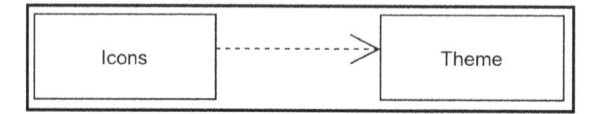

# An example of a class diagram

Let's take a look at an example of a class diagram of a project. Here, we have some grade management software that is used by the teachers and students of a school. The software allows teachers to update the grades of particular students for different subjects. It also allows the students to view their grade. For this software, we have the following classes:

- `Person`:

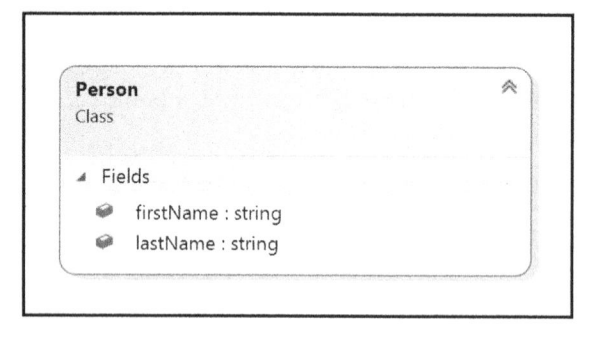

Person class diagram

[ 138 ]

- `Teacher`:

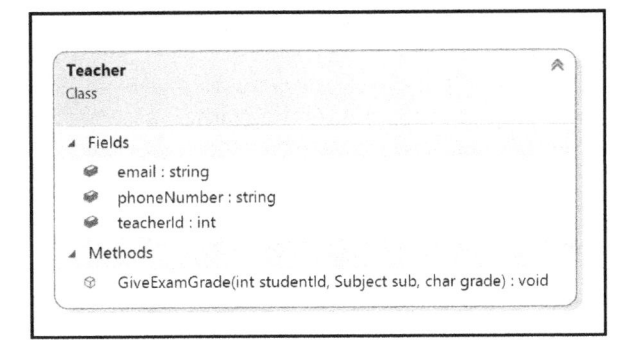

**Teacher**
Class

- Fields
  - email : string
  - phoneNumber : string
  - teacherId : int
- Methods
  - GiveExamGrade(int studentId, Subject sub, char grade) : void

Teacher class diagram

- `Student`:

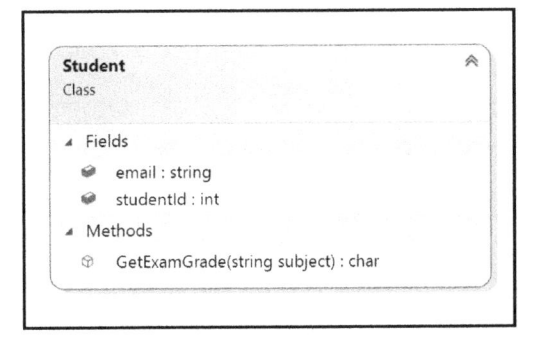

**Student**
Class

- Fields
  - email : string
  - studentId : int
- Methods
  - GetExamGrade(string subject) : char

Student class diagram

- `Subject`:

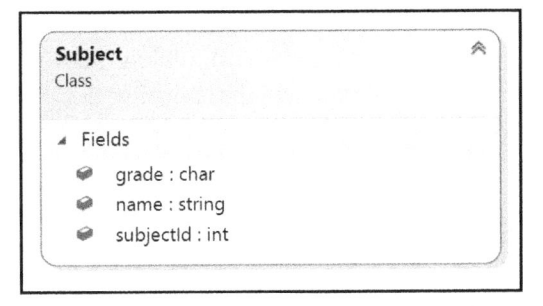

**Subject**
Class

- Fields
  - grade : char
  - name : string
  - subjectId : int

Subject class diagram

*Modeling and Designing Software*

Here, we have used Visual Studio to generate our class diagram, so the arrows might not match the arrows that are given in the previous sections. If you are drawing your class diagrams using other drawing software, or if you are drawing by hand, then use the arrows specified in the previous sections.

Let's take a look at the following complete class diagram:

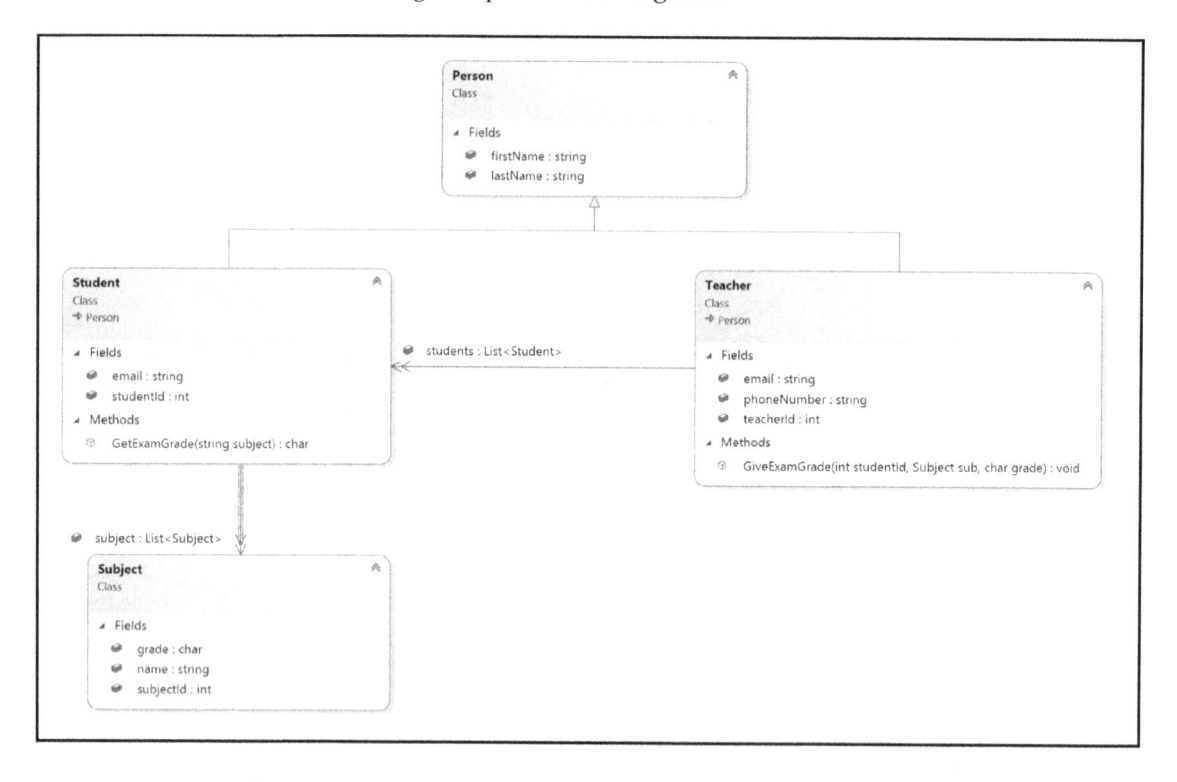

```
Person
Class
  ▲ Fields
    ● firstName : string
    ● lastName : string

Student                                                          Teacher
Class                                                            Class
→ Person                                                         → Person
  ▲ Fields                    ● students : List<Student>           ▲ Fields
    ● email : string                                                 ● email : string
    ● studentId : int                                                ● phoneNumber : string
  ▲ Methods                                                          ● teacherId : int
    ● GetExamGrade(string subject) : char                          ▲ Methods
                                                                     ● GiveExamGrade(int studentId, Subject sub, char grade) : void

● subject : List<Subject>

Subject
Class
  ▲ Fields
    ● grade : char
    ● name : string
    ● subjectId : int
```

Here, we can see that we have a `Person` class that has two attributes, a `FirstName` and a `LastName`. The `Student` and `Teacher` classes inherit the `Person` class, so we can see that the arrow is hollow. The `Student` class has two attributes, `email` and `studentId`. It also has a method called `GetExamGrade` (string subject), which takes the name of the subject and returns the grade in `char` type. We can see that another class, `Subject`, has a composition relationship with `Student`. `Student` has a list of subjects and the `Subject` class has three attributes, `grade`, `name`, and `subjectId`. The `Teacher` class has an `email`, `phoneNumber`, and `teacherId`, which are `string`, `string`, and `int` types respectively. The `Teacher` class has an association relationship with the `Student` class, as a teacher has a group of students under them. The `Teacher` class also has a method called `GiveExamGrade`, which takes three parameters, `studentId`, `subject`, and `grade`. This method will set the grades on the students' subjects.

Just by looking at the class diagram, we get a clear idea of the system. We know how the subject is related to the student and how students are related to teachers. We also know that a subject's object can't exist without a student object, as they have a composition relationship. This is the beauty of the class diagram.

## Use case diagrams

A **use case diagram** is a behavioral diagram that is very commonly used in software development. The main purpose of this diagram is to illustrate the functional usage of a piece of software. It holds the use cases of a system and can be used to provide a high-level view of the functionality or even a very specific low-level module of a software. Normally for a system, there are multiple use case diagrams that focus on the different levels of the system. Use case diagrams shouldn't be used to display the implementation details of a system; they were developed to show only the functional requirements of a system. Use case diagrams are very good diagrams for business people to convey what they need from a system.

There are four main parts of a use case diagram, as shown in the following list:

- The actor
- The use case
- The communication link
- The system boundaries

## The actor

The actor in a use case diagram is not necessarily a person—it is rather the user of the system. It could be a person, another system, or even another module of the system. A visual representation of an actor is given in the following diagram:

An actor is responsible for providing an input. It gives instructions to the system and the system works accordingly. Every action an actor does has a purpose. A use case diagram shows us what an actor can do and what the expectations of the actor are.

## The use case

The visual part or representation of a use case diagram is known as the **use case**. This represents the functionality of the system. An actor will execute a use case to achieve a goal. A use case is represented by an oval with the name of the functionality. For example, in a restaurant app, *placing an order* could be a use case. We can represent this as follows:

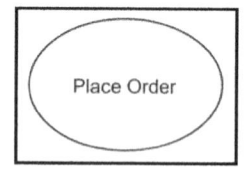

## The communication link

A **communication link** is a simple line from an actor to a use case. This link is used to show that an actor has a relationship with a particular use case. An actor won't have access to all use cases, so communication links are very important when displaying which use cases are accessible by which actor. Let's take a look at an example of a communication link, as shown in the following diagram:

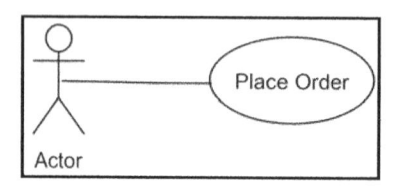

# The system boundaries

**System boundaries** are mainly used to show the scope of a system. It is important to be able to identify which use cases fall in our system and which don't. In a use case diagram, we only focus on the use cases in our system. In large systems, each module of the system is sometimes treated as a boundary if those modules are independent enough to function without each other. This is normally shown with a rectangular box that holds the use cases. An actor is not a part of the system, so the actor will be outside of the system boundary, as shown in the following diagram:

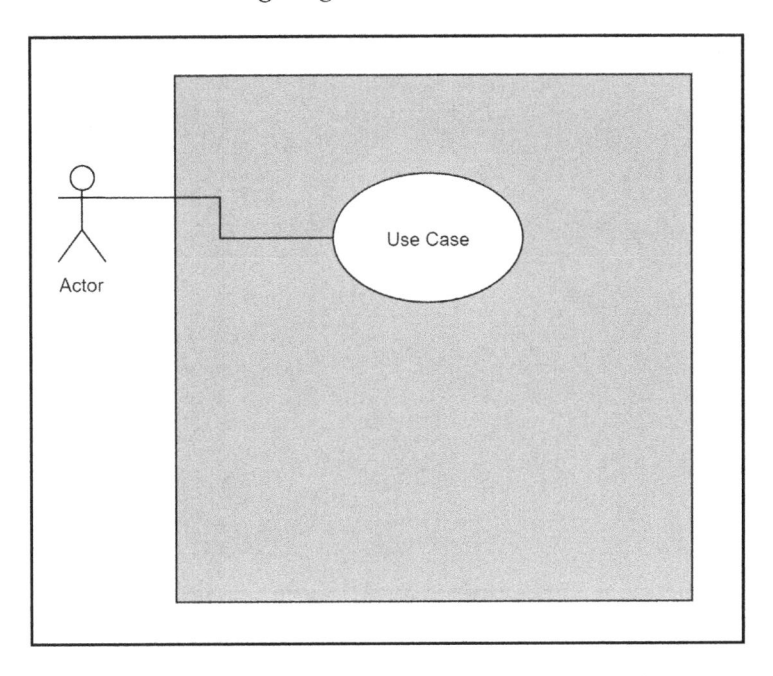

*Modeling and Designing Software*

# An example of a use case diagram

Let's now imagine that we have a restaurant system in which a customer can order food. The chef prepares the food and the manager keeps track of the sales, as shown in the following diagram:

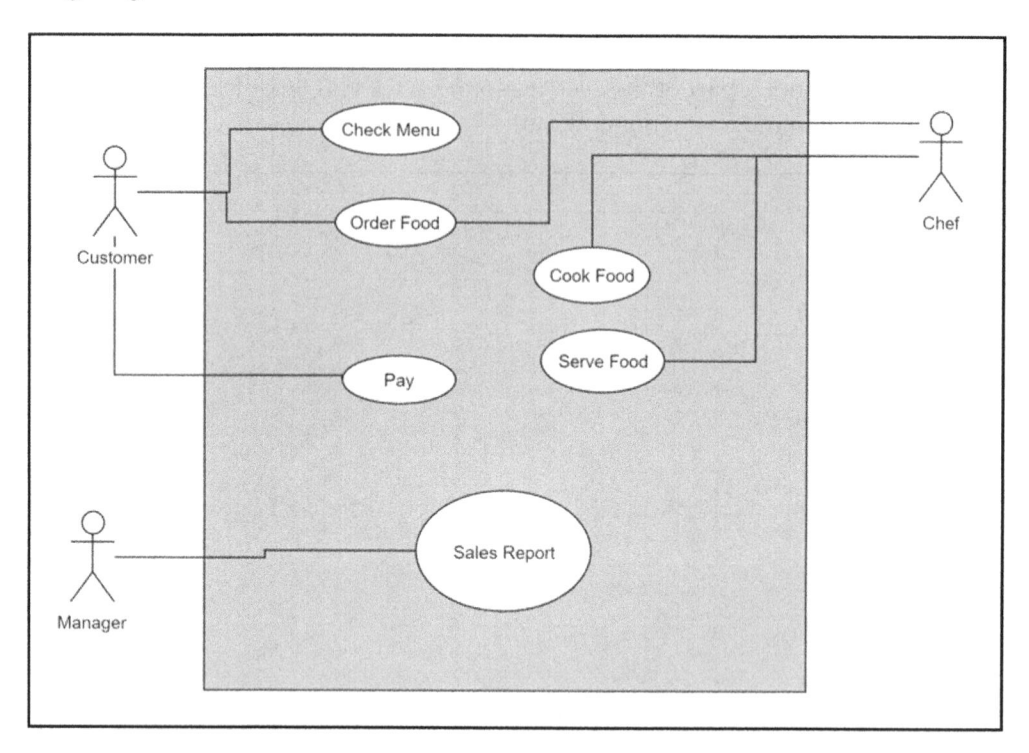

From the preceding diagram, we can see that we have three actors (the **Customer**, the **Chef**, and the **Manager**). We also have different use cases—**Check Menu**, **Order Food**, **Cook Food**, **Serve Food**, **Pay**, and **Sales Report,** which are connected to one or more actors. The **Customer** actor is involved in the **Check Menu**, **Order Food**, and **Pay** use cases. The **Chef** has to access **Order Food** in order to find out about the orders. The **Chef** is also involved in the **Cook Food** and **Serve Food** use cases. Unlike the **Chef** and the **Customer**, the **Manager** is able to see the **Sales Report** of the restaurant.

By looking at this use case diagram, we are able to identify the functionalities of the system. It doesn't give you any implementation details, but we can easily see an overview of the system.

# The system boundaries

**System boundaries** are mainly used to show the scope of a system. It is important to be able to identify which use cases fall in our system and which don't. In a use case diagram, we only focus on the use cases in our system. In large systems, each module of the system is sometimes treated as a boundary if those modules are independent enough to function without each other. This is normally shown with a rectangular box that holds the use cases. An actor is not a part of the system, so the actor will be outside of the system boundary, as shown in the following diagram:

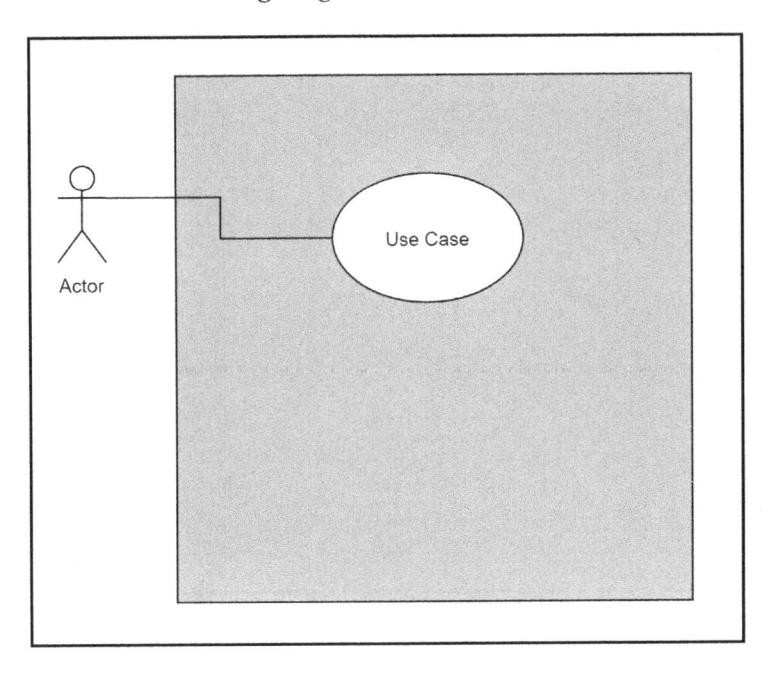

## An example of a use case diagram

Let's now imagine that we have a restaurant system in which a customer can order food. The chef prepares the food and the manager keeps track of the sales, as shown in the following diagram:

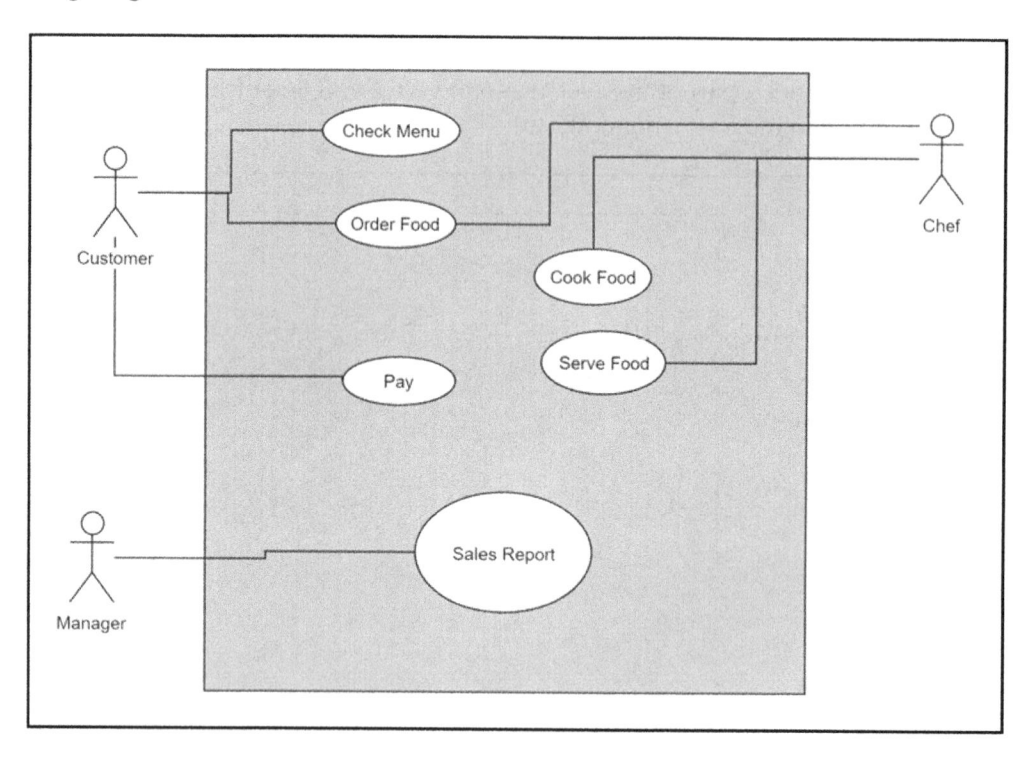

From the preceding diagram, we can see that we have three actors (the **Customer**, the **Chef**, and the **Manager**). We also have different use cases—**Check Menu, Order Food, Cook Food, Serve Food, Pay,** and **Sales Report,** which are connected to one or more actors. The **Customer** actor is involved in the **Check Menu, Order Food,** and **Pay** use cases. The **Chef** has to access **Order Food** in order to find out about the orders. The **Chef** is also involved in the **Cook Food** and **Serve Food** use cases. Unlike the **Chef** and the **Customer**, the **Manager** is able to see the **Sales Report** of the restaurant.

By looking at this use case diagram, we are able to identify the functionalities of the system. It doesn't give you any implementation details, but we can easily see an overview of the system.

# A sequence diagram

A sequence diagram is an interaction diagram that falls under the category of behavioral diagrams. As the name suggests, it shows the sequence of the activities of a system. By looking at a sequence diagram, you can identify which activities happen during a particular time frame and which activities come next. It allows us to understand the flow of a system. The activities it represents might be an interaction between a user and a system, between two systems, or between a system and a subsystem.

The horizontal axis of a sequence diagram shows time passing from left to right, while the vertical axis shows the flow of activity. Different activities are placed in the diagram in a sequential manner. A sequence diagram doesn't necessarily show the duration of time passing but rather the steps from one activity to another.

In the following sections, we'll take a look at the notations that are used in a sequence diagram.

# An actor

An actor in a sequence diagram is very similar to an actor in a use case diagram. It could be a user, another system, or even a user group. An actor is not part of the system and executes commands externally. Different operations are executed upon receiving commands from users. The actor is denoted with a stick figure, as shown in the following diagram:

# A lifeline

A lifeline in sequence diagram is an entity or element of a system. Every lifeline has its own logic and tasks to do. Normally, a system has multiple lifelines, and commands are passed from one lifeline to another.

A lifeline is denoted by a box with a vertical line issuing from the bottom, as shown in the following diagram:

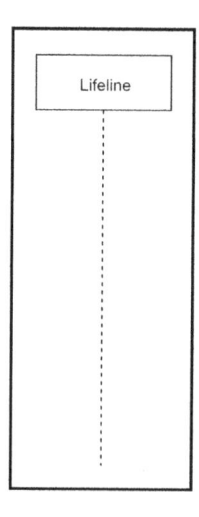

## An activation

An activation is a small rectangular box on a lifeline. This activation box represents the point when an activity was active. The top of the box represents the start of the activity and the end of the box represents the end of the activity.

Let's see how it looks in a diagram:

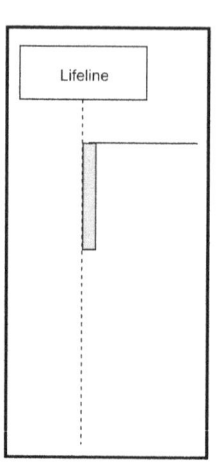

## A call message

A call message indicates an interaction between lifelines. It flows from left to right and is denoted by an arrow at the end of a line, as shown in the following diagram. A message call represents some kind of information or a trigger to the next lifeline:

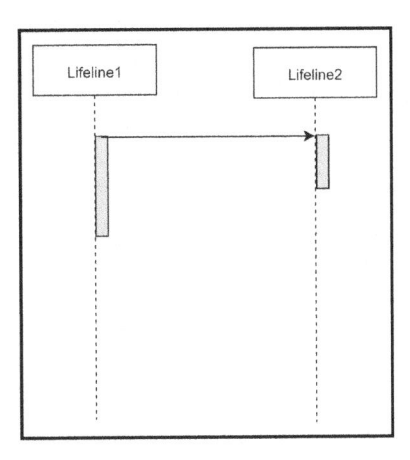

## A return message

The normal message flow in a sequence diagram is from left to right, as this represents the action commands; however, sometimes messages are returned to the caller. A return message flows from right to left and is denoted by a dotted line with an arrow head at the end, as shown in the following diagram:

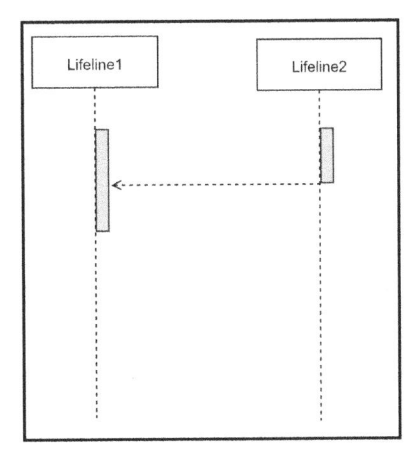

## A self message

Sometimes, messages are passed from a lifeline to itself, such as an internal communication. It will be denoted in a similar way to a message call, but instead of pointing to another activity of another lifeline, it returns to the same activity of the same lifeline, as shown in the following diagram:

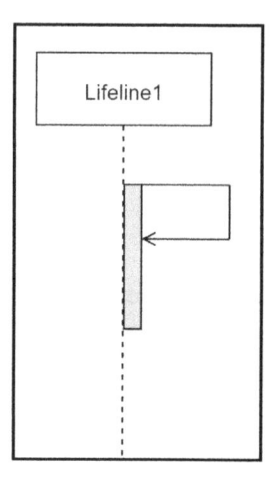

## A recursive message

When a self message is sent for recursive purposes, it is called a recursive message. Another small activity on the same timeline is drawn for this purpose, as shown in the following diagram:

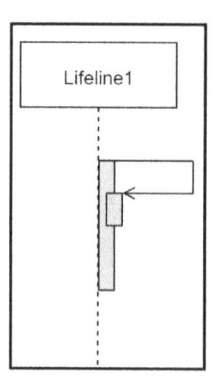

## A create message

This type of message is not a normal message, such as a call message. A create message is used when a lifeline is created by another lifeline, as shown in the following diagram:

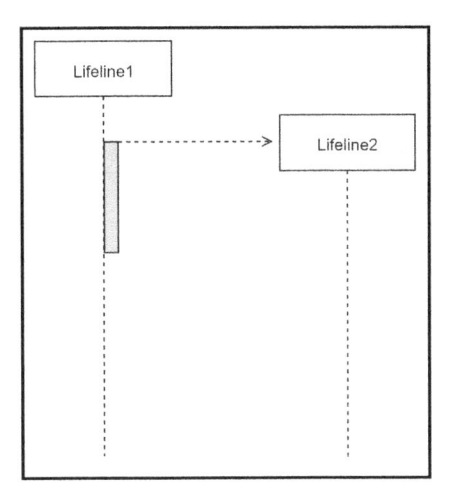

## A destroy message

When a destroy message is sent from an activity to a lifeline, it means that the following lifeline is not going to be executed and the flow will be stopped, as shown in the following diagram. It is called a destroy message because it destroys the activity flow:

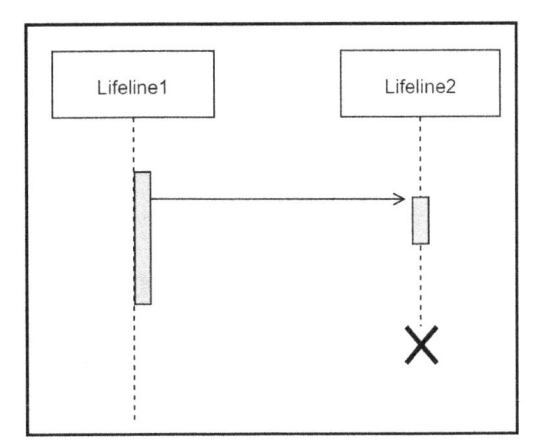

## A duration message

We use a duration message to show when there is a time duration between when an activity passes a message to the next activity and when the next activity receives it. It is similar to a call message, but is angled down, as shown in the following diagram:

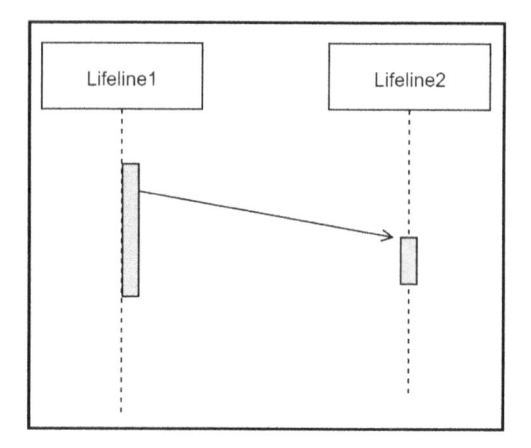

## A note

A note is used to include any necessary remarks to do with an element or an action. It has no particular rules. It can be placed anywhere that is suitable to represent the event clearly. Any type of information can be written in a note. A note is represented as follows:

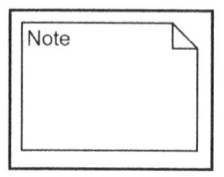

## An example of a sequence diagram

The best way to learn anything is by looking at an example of it. Let's take a look at the following sequence diagram of a simple restaurant system:

*Chapter 8*

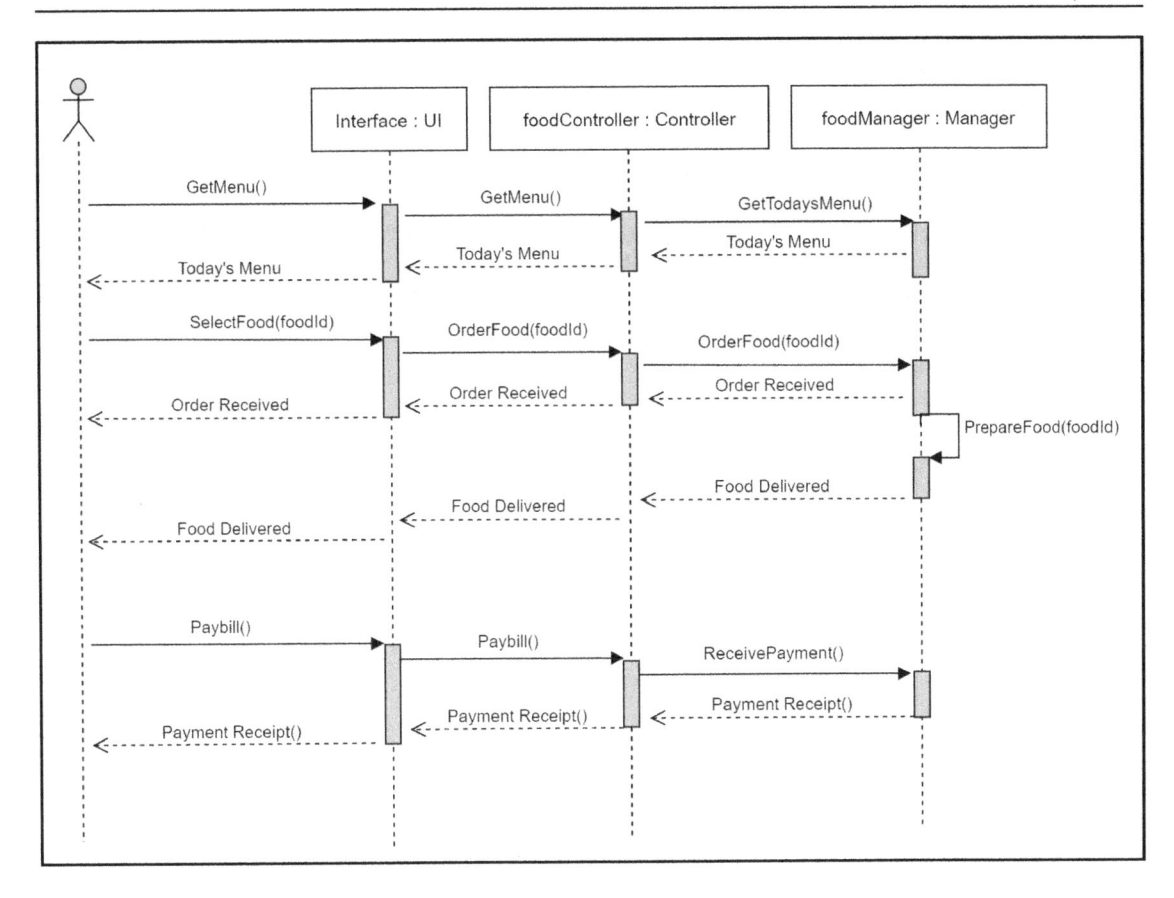

```
[Sequence diagram]
Actor → Interface : UI → foodController : Controller → foodManager : Manager

GetMenu()  →  GetMenu()  →  GetTodaysMenu()
Today's Menu  ←  Today's Menu  ←  Today's Menu

SelectFood(foodId)  →  OrderFood(foodId)  →  OrderFood(foodId)
Order Received  ←  Order Received  ←  Order Received
                                          ↻ PrepareFood(foodId)
Food Delivered  ←  Food Delivered  ←  Food Delivered

Paybill()  →  Paybill()  →  ReceivePayment()
Payment Receipt()  ←  Payment Receipt()  ←  Payment Receipt()
```

Here, we can see that a customer first asks for the menu from the **UI**. The **UI** passes the request to the **Controller** and then the **Controller** passes the request to the **Manager**. The **Manager** gets the menu and responds to the **Controller**. The **Controller** responds to the **UI** and the **UI** displays the menu in the display.

After the **Customer** chooses an item, the order goes step by step to the **Manager**. The **Manager** calls another method to prepare the food and sends a response to the **Customer** notifying them that the order has been received. When the food is ready, it is served to the **Customer**. Upon receiving the food, the **Customer** pays the bill and collects a **Payment Receipt**.

By looking at the sequence diagram, we can see the different activities involved in the process. It's pretty clear how the system is working step by step. This kind of diagram is very useful in showing the flow of a system, and is very popular.

## Summary

In this chapter, you learned the basics of how to model and design your software using UML diagrams. This is very important for every software developer, because we need to be able to communicate with businesses and vice versa. You will also find that these diagrams are useful when discussing systems with other developers or software architects. We haven't covered all the different diagrams that are available for modeling and designing software in this chapter, because this is beyond the scope of this book. We covered class diagrams, use case diagrams, and sequence diagrams in this chapter. We saw an example of each of these diagrams and looked at how to draw them.

In the next chapter, we will look at how to work with Visual Studio. We will see some tips and tricks that will help you increase your productivity while working with Visual Studio.

# Visual Studio and Associated Tools

**9**

Visual Studio is an **integrated development environment (IDE)** from Microsoft. It's computer software, and a tool that can be used to write, debug, and execute code. Visual Studio is one of the most popular IDEs available in the industry, and is mainly used for .NET applications. As it is from Microsoft, it makes .NET development very easy and smooth. You can use Visual Studio for other programming languages, but I can't guarantee that it will be the most useful option; however, for C# developers like me, this is the best IDE available. As a developer, I spend most of my time in Visual Studio.

At the time of writing this book, the latest version of Visual Studio is Visual Studio 2017. Microsoft has introduced different editions of Visual Studio. One of these, the Community edition, is free. There are also two other editions: Visual Studio Professional and Visual Studio Enterprise. The Professional and Enterprise editions are not free, and are more suitable for big projects. In this book, we will explore the features of the Community edition, as that is free and has sufficient functionalities for the purposes of this book.

In this chapter, we will learn about the features of Visual Studio. We will cover the following topics:

- Visual Studio project types and templates
- Visual Studio Editor and the different windows
- Debugging windows
- Breakpoints, Call Stack Trace, and Watch
- Git in Visual Studio
- Refactoring and code-optimization techniques

# Visual Studio project types and templates

Visual Studio is the best IDE for Microsoft-related technology stacks. You can use Visual Studio whether you are planning to develop a desktop application for Windows or a web application for Windows Server. The best part of using Visual Studio is that the IDE will help you with lots of common tasks that you would have to perform manually if you were not using it. For example, if you were planning to create a web application using ASP.NET **Model-View-Controller (MVC)**, Visual Studio can provide you a template for an MVC application. You can start with the template and modify it according to your requirements. Without this, you would have to download the packages, create the folders, and set the web configuration for the application. To get the full benefit of Visual Studio, you have to know the different projects and templates that come with it so that you can speed up your development process.

Let's take a look at the different project types that Visual Studio provides. After opening Visual Studio, if you click **New Project**, the following window will pop up:

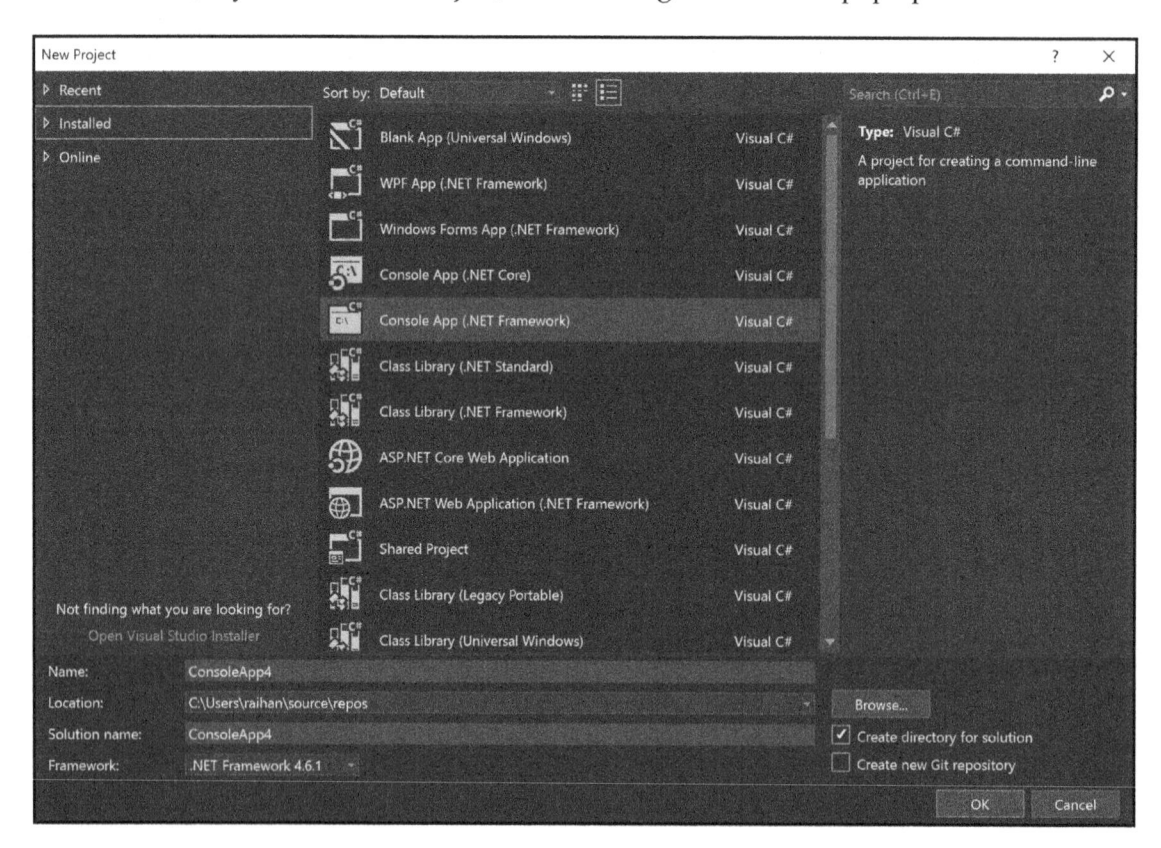

Here, on the left-hand side, we can see the major categories of the projects: **Recent**, **Installed**, and **Online**. In the **Recent** tab, you can see the project types that have been used recently, so you don't have to search for commonly used project types every time. In the **Installed** tab, you will find the project types that are already installed on your computer. When you install Visual Studio, you can choose which workloads you want to install.

The **Workloads** window that will appear while installing Visual Studio looks as follows:

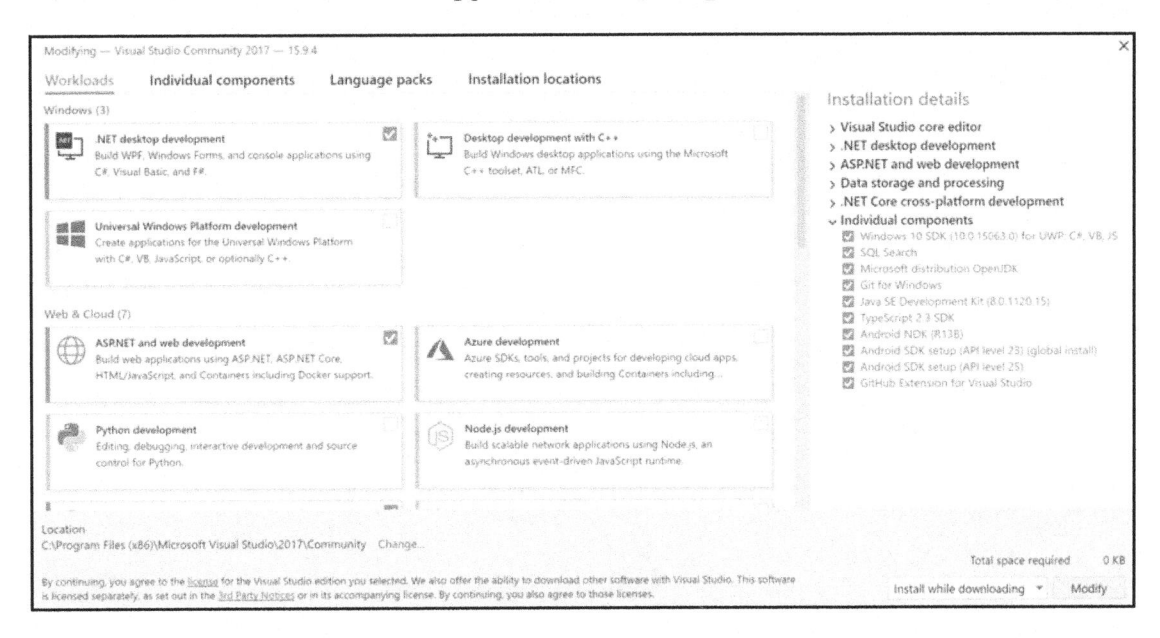

The **Workloads** options you choose have a direct relation to the installed project types. Under the **Online** tab, you will find the projects that were not installed when Visual Studio was installed. There are many project templates available for Visual Studio, which is why they are not all installed at once.

*Visual Studio and Associated Tools*

Now, if we expand the **Installed** tab, we will see that the different programming languages are shown as child tabs: **Visual C#**, **Visual Basic**, **Visual C++**, and so on. As this book relates to C#, we will only focus on the **Visual C#** area, as shown in the following screenshot:

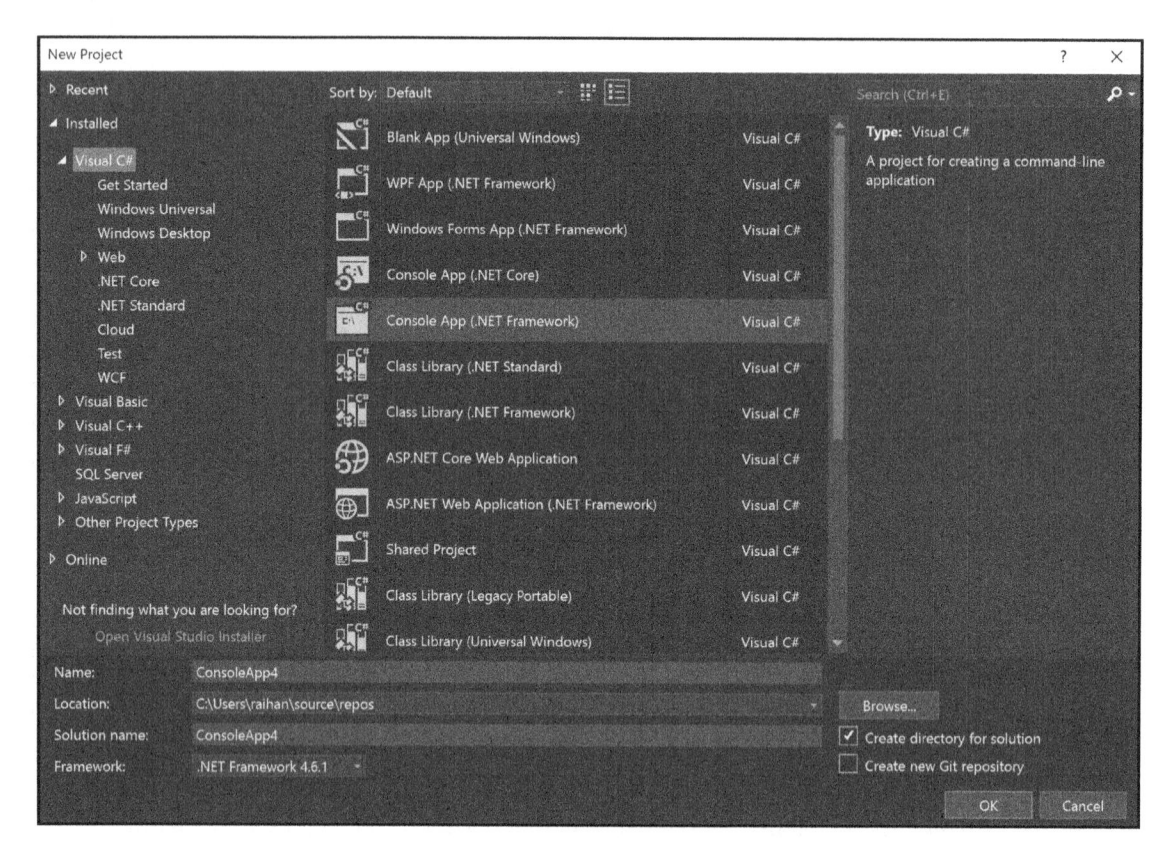

If we expand the **Visual C#** tab, we will see more tabs that relate to more specific types of projects, such as **Windows Desktop**, **Web**, **.NET Core**, **Test**, and so on. But if we focus on the middle part of the window, we will see the different project templates, such as **Windows Forms App (.NET Framework)**, **Console App (.NET Core)**, **Console App (.NET Framework)**, **Class Library (.NET Standard)**, **Class Library (.NET Framework)**, **ASP .NET Core Web Application**, **ASP.NET Web Application (.NET Framework)**, and so on. On the right-hand side of the window, we can see a short description of the project template that you have selected in the middle pane, as shown in the following screenshot:

[ 156 ]

Here, on the left-hand side, we can see the major categories of the projects: **Recent**, **Installed**, and **Online**. In the **Recent** tab, you can see the project types that have been used recently, so you don't have to search for commonly used project types every time. In the **Installed** tab, you will find the project types that are already installed on your computer. When you install Visual Studio, you can choose which workloads you want to install.

The **Workloads** window that will appear while installing Visual Studio looks as follows:

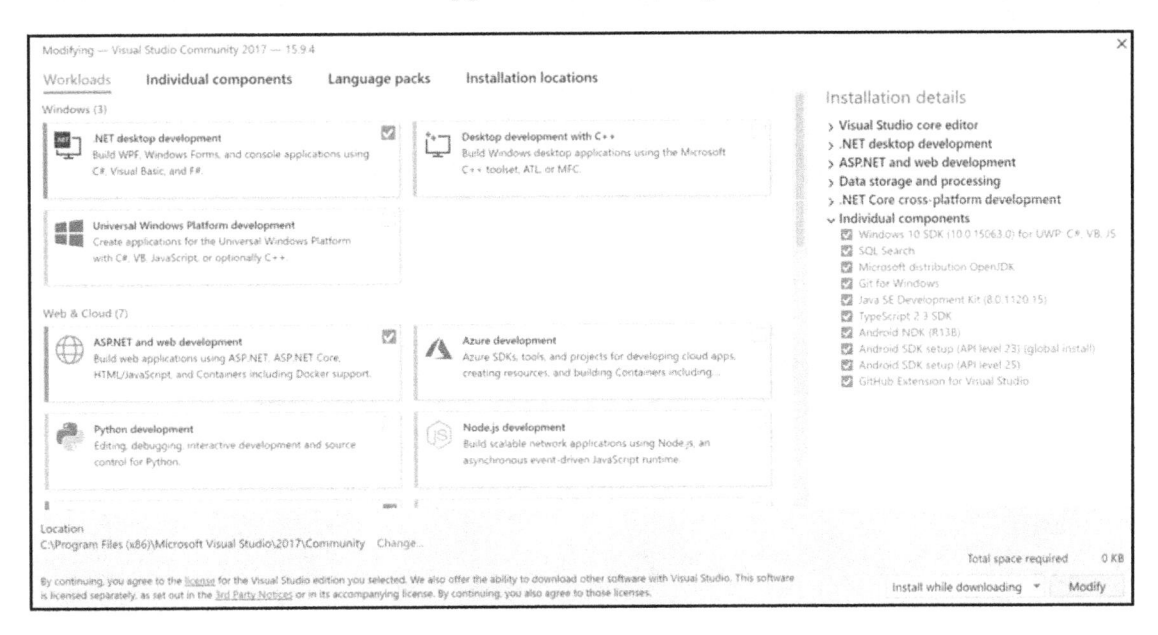

The **Workloads** options you choose have a direct relation to the installed project types. Under the **Online** tab, you will find the projects that were not installed when Visual Studio was installed. There are many project templates available for Visual Studio, which is why they are not all installed at once.

*Visual Studio and Associated Tools*

Now, if we expand the **Installed** tab, we will see that the different programming languages are shown as child tabs: **Visual C#**, **Visual Basic**, **Visual C++**, and so on. As this book relates to C#, we will only focus on the **Visual C#** area, as shown in the following screenshot:

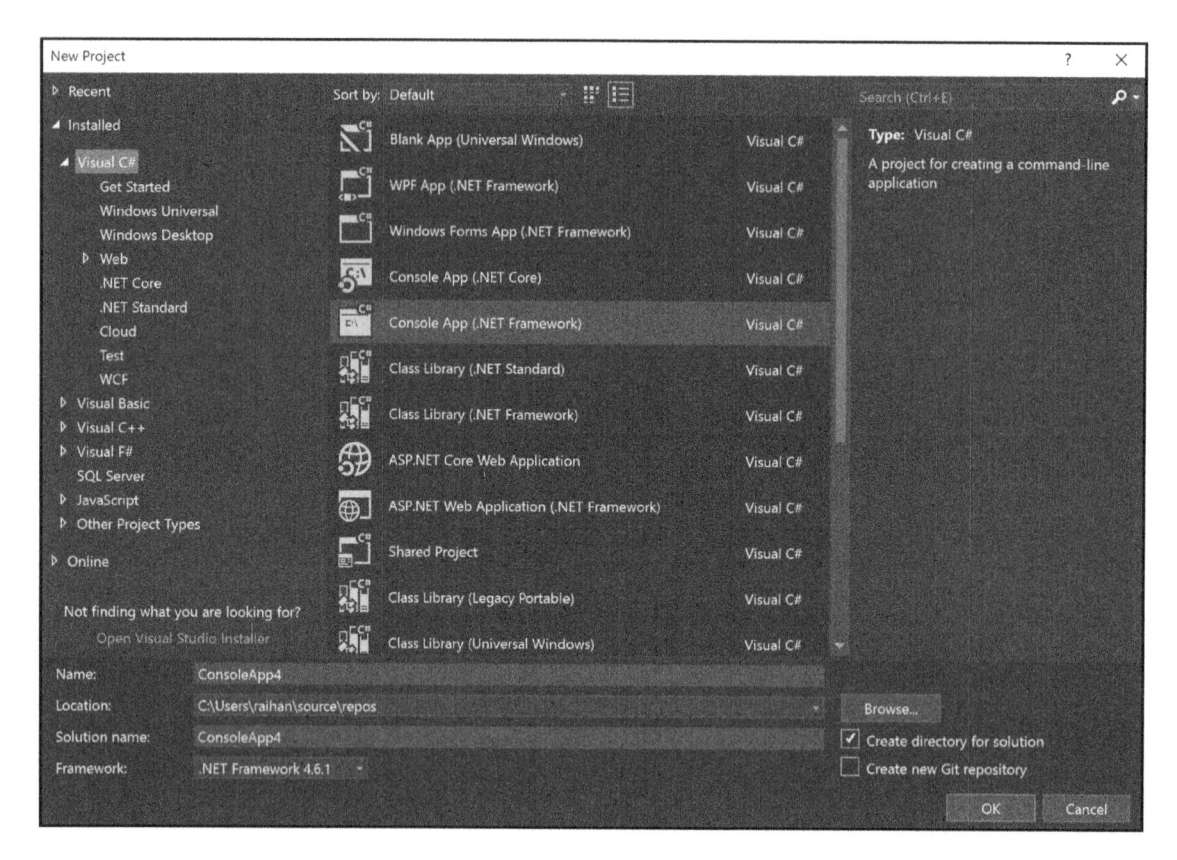

If we expand the **Visual C#** tab, we will see more tabs that relate to more specific types of projects, such as **Windows Desktop**, **Web**, **.NET Core**, **Test**, and so on. But if we focus on the middle part of the window, we will see the different project templates, such as **Windows Forms App (.NET Framework)**, **Console App (.NET Core)**, **Console App (.NET Framework)**, **Class Library (.NET Standard)**, **Class Library (.NET Framework)**, **ASP .NET Core Web Application**, **ASP.NET Web Application (.NET Framework)**, and so on. On the right-hand side of the window, we can see a short description of the project template that you have selected in the middle pane, as shown in the following screenshot:

Chapter 9

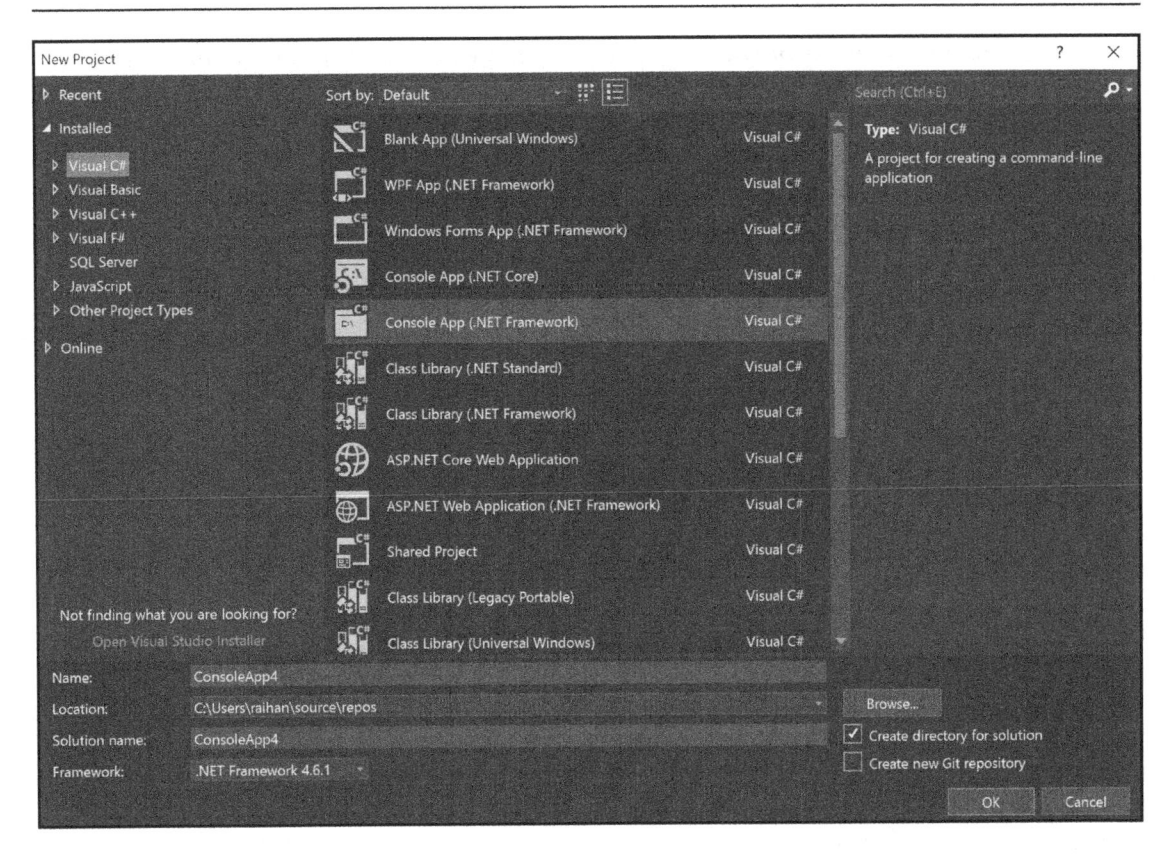

Let's take a look at some of the most common project templates available in Visual Studio 2017:

- **Console App:** A project to create a command-line application. There are two different types of this kind of project: one for .NET Core and another for .NET Framework.
- **Class Library:** You can use this template if you are developing a class library project that can be used as an extension code of another project. In Visual Studio 2017, you again get two options: one for .NET Standard and another for .NET Framework.
- **ASP.NET Core Web Application:** This project is for web applications that use .NET Core, which is platform-independent. You can create MVC, web API, and SPA applications with this type of project.

- **ASP.NET Web Application (.NET Framework):** This project template is used to develop web applications using .NET Framework. Similar to the ASP.NET Core Web Application template, with this project template, you can choose from MVC, web API, or SPA projects.
- **WCF Server Application:** You can use this project type to create a **Windows Communication Foundation** (**WCF**) service.
- **WPF App (.NET Framework):** You can choose this template if you are creating a **Windows Presentation Foundation** (**WPF**) project.
- **Unit Test Project (.NET Framework):** This is a project for unit testing. If you create this project, you will get a premade test class, and you can use it to write your unit tests.

There are many other project templates available that are used by .NET developers. It is always better to start with a project template rather than a blank template if you are sure about your application's purpose.

# Visual Studio Editor and different windows

Visual Studio is not like a simple text editor. It has many tools and features, so it can be a little overwhelming. However, to get started, you don't need to understand every tool and feature: you just need the basics. As you learn more about it, you can take full advantage of its capabilities, making your life easier and making you more productive. Later in this chapter, we will also learn some very useful keyboard shortcuts. We will first take a look at the basics.

## Editor window

After you create or open a project in Visual Studio, you will see a screen that looks like the one shown in the following screenshot, unless you have a different environment setup. On the left-hand side, the window that shows the code is called the **Editor window**. This is the window where you will write your code. This Editor window is very smart; it appears when the file is open in the editor in the upper-left corner. If multiple files are open, the active file will have a blue background and the inactive files will be black, as shown in the following screenshot:

*Chapter 9*

```
using System;
using System.Collections.Generic;
using System.Linq;
using System.Text;
using System.Threading.Tasks;

namespace ExploreVS
{
    class Program
    {
        static void Main(string[] args)
        {
            Console.WriteLine("Hello World!");
        }
    }
}
```

The line numbers are shown on the left-hand side of each code line, and the code is represented in different colors. The words in blue are reserved keywords in C#, the text in white is your active modifiable code, the green text represents a class name, and the orange text refers to string text. There are some other colors, underline marks, and symbols available in Visual Studio to help you understand the code better. If you are reading a black-and-white copy of this book, I would suggest that you open Visual Studio and write the code to check the color representation. For example, take a look at the using statements in the following screenshot. Apart from the System namespace, all other namespaces are in a duller color, which means that those namespaces are not yet in use in this file. The System namespace is bright white because we have used the Console.WriteLine() method in our code, which belongs to the System namespace. You can also see that there are boxes with the - sign inside it, on the left of the code with a horizontal line below it. This shows the code-folding options.

*Visual Studio and Associated Tools*

You can easily fold a code in order to see a particular code more clearly:

```
using System;
using System.Collections.Generic;
using System.Linq;
using System.Text;
using System.Threading.Tasks;

namespace ExploreVS
{
    class Program
    {
        static void Main(string[] args)
        {
            Console.WriteLine("Hello World!");
        }
    }
}
```

The dashed line from an opening curly brace to a closed curly brace shows you which area the braces cover. So even if you have not placed your opening and closing braces in the same vertical line, you will be able to see which lines those braces cover, as shown in the following screenshot:

```
namespace ExploreVS
{
    class Program
    {
        static void Main(string[] args)
        {
            Console.WriteLine("Hello World!"); }
    }
}
```

The Editor window has some other useful features, such as **IntelliSense** and **refactoring**. IntelliSense suggests other options or more details of a component when you write code, including code completion, information about the code, the usage of the code, and the code requirements. For example, if you are writing `Console`, it will suggest different options that you might want to write and will also tell you what that particular code does and how to use it, as shown in the following screenshot. This is very helpful when learning about different methods and how they are used:

Different console methods

Refactoring means improving the code without changing its functionality. Later in this chapter, we will talk about refactoring in detail.

Another very interesting feature available in the Editor window is Quick Action, which is the light bulb on the left-hand side of the selected line of code. This recommends things that Visual Studio thinks you should change about that particular line of code. You can also use this for refactoring your code. For example, if we stop in the middle of writing `Console` and look at the bulb, it will show you a red cross at the bottom of the bulb, which means that this line of code is not valid and Visual Studio has some recommendations. Let's see what it recommends and whether we can use it to fix our code.

*Visual Studio and Associated Tools*

If we click on the bulb, it will show the options that you can see in the following screenshot. From there, **Change 'Conso' to 'Console'** is the option that we want to execute. If we click it, Visual Studio will fix the code for you:

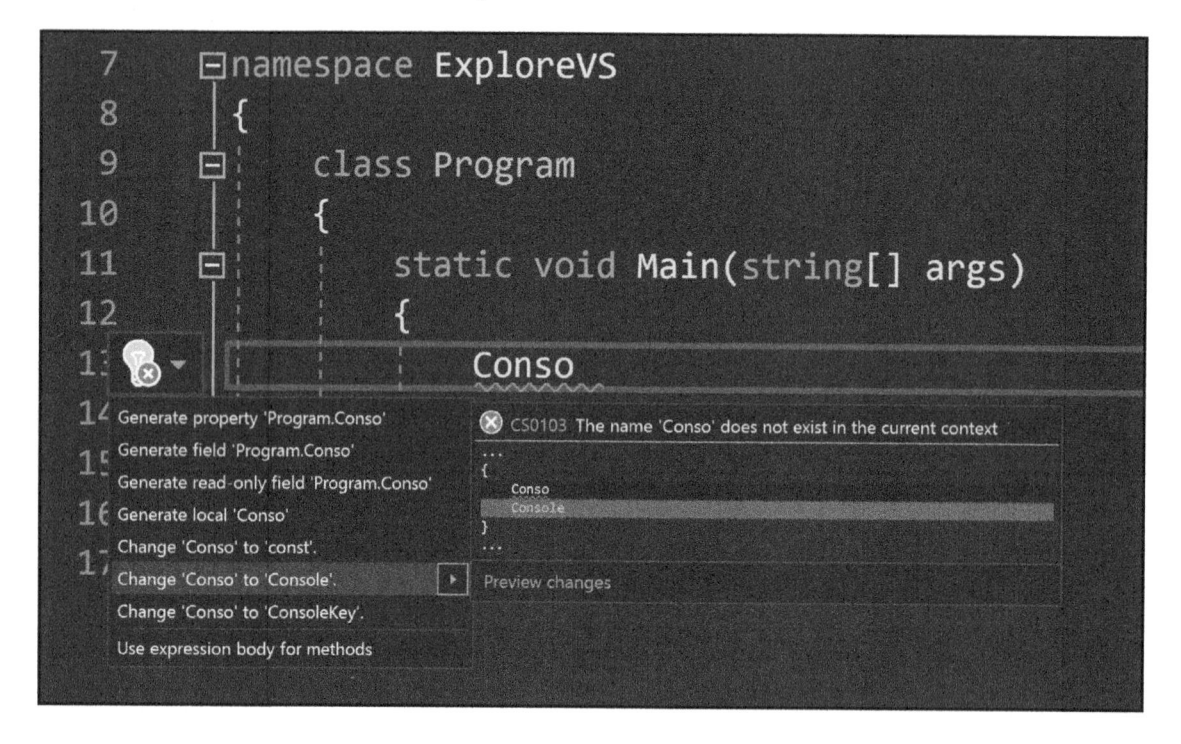

Let's see how we can refactor our code with Quick Action. If we try to create an object of a class that doesn't exist in the code base, it will show you a bulb with a red cross. If you take a look at the options, you will see that Visual Studio is asking whether it should create a class for you, as shown in the following screenshot:

```
 7      ☐namespace ExploreVS
 8      {
 9          ☐class Program
10          {
11              ☐static void Main(string[] args)
12              {
13                  Person person = new Person();
```

There are many other features available in the Editor windows to make your life more productive as a developer. I would suggest that you try more of these and read further documentation to learn more.

# Solution Explorer

If you take a look at the right-hand side of Visual Studio, you will see a window named **Solution Explorer**. This is a very important window in Visual Studio; it displays the files and folders in the solution you are working on. In Visual Studio, we have solutions that are like wrappers of different projects. This term could be a little confusing, as we would normally use the word *project* to identify a particular piece of work. In Visual Studio, solutions are created as wrappers and projects are created inside solutions. A solution can have multiple projects in it. This breakdown helps to make modular applications. In this **Solution Explorer** window, you can see which projects are in the solution and which files are in the projects.

*Visual Studio and Associated Tools*

You can expand or minimize the projects and folders to get a better view, as shown in the following screenshot:

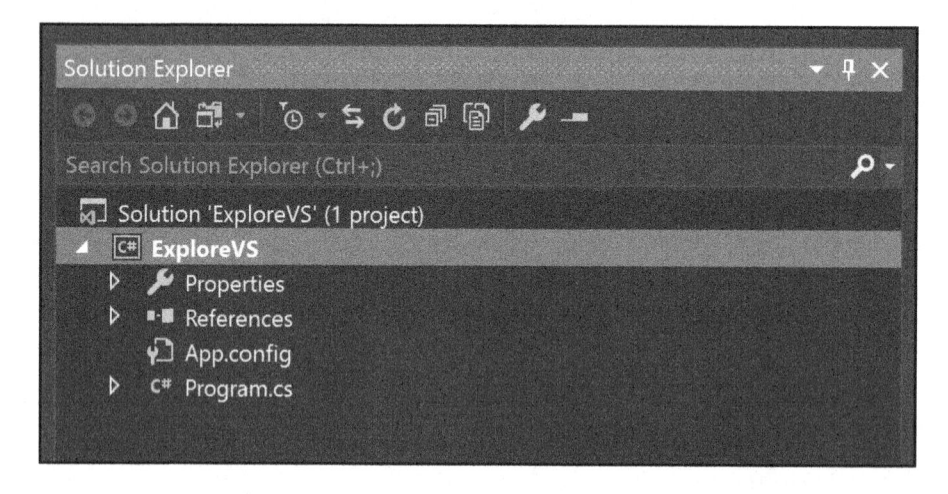

In the preceding screenshot, you can see that we have a solution called **ExploreVS**, and inside that, we have a project called **ExploreVS**. The project and the solution names are the same here because, when we created the solution, we chose to use the same name. If you want, you can have different names for the solution and the project.

In the **Solution Explorer** window, you can right-click on the solution and add another project easily. If you want to add a file or folder to the project, you can right-click on it and add it. In the following screenshot, you can see that we have added another project called **TestApp** to the solution, as well as a class called **Person** in the **ExploreVS** project. You can also see the number of projects that the solutions contain next to the solution name. There is also a search option in the **Solution Explorer** to search files easily in big solutions, in addition to some other features hiding behind the icons at the top. The circular arrow refreshes the **Solution Explorer**. Next to that, the stacked boxes collapse the projects to get a high-level view of the solution. After that, the icon with the three documents shows all the documents in the **Solution Explorer**. This is necessary because not every file is always available for viewing, as Visual Studio gives us the option to exclude files from the solution. This doesn't delete the file from the filesystem, but just ignores it in the solution. Then, next to that icon, we have a view code icon, which will open the code in the code editor. We also have the Properties icon, which will show the properties of a file or project.

On the left, we have the Home icon, which will bring you to the home panel. Next to that, we have the Solutions and Folders switcher. If you click that, instead of seeing the solution, you will see the folder of the filesystem, as shown in the following screenshot:

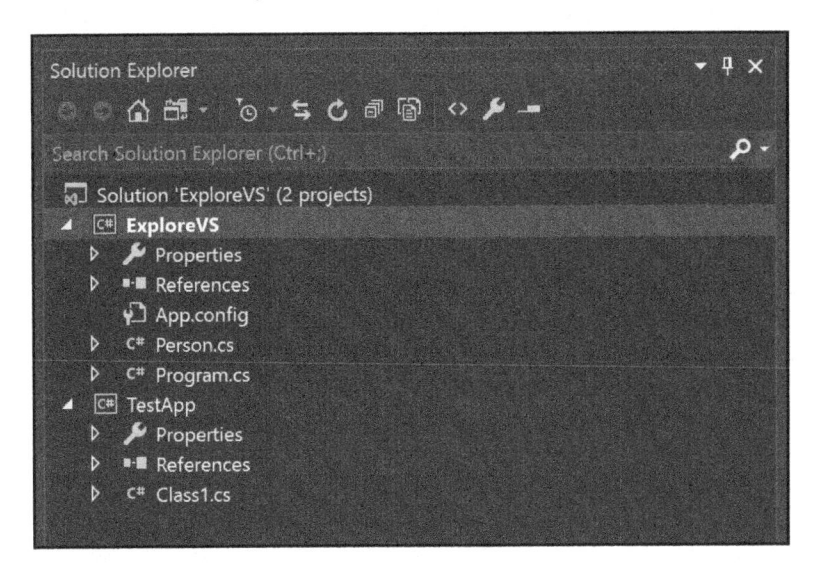

## Output window

The **Output** window is a very important window for a developer, as all the logs and outputs of your build and debugging can be viewed here. If you build your application and it fails, you can use the **Output** window to figure out what went wrong and fix the issue. If your build runs successfully, you will get a message that the build was successful in the **Output** window, as shown in the following screenshot:

*Visual Studio and Associated Tools*

You can view the different types of logs, such as your version control logs, in this window. To change the options, go to the drop-down menu next to the **Show output from** text and view the log of a particular output. You can clear the logs by clicking on the icon that has horizontal lines and a red cross and toggle the word-wrapping function using the next icon.

# Debugging windows

Debugging is a very important part of software development. When you write some code, there is a very high chance that your code won't build the first time. Even if it does build, you may not get the expected results. This is where debugging comes in handy. If you are using a text editor, it can be quite hard to debug some code, because normal text editors don't give you any debugging facilities, and so you might have to use a console. Visual Studio, however, provides some excellent tools and features for debugging, which can make you much more productive. To find these, go to the **Debug** menu from the Visual Studio menu bar and click on **Windows**, as shown in the following screenshot:

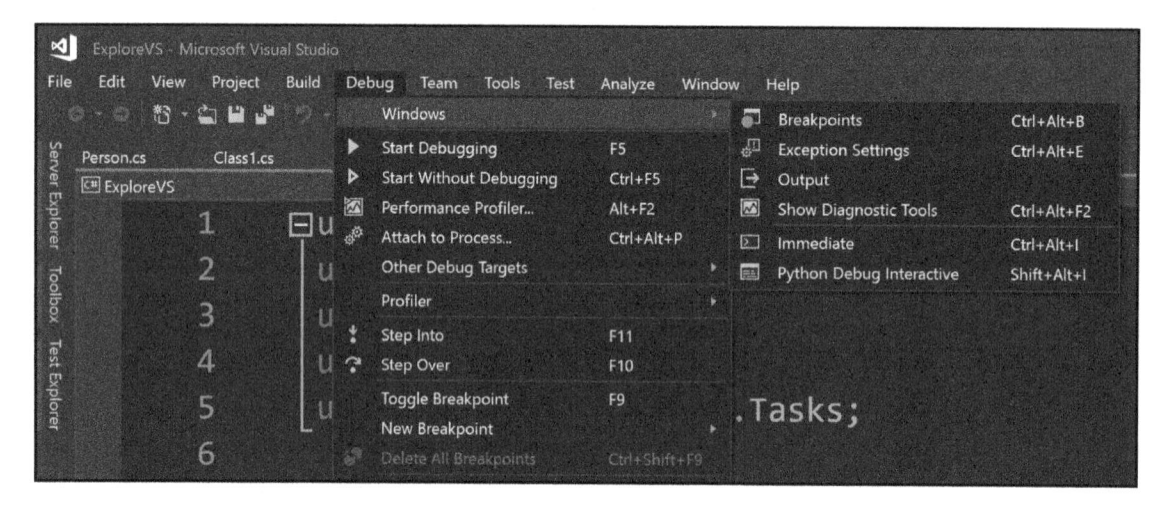

From this list, we can see that the different windows are as follows:

- **Breakpoints**
- **Exception Settings**
- **Output**
- **Show Diagnostic Tools**
- **Immediate**
- **Python Debug Interactive**

[ 166 ]

# Breakpoints window

The **Breakpoints** window lists the breakpoints that you have placed in your code base. It shows you information about the labels, conditions, filters, filenames, function names, and a few other properties in your code base, as shown in the following screenshot:

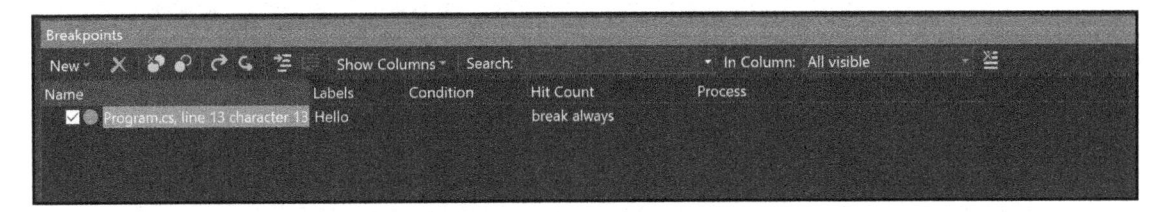

If you are not aware of the labels, conditions, and actions of a breakpoint, let's briefly look at them in the following list:

- **Labels**: You can name a breakpoint or give a label to a breakpoint to easily identify its purpose. You can right-click on a breakpoint and choose **Edit Labels** to add a label or choose from a previous label, as shown in the following screenshot:

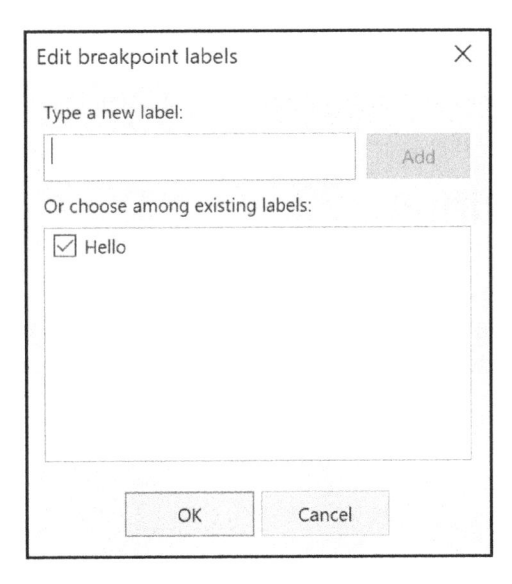

- **Conditions**: You can set the conditions on a breakpoint. This means that the breakpoint will only stop if those conditions are true. To add a condition to a breakpoint, right-click on the breakpoint and then click **Conditions**, as shown in the following screenshot:

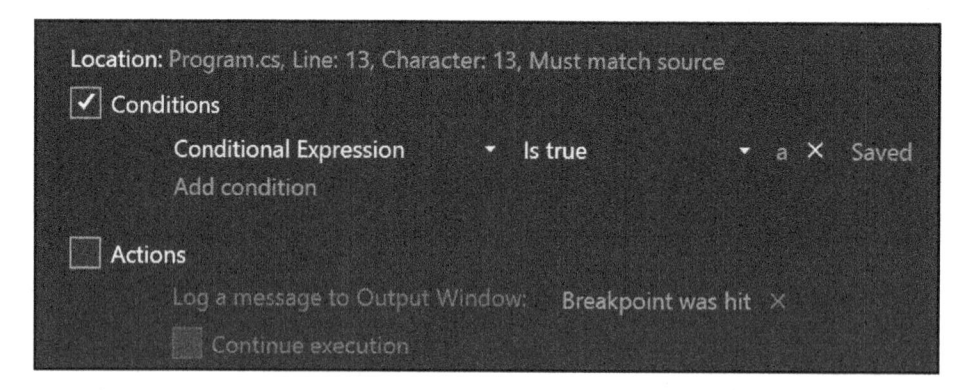

- **Actions**: Like conditions, you can add actions to a breakpoint. An example of an action could be to write in a logging system or console.

There are some other functionalities that the **Breakpoints** window has. You can delete all the breakpoints of the solution, disable or enable breakpoints, import or export breakpoints, go to the code location of a breakpoint, or search for a breakpoint.

# Exception Settings

The **Exception Settings** window displays the different exceptions that are available. If you open the window, you will see a list of exceptions and a checkbox next to each item. You can check a checkbox if you want the debugger to break that exception in Visual Studio, as shown in the following code:

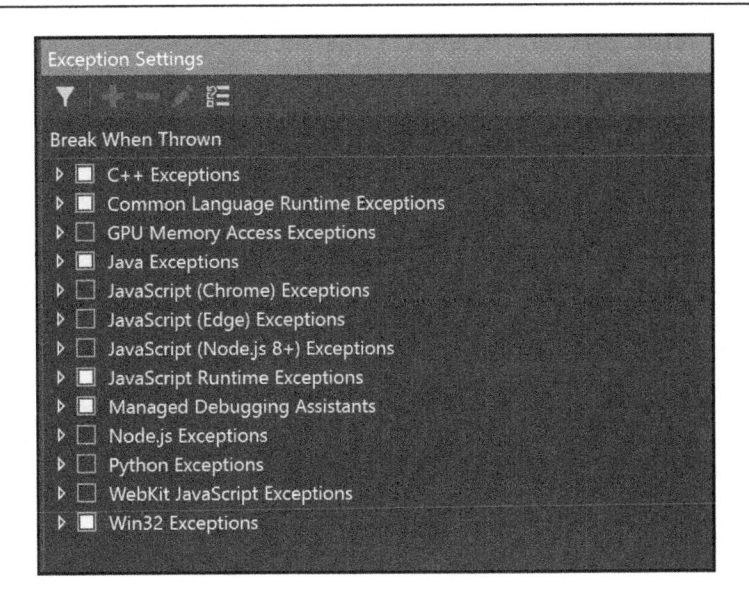

# Output

We have already discussed the **Output** window in the previous section. You can output different values in the **Output** window to check whether they are correct. You can read information about the exceptions in the **Output** window to find out more about the exceptions, as shown in the following screenshot:

*Visual Studio and Associated Tools*

# Diagnostic Tools

The **Diagnostic Tools** window will show you the performance of your application. You can check how much memory and CPU it is using, along with some other performance-related figures, as shown in the following screenshot:

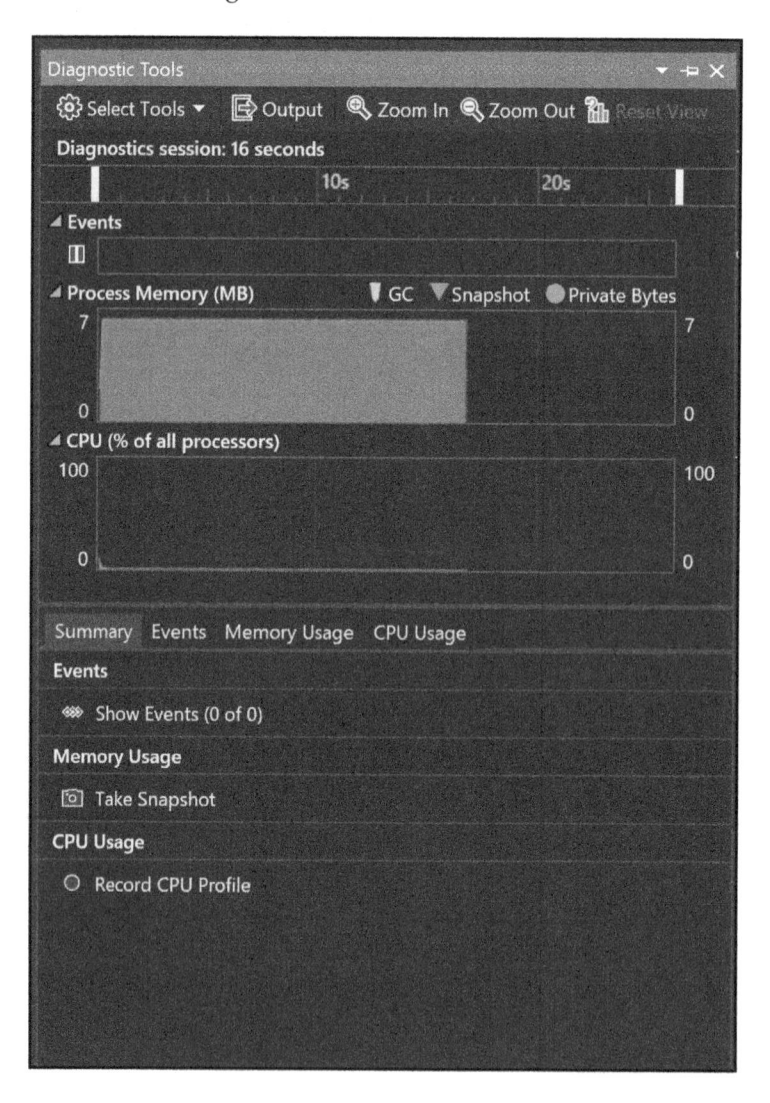

## Immediate window

The **Immediate** window helps you to debug the values of a variable, methods, and other code phrases while running the application. You can manually check the values of different variables at a certain point of a running program. You can check what a method is returning by executing it in this window. In the following screenshot, you can see that we have set a value 1 to an `int` variable called x. Then, we execute a method called Add(x,5), which returns the sum of the two numbers. Here, we pass x and 5 as parameters and get 6 in return:

```
Immediate Window
int x = 1;
Expression has been evaluated and has no value
x
1
Add(x,5)
6
```

## Python debugger window

Using the Python debugger window, you can run Python scripts on the application you are working on in Visual Studio. As this book has nothing to do with the Python programming language, we won't discuss this window in any more detail.

## Breakpoints, Call Stack Trace, and Watch

In the previous section, we looked at the windows that are used for debugging in Visual Studio. We'll now look at some cool features—breakpoints, Call Stack Trace, and Watch—in detail.

Visual Studio and Associated Tools

# Breakpoint

A **breakpoint** is not a feature of the C# programming language—it's a feature of the debugger that comes with Visual Studio. A breakpoint is a spot or place in your code where you want to pause the debugger to examine the code. In Visual Studio, breakpoints can be found in the left-hand pane of the code editor window. To add a breakpoint, click on the appropriate line of code and a red ball will appear, which represents the breakpoint. You can also use the *F9* key (or function 9 key) as a keyboard shortcut to toggle breakpoints.

The following screenshot shows what a breakpoint looks like in Visual Studio:

```
namespace ExploreVS
{
    class Program
    {
        static void Main(string[] args)
        {
            int a = 5;
            int b = a + 4;
            int c = a * 4;
            Console.WriteLine("Hello World! {0} and {1}", b, c);
            Console.ReadKey();
        }
```

After you place a breakpoint, the debugger will pause at that position and give you options to look around the data. When the debugger is paused at the breakpoint, you can choose to **Step Into**, **Step Over**, or **Step Out** to navigate the code, as indicated by the arrows in the top bar. In the circle, you will see an arrow indicating where the debugger is now pointing, as shown in the following screenshot:

*Chapter 9*

```
namespace ExploreVS
{
    class Program
    {
        static void Main(string[] args)
        {
            int a = 5;
            int b = a + 4;
            int c = a * 4;
            Console.WriteLine("Hello World! {0} and {1}", b, c);
            Console.ReadKey();
        }

        public static int Add(int a, int b)
        {
            return a + b;
```

The main purpose of breakpoints is to check the data and see how a particular piece of code reacts when it is run. Visual Studio provides a very easy way to debug code using breakpoints.

## Call Stack Trace

**Call Stack** is a window that is very useful when debugging your application. It shows you the flow of your application and tells you which methods have been called to reach a certain point. For example, if you have a method that can be called by two different sources, then, by looking at the call stack, you can easily identify which source called the method and get a better idea of the program flow.

# Watch window

The **Watch** window is another very useful feature for debugging in Visual Studio. In your code base, you might face a situation where you need to check the value of a particular variable. Hovering over to check the value every time is time-consuming. Instead, you can add those variables to your watch list and keep the **Watch** window open in Visual Studio to see the values of those variables at that moment.

In the following screenshot, you can see how the **Watch** window is used to watch the variable values:

```
namespace ExploreVS
{
    class Program
    {
        static void Main(string[] args)
        {
            Calc calc = new Calc();
            int a = 5;
            int b = a + 4;
            int c = calc.Calculate(a, b);
            Console.WriteLine("Hello World! {0} and {1}", b, c);
            Console.ReadKey();
        }
    }
}
```

| Name | Value | Type |
|------|-------|------|
| a    | 5     | int  |
| b    | 9     | int  |

# Git in Visual Studio

Version control is now an essential part of software development. It doesn't matter how big or small a project is, version control is a must for every software application. There are many version control systems available, but Git is the most popular. For the remote repository, you can use Microsoft Team Foundation Server, Microsoft Azure, GitHub, or any other remote repository. As GitHub is also the most popular remote repository, we will take a look at how to integrate it with Visual Studio in this section.

Currently, by default, Visual Studio doesn't have the functionality to connect with GitHub, and so you have to use an extension. To get the extension, go to **Tools** | **Extensions and Updates**. Then, in the **Online** category, search for GitHub. You will see an extension called **Github Extension for Visual Studio**, as shown in the following screenshot. Install the extension and restart Visual Studio:

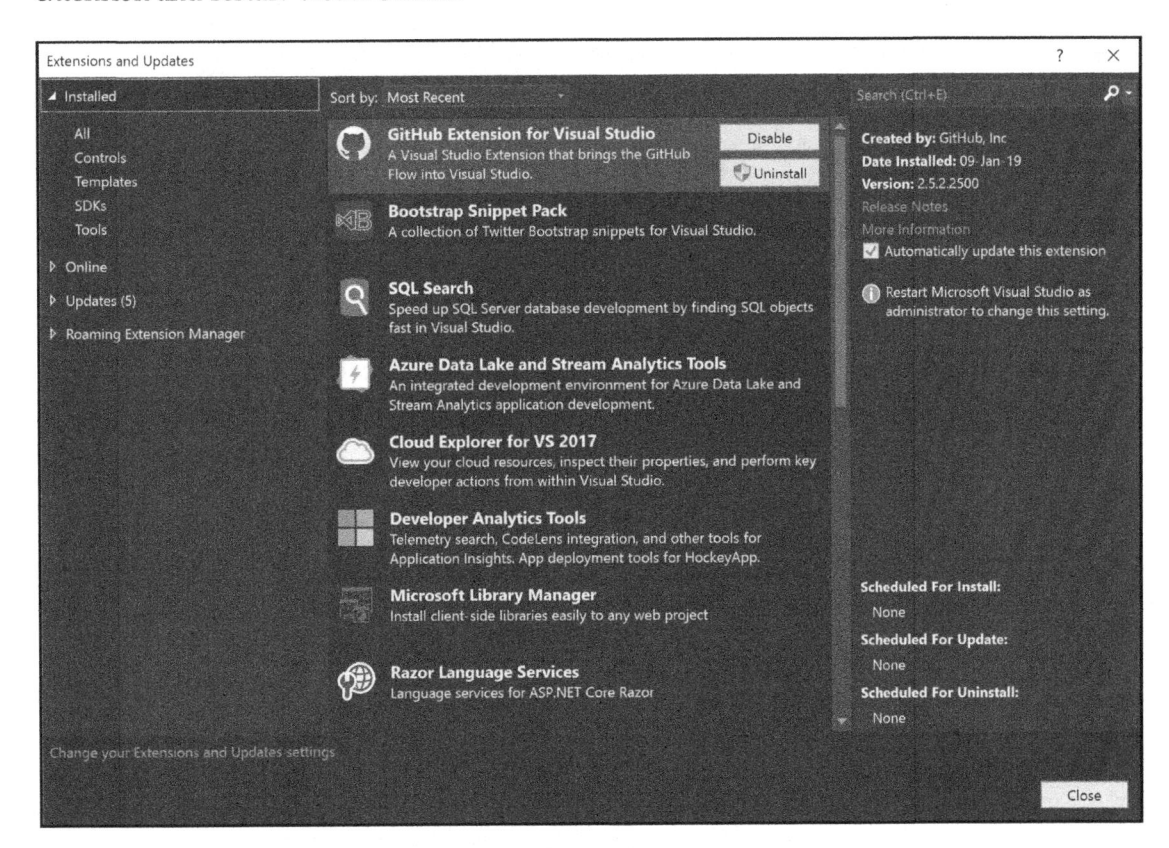

*Visual Studio and Associated Tools*

Now, if you open the **Team Explorer** window, you can see a section for **GitHub**. Enter your GitHub credentials and connect, as shown in the following screenshot. After the connection is confirmed, you will be all set to communicate with GitHub through Visual Studio:

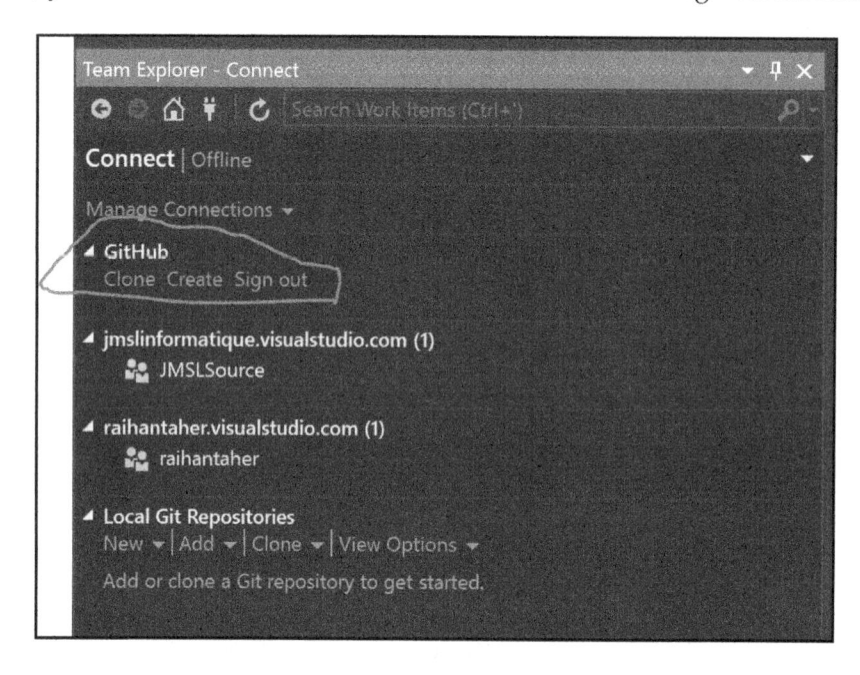

You can create or clone repositories from Visual Studio and keep committing your code and pushing it to the remote repository in GitHub. You can also carry out all major Git tasks in Visual Studio. You can create branches, push and pull code, and send pull requests.

The following screenshot shows the Git panel in the Visual Studio **Team Explorer** window:

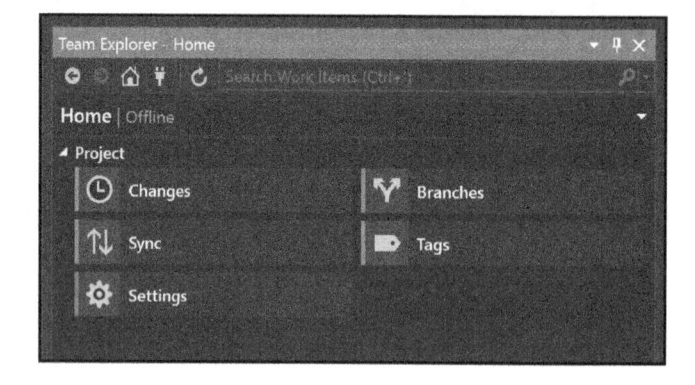

It's really useful to be able to use your IDE to handle version control without having to use any external software. You don't need to use the CLI for your version control either.

# Refactoring and code-optimization techniques

If you're not aware of the concept of refactoring, I recommend that you carry out some further research; it is a very interesting topic, and crucial for quality software development. Basically, refactoring refers to the process of modifying existing code for the sake of code improvement without changing its functionality.

Visual Studio provides some excellent features and tools for refactoring. We'll take a look at a few of these in the following sections.

## Rename

You can change the name of a method, field, property, class, or anything else by using the **Rename** feature of Visual Studio, as shown in the following screenshot. To do this, highlight the entity and press *Ctrl + R* twice. Alternatively, go to **Edit | Refactor | Rename**. When you change the name this way, it will be updated wherever it is used. This simple refactoring step allows you to change the name of something anytime you like:

## Changing the method signature

Imagine that you have a method that is used in many places in your solution. Now, if you change the parameters of that method, your code will break until you fix the method everywhere it is used. Doing this manually is time-consuming, and is likely to generate errors. Visual Studio provides a refactoring feature that can be used to refactor a method signature wherever it is used in the code, as shown in the following screenshot.

If you want to change the parameter sequence in a method, you can use *Ctrl + R* and *Ctrl + O* or click **Edit | Refactor | Reorder Parameter** from the menu. To remove a parameter from the method, you can use *Ctrl + R* and *Ctrl + V* or click **Edit | Refactor | Remove Parameters**:

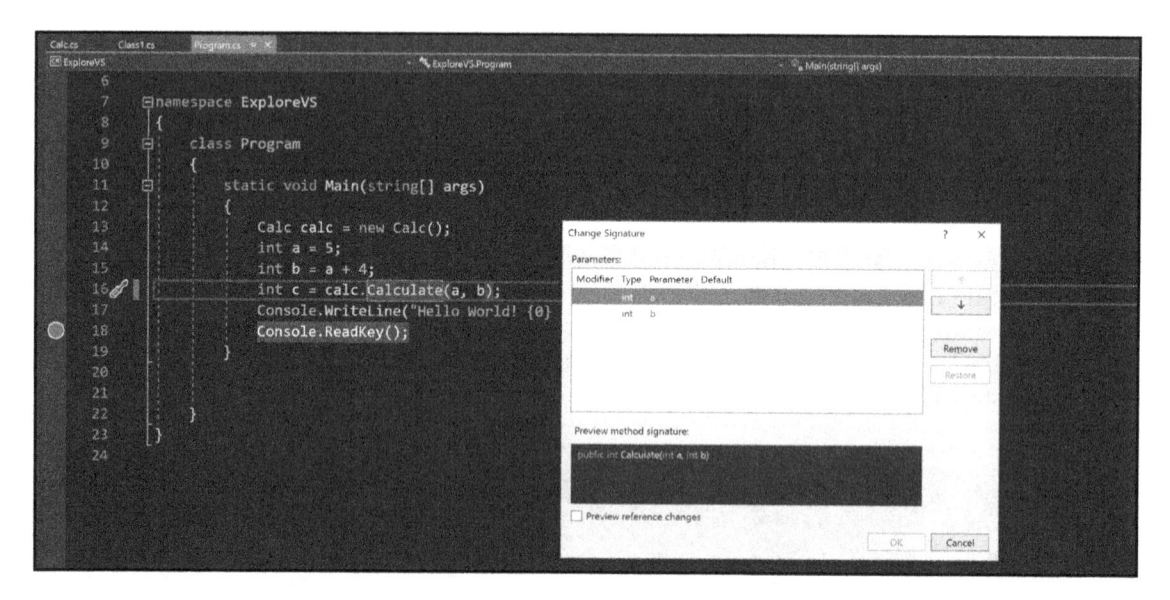

It is always recommend that you use Visual Studio refactoring tools rather than refactoring manually.

# Encapsulate Field

You can use the Visual Studio refactoring tool to convert a field to a property, instead of doing it manually. Highlight the field and press *Ctrl + R* and *Ctrl + E*, or go to **Edit | Refactor | Encapsulate Field**.

This will change all the places in the code in which the variable has been used, as shown in the following screenshot:

*Visual Studio and Associated Tools*

# Extract Method

If you see a piece of code and you think it should be in a method, you can use **Extract Method** refactoring to extract the selected code and create a new method for it, as shown in the following screenshot. The refactoring tool is so smart that it can also identify whether the method should return a particular value or not. To do this, select the code you want to extract to a method, then press *Ctrl + R* and *Ctrl + M*, or go to **Edit** | **Refactor** | **Extract Method**:

There are many other refactoring features available in Visual Studio. It isn't possible to cover them all here; I recommend that you look at the Visual Studio documentation for more information.

# Encapsulate Field

You can use the Visual Studio refactoring tool to convert a field to a property, instead of doing it manually. Highlight the field and press *Ctrl + R* and *Ctrl + E*, or go to **Edit | Refactor | Encapsulate Field**.

This will change all the places in the code in which the variable has been used, as shown in the following screenshot:

*Visual Studio and Associated Tools*

# Extract Method

If you see a piece of code and you think it should be in a method, you can use **Extract Method** refactoring to extract the selected code and create a new method for it, as shown in the following screenshot. The refactoring tool is so smart that it can also identify whether the method should return a particular value or not. To do this, select the code you want to extract to a method, then press *Ctrl + R* and *Ctrl + M*, or go to **Edit | Refactor | Extract Method**:

There are many other refactoring features available in Visual Studio. It isn't possible to cover them all here; I recommend that you look at the Visual Studio documentation for more information.

# Summary

Visual Studio is an essential tool for a C# developer; understanding it properly will increase your productivity. In this chapter, we discussed various concepts related to Visual Studio, including its project and templates, its different editors and windows, and its debugging facilities. We also looked at breakpoints, Call Stack Trace, and the Watch window, and how to use these to optimize your debugging process. After that, we explored Git and GitHub integration with Visual Studio. Finally, we talked about the different refactoring features that are available in Visual Studio. It's very hard to cover all of the concepts that are related to such an extraordinary IDE in one chapter of a book; I would recommend that you play with it and explore it further in order to learn how to use it in the best way possible. In the next chapter, we will talk about databases and ADO.NET.

# 10
# Exploring ADO.NET with Examples

If you have any exposure to web development, you might have heard of ASP.NET, which is a framework for web development. Similarly, if you have worked with databases before in .NET projects, you should have heard of or used ADO.NET. ADO.NET is a framework that's similar to ASP.NET, but instead of web development, this framework is used for database-related work. **ActiveX Data Object (ADO)** was an old technology created by Microsoft, but the evolution to ADO.NET has been extraordinary. ADO.NET contains classes and methods that can be used to easily establish a connection with a database management system such as SQL Server or Oracle. Not only that, it also provides methods and objects that help to execute commands in the database, such as select, insert, update, and delete.

We need a separate framework for database connection and activity because there are a lot of different database systems that can be used when developing an application. Databases are a very important part of an application; applications need data and data needs to be stored in a database. Because databases are so important and there are so many databases available, it would be very hard for a developer to write all of the necessary code. It's not worth writing separate bits of code when we could write one piece of code that is reusable. This is why Microsoft came up with the ADO.NET framework. This framework has different data providers, datasets, data adapters, and various other things that are related to databases.

This chapter will cover the following topics:

- The fundamentals of ADO.NET
- `DataProvider`, `Connection`, **Command**, `DataReader`, and `DataAdapter`
- Connecting SQL Server Database and the Oracle Database

- Stored Procedures
- Entity Frameworks
- Transactions in SQL

# The fundamentals of ADO.NET

To learn about ADO.NET, we need to know how an application works with a database. Then, we need to know how ADO.NET provides support for this process. Let's start by learning about some important concepts.

## Data providers

There are different kinds of data providers available in ADO.NET. The most popular data providers are SQL Server, **Open Database Connectivity (ODBC)**, **Object Linking and Embedding Database (OLE DB)**, and **Java Database Connectivity (JDBC)**. These data providers have a very similar code structure, which makes a developer's life much easier. If you have used one in the past, you will be able to use any of the others without much difficulty. These data providers can be divided into different components: Connection, Command, DataReader, and DataAdapter.

## Connection objects

Connection is a component that establishes a connection with a database to execute a command on the database. It doesn't matter which database you want to connect, you can use ADO.NET for them all. Even if there is no specific data provider for a particular database, you can use the OLE DB data provider to connect with any database. This connection object has a property called `connectionstring`. That is one of the most important elements of connection. The `connection` string is a string that holds data as key-value pairs. For example, a `connection` string contains information about the server in which the database is located, the name of the database, the user credentials, and some more information. If the database is in the same computer, you have to use `localhost` as the server. `ConnectionString` contains the database name and the authorization data, such as the username and password required to access the database. Let's see an example of `connectionString` for SQL Server:

```
SqlConnection con = new SqlConnection();
Con.connectionString = "Data Source=localhost; database=testdb; Integrated Security=SSPI";
```

Here, `Data Source` is the server name as the database is located in the same computer. The `database` keyword in the `connection` string holds the name of the database, which is `testdb` in this example. You will see in some `connection` strings that `Initial Catalog` is used instead of the `database` keyword in the `connection` string to store the name of the database. You can use either `Initial Catalog` or `database` to specify the name of the database in `connection` string. The last part of the `connectionString` property that we have here is `Integrated Security`, which is used as authentication. If you set it as `TRUE` or `SSPI`, this means that you are instructing the program to use Windows authentication to access the database. If you have a specific database user that you want to use, you can specify that by adding a `user` key and a `password` key in the `connection` string. You can provide some other data as well, including connection timeout and connect timeout. This `connection` string contains the minimum information required.

## The Command object

The Command object is used to give instructions to the database. Every data provider has its own `command` object that is inherited from the `DbCommand` object. The `command` object in the SQL data provider is `SqlCommand`, whereas the OLE DB provider has an `OleDbCommand` object. The command object is used to execute any kind of SQL statement, such as `SELECT`, `UPDATE`, `INSERT`, or `DELETE`. Command objects can also execute Stored Procedures. Later in the *Working with stored procedures* section, we will look at how to do that. They also have a few methods that are used to let the compiler know what type of command we are executing. For example, the `ExecuteReader` method queries in the database and returns a `DataReader` object:

```
using System.Data.SqlClient;
using System;
using System.Data;

public class Program
{
    public static void Main()
    {
        string connectionString = "Data source = localhost;Initial Catalog=TestDBForBook;Integrated Security = SSPI;";
        SqlConnection conn = new SqlConnection(connectionString);
        string sql = "SELECT * FROM Person";
        SqlCommand command = new SqlCommand(sql, conn);
        conn.Open();
        SqlDataReader reader = command.ExecuteReader();
        while (reader.Read())
        {
            Console.WriteLine("FirstName " + reader[1] + " LastName " +
```

*Exploring ADO.NET with Examples*

```
    reader[2]);
        }
            conn.Close();
    }
}
```

The output is as follows:

```
C:\WINDOWS\system32\cmd.exe
FirstName John LastName Nash
FirstName John LastName Doe
FirstName John LastName Wall
Press any key to continue . . .
```

The database table appears as follows:

|   | Id | FirstName | LastName | Age |
|---|----|-----------|----------|-----|
| 1 | 1  | John      | Nash     | 34  |
| 2 | 2  | John      | Doe      | 36  |
| 3 | 3  | John      | Wall     | 28  |

`ExecuteNonQuery` is another method that is mainly used to execute non-query methods, such as INSERT, UPDATE, and DELETE. When you insert some data into a database, you are not querying anything in the database, you just want to insert the data. The same goes for update and delete. The `ExecuteNonQuery` method returns an INT value, which represents how many rows in the database were affected by the command. For example, if you are inserting a person in a Person table, you are inserting one new row in the table, so only one row is getting affected. The method will therefore return 1 to you.

Let's see an example code of the `ExecuteNonQuery()` method:

```
using System.Data.SqlClient;
using System;
using System.Data;
public class Program
{
    public static void Main()
    {
```

```
            string connectionString = "Data source = localhost;Initial Catalog=
    TestDBForBook;Integrated Security = SSPI;";
            SqlConnection conn = new SqlConnection(connectionString);
            string sql = "INSERT INTO Person (FirstName, LastName, Age) VALUES
    ('John', 'Nash', 34)";
            SqlCommand command = new SqlCommand(sql, conn);
            conn.Open();
            int rowsAffected = command.ExecuteNonQuery();
            conn.Close();
            Console.WriteLine("Number of rows inserted: " + rowsAffected);
        }
    }
```

The output is as follows:

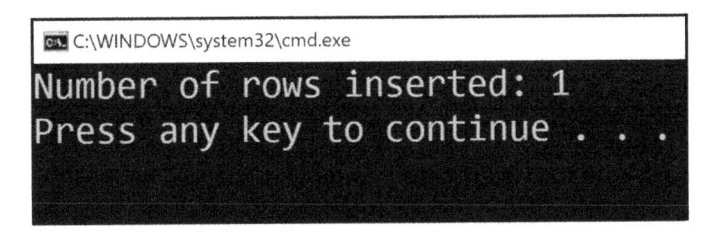

```
C:\WINDOWS\system32\cmd.exe
Number of rows inserted: 1
Press any key to continue . . .
```

Let's say you want to update the Age of Mr. John Nash. When you execute the UPDATE query, it will affect only one row of the table, so it will return 1. But, for example, if you execute a query in which the condition matches several different rows, it will update all of the rows and return the total number of rows that were affected. Take a look at the following example. Here, we have a Food table that has different food items. Every item has a category:

|   | Id | Name | Category | Price | Discount |
|---|----|------|----------|-------|----------|
| 1 | 1 | Chicken Burger | Lunch | 10 | 0 |
| 2 | 2 | Beef Burger | Lunch | 12 | 0 |
| 3 | 3 | Mixed Rice | Dinner | 8 | 0 |
| 4 | 4 | Pizza | Dinner | 10 | 0 |
| 5 | 5 | Egg | Breakfast | 2 | 0 |
| 6 | 6 | Tea | Breakfast | 1 | 0 |

Here, we can see that there is no discount on any food items. Let's say that we now want to give a discount of 5% on every breakfast item. To change the `Discount` value, you will have to execute an UPDATE command to update all of the rows. From the table, we can see that there are two breakfast items in the table. If we run an UPDATE command with a condition that applies only to `Category= 'Breakfast'`, it should affect two rows. Let's see the C# code for this process. We are going to use the `ExecuteNonQuery` command here:

```
using System.Data.SqlClient;
using System;
using System.Data;
public class Program
{
    public static void Main()
    {
        string connectionString = "Data source = localhost;Initial Catalog= TestDBForBook;Integrated Security = SSPI;";
        SqlConnection conn = new SqlConnection(connectionString);
        string sql = "UPDATE Food SET Discount = 5 WHERE Category = 'Breakfast'";
        SqlCommand command = new SqlCommand(sql, conn);
        conn.Open();
        int rowsAffected = command.ExecuteNonQuery();
        conn.Close();
        Console.WriteLine("Number of rows inserted: " + rowsAffected);
    }
}
```

The output is as follows:

```
Number of rows inserted: 2
Press any key to continue . . .
```

We can see from the output that 2 rows were affected. Now, let's take a look at the database table:

| | Id | Name | Category | Price | Discount |
|---|---|---|---|---|---|
| 1 | 1 | Chicken Burger | Lunch | 10 | 0 |
| 2 | 2 | Beef Burger | Lunch | 12 | 0 |
| 3 | 3 | Mixed Rice | Dinner | 8 | 0 |
| 4 | 4 | Pizza | Dinner | 10 | 0 |
| 5 | 5 | Egg | Breakfast | 2 | 0 |
| 6 | 6 | Tea | Breakfast | 1 | 0 |

We can see that two rows were changed.

If you execute a `DELETE` command using the `ExecuteNonQuery` method, it will return the amount of rows that were affected. If you get 0 as a result, this means that your command wasn't successfully executed.

There are many other methods in the `SQLCommand` object. `ExecuteScalar` returns a scalar value from the query. `ExecuteXMLReader` returns an `XmlReader` object. There are other methods that work in an asynchronous way. All of these methods work in a similar way to the examples shown here.

There is a property in the Command object called `CommandType`. `CommandType` is an `enum` type that states how the command is provided. The enum values are `Text`, `StoredProcedure`, and `TableDirect`. If text is selected, the SQL command will be executed as an SQL query in the data source directly. In `StoredProcedure`, you can set parameters and execute `storedprocedures` to execute a command in the database. By default, the value is set as `TEXT`. This is why, in the earlier examples, we didn't set the value of `CommandType`.

*Exploring ADO.NET with Examples*

## The DataReader object

DataReader objects provide a way of reading a forward-only stream of rows from database. Like the others, a DataReader is an object of a data provider. Every data provider has different DataReader objects that inherit from `DbDataReader`. When you execute an `ExecuteReader` command, it returns a `DataReader` object. You can process this `DataReader` object to collect the data you have queried for. If you are using SQL Server as your database, you should use the `SqlDataReader` object. `SqlDataReader` has a method called `Read()`, which returns `true` when you have available data in the `DataReader` object to read. If there is no data in the `SqlDataReader` object, the `Read()` method will return `false`. It's a common practice to first check whether the `Read()` method is `true` and then read the data. The following example shows how `SqlDataReader` is used:

```
using System.Data.SqlClient;
using System;
using System.Data;

public class Program
{
    public static void Main()
    {
        string connectionString = "Data source = localhost;Initial Catalog=TestDBForBook;Integrated Security = SSPI;";
        SqlConnection conn = new SqlConnection(connectionString);
        string sql = "SELECT * FROM Person";
        SqlCommand command = new SqlCommand(sql, conn);
        conn.Open();
        SqlDataReader reader = command.ExecuteReader();
        while (reader.Read())
        {
            Console.WriteLine("FirstName " + reader[1] + " LastName " + reader[2]);
        }
        conn.Close();
    }
}
```

Here, the `command.ExecuteReader()` method returns an `SqlDataReader` object, which holds the result of the query:

```
SELECT * FROM Person
```

First, we hold the returned object in a variable called **reader**, which is of
the `SqlDataReader` type. Then, we check whether its `Read()` method is `true`. If it is, we
execute the following statement:

```
Console.WriteLine("FirstName " + reader[1] + " LastName " +  reader[2]);
```

Here, the reader is working as an array and we get the value of the database table columns sequentially from the index. As we can see from the following table structure in the database, it has four columns, **Id**, **FirstName**, **LastName**, and **Age**:

| Column Name | Data Type | Allow Nulls |
|---|---|---|
| Id | int | ☐ |
| FirstName | nvarchar(50) | ☐ |
| LastName | nvarchar(50) | ☐ |
| Age | int | ☑ |
| | | ☐ |

These columns will be mapped one after another. `reader[0]` refers to the **Id** column, `reader[1]` refers to the **Firstname** column, and so on.

The statement we have written will print the value of the **FirstName** column, where it will find `reader[1]`. It will then print the value of the **LastName** column, where it will find `reader[2]`.

If this array index is confusing for you and if you want more readability, feel free to use named indexes instead of numbers:

```
Console.WriteLine("FirstName " + reader["FirstName"] + " LastName " + 
reader["LastName"])
```

This will print the same thing. Instead of putting `reader[1]`, we have written `reader["FirstName"]`, so it's clearer which column we are accessing. If you use this approach, make sure the name is written correctly.

# DataAdapter

`DataAdapter` is another way to read and use data from a data source. DataAdapter gives you an easy way to store the data directly to a dataset. You can also use DataAdapter to write back in the data source from the dataset. Every provider has its own DataAdapter. An SQL data provider, for example, has `SqlDataAdapter`.

*Exploring ADO.NET with Examples*

# Connecting to various databases

Let's see some examples of how to connect to different databases using ADO.NET. If you are using ADO.NET, the most probable database system you are going to use is SQL Server Database as that is the best match when you are using a Microsoft stack. You won't, however, have any reduction in performance or encounter problems if you use any other source. Let's see how we can connect with other databases with ADO.NET.

## SQL Server

To connect to SQL Server, we need to use the SQL Server provider in ADO.NET. Take a look at the following code:

```
using System.Data.SqlClient;
using System;
using System.Data;
public class Program
{
    public static void Main()
    {
        string connectionString = "Data source = localhost;Initial Catalog= TestDBForBook;Integrated Security = SSPI;";
        SqlConnection conn = new SqlConnection(connectionString);
        string sql = "SELECT * FROM Person";
        SqlCommand command = new SqlCommand(sql, conn);
        conn.Open();
        SqlDataReader reader = command.ExecuteReader();
        while (reader.Read())
        {
            Console.WriteLine("FirstName " + reader["FirstName"] + " LastName " +  reader["LastName"]);
        }
        conn.Close();
    }
}
```

## The Oracle database

To connect to the Oracle database, we need to use the ODBC provider in ADO.NET. Take a look at the following code:

```
using System.Data.SqlClient;
using System;
using System.Data;
using System.Data.Odbc;
public class Program
{
    public static void Main()
    {
        string connectionString = "Data Source=Oracle9i;User ID=*****;Password=*****;";
        OdbcConnection odbcConnection = new OdbcConnection(connectionString);
        string sql = "SELECT * FROM Person";
        OdbcCommand odbcCommand = new OdbcCommand(sql, odbcConnection);
        odbcConnection.Open();
        OdbcDataReader odbcReader = odbcCommand.ExecuteReader();
        while (odbcReader.Read())
        {
            Console.WriteLine("FirstName " + odbcReader["FirstName"] + " LastName " + odbcReader["LastName"]);
        }
        odbcConnection.Close();
    }
}
```

# Working with DataReaders and DataAdapters

DataReaders and DataAdapters are core objects of a data provider. These are some of the most important features that ADO.NET provides. Let's see how to work these objects.

*Exploring ADO.NET with Examples*

# DataReaders

Every provider has DataReaders. Underneath, all classes do the same thing. `SqlDataReader`, `OdbcDataReader`, and `OleDbDataReader` all implement the `IDataReader` interface. The main use of DataReader is to read data from a data source when it is coming from a stream. Let's take a look at the different properties that a data reader has:

| Property | Description |
| --- | --- |
| Depth | The depth of nesting for a row |
| FieldCount | Returns the number of columns in a row |
| IsClosed | Returns TRUE if DataReader is closed |
| Item | Returns the value of a column |
| RecordsAffected | The number of rows affected |

A DataReader has the following methods:

| Method | Description |
| --- | --- |
| Close | This method will close the DataReader object. |
| Read | This method will read the next piece of data in DataReader. |
| NextResult | This method will move the head to the next result. |
| GetString, GetChar, and so on | The GetString method will return the value in string format. GetChar will return the value in Char format. There are other methods that will return a value in that particular type. |

The following code snippet shows an example of DataReader:

```
using System;
using System.Collections.Generic;
using System.Text;
using System.Data.SqlClient;
namespace CommandTypeEnumeration
{
    class Program
    {
        static void Main(string[] args)
        {
            // Create a connection string
            string ConnectionString = "Integrated Security = SSPI; " +
            "Initial Catalog= Northwind; " + " Data source = localhost; ";
```

```csharp
            string SQL = "SELECT * FROM Customers";
            // create a connection object
            SqlConnection conn = new SqlConnection(ConnectionString);
            // Create a command object
            SqlCommand cmd = new SqlCommand(SQL, conn);
            conn.Open();
            // Call ExecuteReader to return a DataReader
            SqlDataReader reader = cmd.ExecuteReader();
            Console.WriteLine("customer ID, Contact Name, " + "Contact Title, Address ");
            Console.WriteLine("==============================");
            while (reader.Read())
            {
                Console.Write(reader["CustomerID"].ToString() + ", ");
                Console.Write(reader["ContactName"].ToString() + ", ");
                Console.Write(reader["ContactTitle"].ToString() + ", ");
                Console.WriteLine(reader["Address"].ToString() + ", ");
            }
            //Release resources
            reader.Close();
            conn.Close();
        }
    }
}
```

# DataAdapters

DataAdapters work like a bridge between disconnected ADO.NET objects and the data source. This means that they help to establish a connection and execute commands in the database. They also map back the query results to the disconnected ADO.NET objects. Data Adapters use `DataSet` or `DataTable` to store data after its retrieval from a data source. `DataAdapter` has a method called `Fill()`, which collects data from a data source and populates `DataSet` or `DataTable`. If you want to retrieve the schema information, you can use another method called `FillSchema()`. A further method, named `Update()`, transfers all changes made in `DataSet` or `DataTable` to the data source.

One of the benefits of using Data Adapters is that no information about the connection, database, tables, columns, or any other information related to the data source is passed to the disconnected object. It's therefore safe to use when passing a value to an external source.

# Working with stored procedures

**Stored Procedures** are batches of SQL statements that are stored in a database for the purpose of reuse. ADO.NET has support for Stored Procedures, which means that we can use ADO.NET to call stored procedures in a database and get results from them. It is a very common practice to pass parameters, which could be input or output parameters, to stored procedures. The ADO.NET command object has parameters that are objects of the parameter type. Depending on the provider, the parameter object changes, but they all follow the same base. Let's take a look at how to use stored procedures instead of normal SQL statements in ADO.NET.

To use a stored procedure, the SQL string that is passed in `SQLCommand` should be the name of the Stored Procedure:

```
string ConnectionString = "Integrated Security = SSPI;Initial Catalog=Northwind;Data source=localhost;";
SqlConnection conn = new SqlConnection(ConnectionString);
String sql = "InsertPerson";
SqlCommand command = new SqlCommand(sql, conn);
```

We normally pass parameters to stored procedures as follows:

```
using System.Data.SqlClient;
using System;
using System.Data;

public class Program
{
    public static void Main()
    {
        string ConnectionString = "Integrated Security = SSPI; Initial Catalog= Northwind; Data source = localhost; ";
        SqlConnection conn = new SqlConnection(ConnectionString);
 String sql = "InsertPerson";
 SqlCommand command = new SqlCommand(sql, conn);
 command.CommandType = CommandType.StoredProcedure;
 SqlParameter param = command.Parameters.Add("@FirstName", SqlDbType.NVarChar, 11);
 param.Value = "Raihan";
 param = command.Parameters.Add("@LastName", SqlDbType.NVarChar, 11);
 param.Value = "Taher";
 conn.Open();
 int rowsAffected = command.ExecuteNonQuery();
 conn.Close();
```

```
  Console.WriteLine(rowsAffected);
    }
}
```

Let's now see the stored procedure to get an idea of how the parameter is used:

```
CREATE procedure InsertPerson (
@FirstName nvarchar (11),
@LastName nvarchar (11)
)
AS
INSERT INTO Person (FirstName, LastName) VALUES (@FirstName, @LastName);
GO
```

# Working with the Entity Framework

**The Entity Framework (EF)** is an **Object Relational Mapper (ORM)** framework developed by Microsoft. It was developed for .NET developers to work with databases easily using entity objects. It sits in the middle of your backend code or business logic and the database. It allows the developer to write code in the application language, C#, to talk with the database. This means that there is no need to use and write the ADO.NET code manually, which we did in the preceding sections. EF has different kinds of commands to the normal SQL commands. EF commands, which look very similar to C# code, will communicate with the database using SQL in the background. It can communicate with any type of data source, so you don't have to worry about setting up or writing different code for each DBMS.

# What is an entity in the Entity Framework?

An entity is a class in the application domain that is also included as a `DbSet` property in the derived `DbContext` class. An entity is transformed into a table and the properties of an entity are transformed as columns when EF executes it:

```
public class Student{
}

public class StudentClass{
}

public class Teacher{
}

public class SchoolContext : DbContext {
```

*Exploring ADO.NET with Examples*

```
    public SchoolContext(){}
    public DbSet<Student> Students { get; set; }
    public DbSet<StudentClass> StudentClasses { get; set; }
    public DbSet<Teacher> Teachers { get; set; }
}
```

# Different types of Entity properties

Let's see what different types of properties an Entity can have:

- Scalar properties
- Navigation properties. These include the following:
    - Reference Navigation properties
    - Collection Navigation properties

# Scalar properties

These are the properties that are used as columns in the database directly. They are used to save and query in the database. Let's see an example of these properties:

```
public class Student{
    public int StudentID { get; set; }
    public string StudentName { get; set; }
    public DateTime? DateOfBirth { get; set; }
    public byte[]  Photo { get; set; }
    public decimal Height { get; set; }
    public float Weight { get; set; }
    public StudentAddress StudentAddress { get; set; }
    public Grade Grade { get; set; }
}
```

The following properties are scalar properties:

```
public int StudentID { get; set; }
public string StudentName { get; set; }
public DateTime? DateOfBirth { get; set; }
public byte[]  Photo { get; set; }
public decimal Height { get; set; }
public float Weight { get; set; }
```

## Navigation properties

This type of property represents relationships between entities. They are not related directly to particular columns. There are two types of navigation properties:

- **Reference navigation property:** If another entity type is used as a property, it is called a reference navigation property
- **Collection navigation property:** If an entity is included as a collection type, it is called a collection navigation property

An example of navigation properties is as follows:

```
public Student Student { get; set; }
public ICollection<Student> Students { get; set; }
```

Here, `Student` is a reference navigation property and `Students` is a collection navigation property.

Now let's see the two approaches of using EF: the **code-first approach** and the **database-first approach**.

## The code-first approach

This can be thought of as similar to domain-driven design. In this approach, you write the entity objects and the domain and then use the domain to generate a database using EF. Using different attributes in the entity objects, EF can understand what to do with the database and how. For example, if you want a particular property in your model to be treated as a primary key, you can use data annotations or a fluent API to indicate to the EF that it should treat this column as a primary key when creating the table in the database.

## The database-first approach

In this approach, you create the database first and then ask EF to generate the entity for you. You make all of your changes at the database level and not in your entities in the backend application. Here, the EF does a different job to in the code-first approach. In the database-first approach, EF reads through the database tables and columns and generates C# classes models in which each column is treated as a property. The EF also takes care of the relationship between different database tables and creates the same kind of relationship in the generated models.

## Using the Entity Framework

Both approaches have their benefits, but the code-first approach is more popular among developers as you have to deal less with the database and work more in C#.

An EF doesn't comes with the .NET framework by default. You have to download the library from the NuGet package manager and install it in the project you are working with. To download and install the entity framework, you can open the Nuget **Package Manager Console** and write the following command:

```
Install-Package EntityFramework
```

This command will download and install the Entity Framework in your project:

If you are not comfortable with the **Package Manager Console**, you can also use the GUI's **Manage Packages for Solution** window to install entity framework. Go to the **Browse** tab and search for **Entity Framework**. You will see it at the top of the search results. Click it and install it in your project:

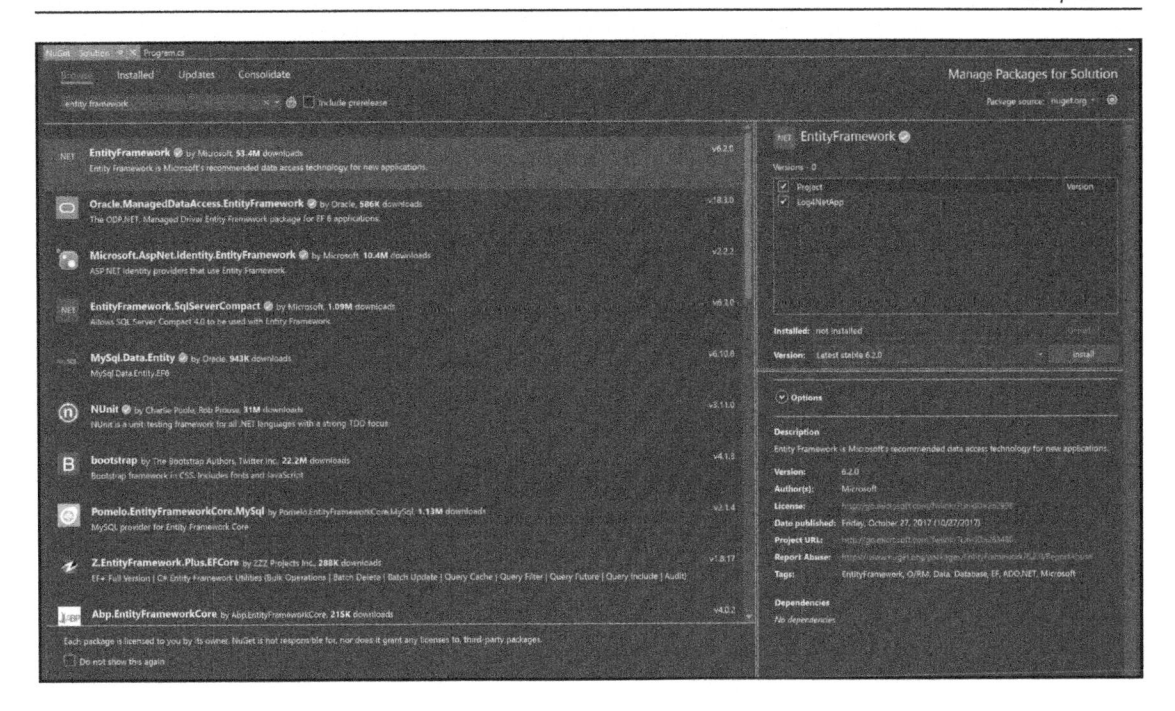

*Installing Entity Framework using Nuget Package Manager*

In this book, we are focusing more on C#, so we will look more closely at the code-first approach than the database-first approach. In the code-first approach, as we don't touch the database code, we need to make our entity objects in a way that can be followed when creating a database. After we have created the database tables, if we want to update the tables or change the tables, we need to use migrations. Database migration creates a new instance of the database and applies the new changes in the new instance. By using migrations, it's easier to manipulate the database.

Let's now learn a little bit more about the history and the flow of EF. It was first published in the year 2008 with .NET 3.5. At the time of writing this book, the latest version of EF is version 6. EF also has a .NET Core version that is called **Entity Framework Core**. Both frameworks are open source. When you install an entity framework in your project and write a **Plain Old CLR Object** (**POCO**) class, that POCO class is used by the entity framework. First, EF creates an **Entity Data Model** (**EDM**) from it. This EDM is used later to save and query in the database. **Language Integrated Queries** (**LINQs**) and SQL can both be used to give instructions to EF. When one entity object is used in EDM, it is tracked. When it is updated, the database will also be updated.

We can use the `SaveChanges()` method to execute insert, update, and delete activity in the database. For asynchronous programming, the `SaveChangesAsync()` method is used. For a better query experience, EF has first-level caching, so when repeated queries are executed, EF returns the results from the cache instead of going to the database to collect the same result.

An EF API mainly does four things:

- Maps classes to the database schema
- Translates LINQs into Entity Queries to SQL and executes them
- Tracks changes
- Saves changes in the database

EF converts entity objects and context classes into EDM, and EDM is used in the database. For example, let's say we have the following class:

```
public class Person {
    public int PersonId { get; set; }
    public string FirstName { get; set; }
    public string LastName { get; set; }
}
```

The EF will convert it into EDM, which looks as follows:

```
Table Name: Person
PersonId(PK,int,not null)
FirstName (nvarchar(50),null)
LastName (nvarchar(50),null)
```

Then, this EDM will be used to create or update the `Person` database table.

# Transactions in SQL

A transaction is a single unit of work that either has to complete the whole work or roll back to its previous state. A transaction can't stop in the middle of a piece of work. It's a very important feature for sensitive data-handling. One of the best uses of transactions is when dealing with money-transfer processes. When a person transfers some money to another person's account, if any error occurs in the middle of the process, the whole process should be cancelled or rolled back.

There are four properties of a transaction in SQL: **Atomic, Consistent, Isolated, and Durable (ACID)**.

## Atomic

Atomic means that all statements in a group must be executed. If one of the statements in a group doesn't get executed, none of the statement should be executed. The whole group of the statement should work as a single unit.

## Consistent

When a transaction is executed, the database should reach from one state to another. We call the initial point the starting point and the point after execution the end point. In a transaction, the start and end points should be clear. If the transaction is successful, the database state should be at the end point, otherwise it should be at the start point. Maintaining this consistency is what this property is about.

## Isolated

A group of a statements that are part of a transaction should be isolated from other statements in another transaction or manual statements. While a transaction is running, if another statement changes a particular piece of data, the whole transaction would produce bad data. When a transaction is run, all other outside statements are not allowed to run on that particular piece of data in the database.

## Durable

After a group of statements is executed, the result needs to be stored in a permanent place. If, in the middle of a transaction, an error occurs, the statements can be rolled back and the database goes to its previous position.

Transactions plays a very important role in SQL, so the SQL data provider provides the SQLTransaction class, which can be used to execute transactions using ADO.NET.

# Summary

Data is a very important part of a software application. To maintain data, we need some kind of database that will store the data in a structured way, so that it can be easily retrieved, saved, updated, and deleted. It's essential that our software is able to communicate with a data source to use the data. The ADO.NET framework provides this facility to .NET developers. Learning and understanding ADO.NET is one of the basic requirements of any .NET developer. In this chapter, we covered the fundamentals of ADO.NET elements, such as `DataProviders`, `Connection`, **Command**, `DataReader`, and `DataAdapter`. We also learned how to connect with the SQL Server database and the Oracle Database using ADO.NET. We discussed stored procedures and explained what the Entity Framework is and how to use it.

In the next chapter, we will be talking about a very interesting topic: Reflection.

# 11
# New Features in C# 8

For decades, we have seen the development of a wide variety of programming languages. Some are now almost dead, some are used by few companies, and others have remained dominant in the market for many years. C# belongs to the third category. The first version of C# was released in the year 2000. When C# was released, many people said that it was a clone of Java. Over time, however, C# became more mature and started dominating the market. This is especially the case for the Microsoft technology stack, where C# is undoubtedly the number one programming language. With every new release, Microsoft has introduced amazing features and made the language very powerful.

At the end of 2018, Microsoft announced some exciting features that will be available in C# 8. At the time of writing, C# 8 is still yet to be officially released, so I can't guarantee that all of these features will be available in the final release. However, there is a very high chance that these features will be available in the final release. In this chapter, we will look at these features and try to understand how the language is evolving into an extraordinary programming language. Let's take a look at the features that we are going to discuss:

- Nullable reference types
- Async streams
- Ranges and indices
- Default implementation of interface members
- Switch expressions
- Target-typed new expressions

# Environment Setup

To execute the code of this chapter you will need **Visual Studio 2019**. At the time of my writing this book, Visual Studio 2019 is not yet released officially. However, the preview version is available and to execute the code of this chapter, you will need Visual Studio 2019 preview version at least. Another thing to keep in mind is to create **.NET Core** Console App projects when testing the code of this chapter.

To download Visual Studio 2019 Preview Version, go to this link: `https://visualstudio.microsoft.com/vs/preview/`.

Visual Studio 2019 Preview download page

# Nullable reference types

If you have ever faced an exception while coding in C#, it is likely to have been a null reference exception. Null reference exceptions are one of the most common exceptions a programmer will face while developing applications, so the C# language development team has worked hard to make them easier to understand.

In C#, there are two types of data: **value types** and **reference types**. Value types normally have default values when you create them, whereas reference types are, by default, null. Null means that the memory address does not point to any other memory address. When the program tries to find a reference and can't find any, it throws an exception. As developers, we want to ship software that is exception-free, so we try to handle all the exceptions in our code; however, sometimes, it can be really hard to find a null reference exception when developing applications.

In C# 8, the language development team came up with nullable reference types, which means that you can make a reference type nullable. If you do this, the compiler will not allow you to set null to non-nullable reference variables. If you are using Visual Studio, you will also get a warning if you try to set a null value to a non-nullable reference variable.

As this is a new feature and not available in old versions of C#. The C# programming language team came up with the idea of enabling the feature by writing a piece of code, so that the old systems do not crash. You can enable this feature for the whole project or for an individual file.

To enable nullable reference types in a code file, you have to place the following code at the top of the source code:

```
#nullable enable
```

Let's take a look at an example of a nullable reference type:

```
class Hello {
    public string name;
    name = null;
    Console.WriteLine($"Hello {name}");
}
```

If you run the preceding code, you get an exception when trying to print the statement. Try to enable nullable reference types by using the following code:

```
#nullable enable

class Hello {
    public string name;
    name = null;
    Console.WriteLine($"Hello {name}");
}
```

The preceding code will show you a warning to the effect that the name can't be null. To make this workable, you have to change the code as follows:

```
#nullable enable

class Hello {
    public string? name;
    name = null;
    Console.WriteLine($"Hello {name}");
}
```

By changing the string name to `nullable`, you are telling the compiler that it's OK to make this field nullable.

## Async streams

If you have worked with async methods in C#, you might have noticed that returning streams is not possible, or is hard to achieve with existing features. This would, however, be a helpful feature, which would make development tasks much simpler. This is why C# 8 has introduced a new interface called `IAsyncEnumerable`. With this new interface, asynchronous streams of data can be returned. Let me explain a little bit more about this.

Before async streams, in the C# programming language an async method was not able to return a stream of data—it could could only return a single value.

Let's take a look at an example of code that doesn't use an async stream:

```
using System;
using System.Collections.Generic;
using System.Linq;
using System.Text;
using System.Threading.Tasks;
namespace ExploreVS
{
 class Program
 {
 public static void Main(string[] args)
 {
 var numbers = GetNumbersAsync();
 foreach(var n in GetSumOfNums(numbers))
 {
 Console.WriteLine(n);
 }
 Console.ReadKey();
 }
```

```
public static IEnumerable<int> GetNumbersAsync()
{
List<int> a = new List<int>();
a.Add(1);
a.Add(2);
a.Add(3);
a.Add(4);
return a;
}
public static IEnumerable<int> GetSumOfNums(IEnumerable<int> nums)
{
var sum = 0;
foreach(var num in nums)
{
sum += num;
yield return sum;
}
}

}
}
```

With async streams, a stream of data can now be returned using `IAsyncEnumerable`. Let's take a look at the following code:

```
using System;
using System.Collections.Generic;
using System.Linq;
using System.Text;
using System.Threading.Tasks;
namespace ExploreVS
{
 class Program
 {
 public static async void Main(string[] args)
 {
 var numbers = GetNumbersAsync();
 await foreach(var n in GetSumOfNums(numbers))
 {
 Console.WriteLine(n);
 }
 Console.ReadKey();
 }
 public static IEnumerable<int> GetNumbersAsync()
 {
 List<int> a = new List<int>();
 a.Add(1);
 a.Add(2);
```

```
            a.Add(3);
            a.Add(4);
            return a;
        }
        public static async IAsyncEnumerable<int>
GetSumOfNums(IAsyncEnumerable<int> nums)
        {
        var sum = 0;
        await foreach(var num in nums)
        {
        sum += num;
        yield return sum;
        }
        }

    }
}
```

From the preceding example, we can see how we can use this new feature of C# to return asynchronous streams.

# Ranges and indices

C# 8 comes with ranges, which allow you to take a slice of an array or string. Before, if you wanted to get only the first three numbers of an array, you had to iterate through the array and use a condition to find out which values you wanted to use. Let's take a look at an example:

```
using System;
namespace ConsoleApp6
{
    class Program
    {
        static void Main(string[] args)
        {
            var numbers = new int[] { 1, 2, 3, 4, 5 };
            foreach (var n in numbers)
            {
                if(numbers[3] == n) { break; }
                Console.WriteLine(n);
            }
            Console.ReadKey();
        }
    }
}
```

With ranges, you can easily slice the array and take whatever value you want, as shown in the following code:

```
using System;
namespace ConsoleApp6
{
 class Program
 {
 static void Main(string[] args)
 {
 var numbers = new int[] { 1, 2, 3, 4, 5 };
 foreach (var n in numbers[0..3])
 {
 Console.WriteLine(n);
 }
 Console.ReadKey();
 }
 }
}
```

In the preceding example, we can see that we gave a range (`[0..3]`) in the `foreach` loop next to the numbers. This means that we should only take the values of index 0 to index 3 in the array.

There are other ways to slice an array. You can use ^ to say that indexes should be taken backward. For example, if you want to get values from the second element to the second-from-last element, you can use `[1..^1]`. If you apply this, the result you will get is 2, 3, 4.

Let's take a look at the use of ranges in the following code:

```
using System;
namespace ConsoleApp6
{
 class Program
 {
 static void Main(string[] args)
 {
 var numbers = new int[] { 1, 2, 3, 4, 5 };
 foreach (var n in numbers[1..^1])
 {
 Console.WriteLine(n);
 }
 Console.ReadKey();
 }
 }
}
```

When running the above code you will need a special Nuget package in your project. The name of the package is `Sdcb.System.Range`. To install this package you can go to **Nuget Package Manager** in Visual Studio and install it.

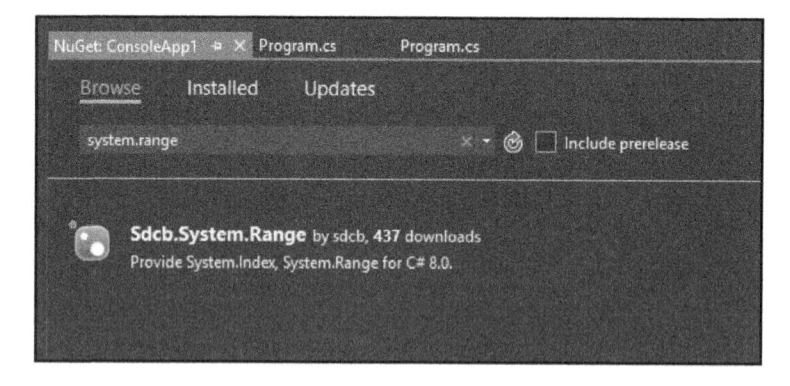

Installing Sdcb.System.Range Nuget package

If you are still having build errors, there is a possibility that your project is still using C# 7 and, to upgrade to C# 8, you hover over the place which is marked with a red underline and click the light bulb that will popup. Then, Visual Studio will ask if you want to use C# 8 for your project. You need to click on **Upgrade this project to C# language version '8.0 *beta*'**. This will upgrade your project from C# 7 to C# 8 and you will be able to run your code.

Figure: Upgrade project to C# 8

# Default implementation of interface members

We all know that, in C#, interfaces don't have any method implementations; they only contain the method signature. In C# 8, however, interfaces are allowed to have implemented methods. These methods can be overridden by classes if they need to be. Interface methods will also have access to modifiers, such as public, virtual, protected, or internal. By default, the access level is set to virtual unless it is fixed as sealed or private.

There is another important thing to note. No attributes or fields are yet allowed in an interface. This means that interface methods can't use any instance fields in the methods. Interface methods can take parameters as input and use those, but not instance variables. Let's take a look at an example of an interface method:

```csharp
using System;
namespace ConsoleApp7
{
 class Program
 {
 static void Main(string[] args)
 {
 IPerson person = new Person();
 person.PrintName("John", "Nash");
 Console.ReadKey();
 }
 }
 public class Person : IPerson
 {
 }
 public interface IPerson
 {
 public void PrintName(string FirstName, string LastName)
 {
 Console.WriteLine($"{FirstName} {LastName}");
 }
 }
}
```

> At this time of writing the book, this feature has not yet been available in the C# 8 preview version. This is still marked as a proposed feature but, hopefully, it will be implemented in the final release. Therefore, the above given code might not work even if you use Visual Studio 2019 preview version.

## Switch expressions

We have been using switch statements for many years now. Whenever we think of or hear about switches, we think about case and break. C# 8, however, will force us to change that mindset through the introduction of switch expressions. This means that switch statements will not be the same as they were in the past.

# New Features in C# 8

Let's take a look at what our old `switch` statement used to look like:

```csharp
using System;
namespace ConsoleApp7
{
    class Program
    {
        static void Main(string[] args)
        {
            string person = "nash";
            switch (person)
            {
                case "john":
                    Console.WriteLine("Hi from john!");
                    break;
                case "smith":
                    Console.WriteLine("Hi from smith!");
                    break;
                case "nash":
                    Console.WriteLine("Hi from nash!");
                    break;
                case "harrold":
                    Console.WriteLine("Hi from harrold!");
                    break;
                default:
                    Console.WriteLine("Hi from None!");
                    break;
            }
            Console.ReadKey();
        }
    }
}
```

With the new approach, we won't place the `person` in parentheses after the `switch`, but we will place the `switch` to the right of the `person` variable, and no `case` keywords will be needed. Let's take a look at how we can use `switch` expressions in a new way:

```csharp
{
  "john"   j => Console.WriteLine("Hi from john!"),
  "smith"  s => Console.WriteLine("Hi from smith!"),
  "nash"   n => Console.WriteLine("Hi from nash!"),
  "harrold" h => Console.WriteLine("Hi from harrold!"),
  _ => Console.WriteLine("Hi from None!")
};
```

Here, we can also see that, for the default case, we just use the underscore (_).

# Target-typed new expressions

In C# 8, another new feature is target-typed new expressions. This feature will make code assignment much cleaner. Let's start with some example code in which we are creating a dictionary with a value:

```
person switch
Dictionary<string, List<int>> student = new Dictionary<string, List<int>> {
    { "john", new List<int>() { 98, 75 } }
};
```

With target-typed new expressions, the preceding code can be written as follows:

```
Dictionary<string, List<int>> student = new() {
    { "john", new() { 98, 75 } }
};
```

When you place `new()`, the variable takes the type that is on the left-hand side and creates a new instance of it.

# Summary

Every time Microsoft announces a new release of the C# programming language, I get excited to see what they are bringing to the table, and every time, I am impressed with the results. C# 8 was no exception. The nullable reference type in particular is an amazing feature because it allows us to prevent a very common exception. Async streams are another fantastic feature, especially for the development of IoT. Ranges, interface members, switch expressions, and all the other additions are small steps towards significant progress. New features such as these make a developer's life much easier, and bring benefits to businesses by reducing software crashes. In the next chapter, we are going to discuss design principles and different design patterns.

# Target-typed new expressions

In C# 8, another new feature is target-typed new expressions. This feature will make code assignment much cleaner. Let's start with some example code in which we are creating a dictionary with a value:

```
person switch
Dictionary<string, List<int>> student = new Dictionary<string, List<int>> {
    { "john", new List<int>() { 98, 75 } }
};
```

With target-typed new expressions, the preceding code can be written as follows:

```
Dictionary<string, List<int>> student = new() {
    { "john", new() { 98, 75 } }
};
```

When you place `new()`, the variable takes the type that is on the left-hand side and creates a new instance of it.

# Summary

Every time Microsoft announces a new release of the C# programming language, I get excited to see what they are bringing to the table, and every time, I am impressed with the results. C# 8 was no exception. The nullable reference type in particular is an amazing feature because it allows us to prevent a very common exception. Async streams are another fantastic feature, especially for the development of IoT. Ranges, interface members, switch expressions, and all the other additions are small steps towards significant progress. New features such as these make a developer's life much easier, and bring benefits to businesses by reducing software crashes. In the next chapter, we are going to discuss design principles and different design patterns.

# 12
# Understanding Design Patterns and Principles

Over the years, software has become increasingly complicated. Now, software is not only used for mathematical calculations or simple **create, read, update, and delete** (**CRUD**) operations: we are employing it to carry out complex tasks, such as controlling rocket engines or managing huge amounts of data every day. Businesses from a vast range of sectors have started to adopt software systems, including banks, insurance companies, research institutes, education institutes, and government agencies. The higher the demand for software, the more people begin to build careers in software development. From assembly-language programming, came procedural programming, before the introduction of the era of **Object-oriented programming** (**OOP**), which is still the most popular model, despite the emergence of other types of programming, such as functional programming. OOP has helped developers write good, modular software that is easy to maintain and extend. In this chapter, we are going to discuss some of the most important design principles and patterns that are followed by thousands of developers, and we are going to cover the following topics:

- Design principles in software development
- Different design patterns in software development
- Creational design patterns
- Behavioral design patterns
- Structural design patterns
- The **Model-View-Controller** (**MVC**) pattern

# Design principles

Before we start discussing design principles, let's think about what we mean by **design principles** in software development. When we develop software, we first design its architecture, and then we start writing its code. We want to write our code in such a way that it generates no bugs, or so it is easy to find bugs if there are any. We also want the code to be easily understandable when we read it and we want it to be structured in such a way that it can be changed later if required. Although it is difficult to write the best-possible code, there are various principles in software development that have been developed by experienced computer scientists. Using these, developers can write very clean code.

The software developer Robert C. Martin, also known as Uncle Bob, came up with five software design principles. These principles are so effective and helpful for developers that they have become a norm in the software industry. Collectively, they are known as the SOLID principle, which represents the following different definitions:

- S stands for the **single responsibility principle**
- O stands for the **open-closed principle**
- L stands for the **Liskov substitution principle**
- I stands for the **interface segregation principle**
- D stands for the **dependency inversion principle**

Let's discuss these principles one by one.

## The single responsibility principle

> *"A class should have one, only one reason to change."*
>
> – *Robert C. Martin*

This means that when we write a class, we should design it in such a way that it has only one responsibility. You should only need to change the class for one reason. If you have multiple reasons to change the class, it is violating the single responsibility principle.

If a class has more than one responsibility and you make changes to a piece of code, this might break another piece of code, as they are in the same class and share some dependencies. Your code might not be very decoupled.

## The open-closed principle

Code needs to be written in such a way that adding new things in a software entity, such as classes, modules, or functions, is good, but modifying the entity itself should not be allowed. This reduces the possibility of bugs being generated.

## The Liskov substitution principle

*"Derived types must be completely substitutable for their base types."*

*– Barbara Liskov*

This principle states that when you write a class, if it is derived from another class, it should be replaceable with the base class. Otherwise, your code will be very fragile and coupled. This principle was first discovered by Barbara Liskov, so it is named after her.

## The interface segregation principle

Sometimes, developers create large interfaces that contain too much information. Many classes might use this interface, but they might not need everything in it. This is what you should avoid in order to follow this principle. This principle supports small interfaces instead of big interfaces and, if necessary, a class can inherit multiple small interfaces that are actually applicable for the class.

## The dependency inversion principle

*"High-level modules should not depend on low-level modules; both should depend on abstractions. Abstractions should not depend on details. Details should depend upon abstractions"*

*– Robert C. Martin*

We know that, in software development, we work with layers. To make the layers decoupled, we have to design the dependencies of these layers in such a way that, instead of depending on each other, the layers should depend on abstraction. Therefore, if you change something in a high-level module or a low-level module, it won't harm the system. When we create these abstractions, we have to design them in such a way that they are not dependent on the implementation details. The abstractions should be independent and the classes that implement these interfaces or abstract classes should depend on those abstractions.

# Creational design patterns

In OOP, where all things are treated as objects, it's very important to keep track of how an object is created and managed. If a developer doesn't pay much attention to this topic, the objects of the software could make the software fragile and coupled. It's important to maintain the objects appropriately to keep the application easily extendable. Creational design patterns are patterns that help create objects in a manner where the most common problems regarding object creation can be avoided.

There are two main concepts that exist in creational design patterns:

- Encapsulating knowledge about the concrete classes the system uses
- Hide creating and combining instances of the concrete classes

Creational design patterns are classified into object-creational patterns and class-creational patterns, in which **object-creational patterns** deal with the creation of objects and **class-creational patterns** deal with the discovery of classes.

There are five main creational design patterns in the industry:

- The abstract factory pattern
- The builder pattern
- The factory method pattern
- The prototype pattern
- The singleton pattern

# The abstract factory pattern

The definition of this pattern from *Design Patterns: Elements of Reusable Object-Oriented Software* by the Gang of Four is to provide a combination to build families of similar or reliant objects without specifying their concrete classes.

The most important thing that this pattern offers is separation or abstraction of object creation. If you are not following any pattern, the simplest thing that comes to mind when you are creating an object is to use the `new` keyword and create an object wherever you need it. For example, if I need a `Person` object in my `Bank` class, the easiest way to do this would be to instantiate a `Person` object using a `new` keyword in the `Bank` class. However, using this approach sometimes creates complexity in the software. To avoid that, we can use the abstract factory pattern.

The abstract factory pattern is mainly used in cases where you have objects from the same family, or that are related or dependent in some way. The idea is to create factory classes to carry out the work of object creation. If an object `A`, needs an instance of another object `B`, object `A` should ask the factory of object `B` to create an object of `B` and pass it to object `A`. In this way, object `A` is independent of the creation of object `B`. Now, in the abstract factory pattern, there is another layer of abstraction. The factory classes are also abstracted. This means that object `A` won't call the factory of object `B` directly, but instead use an abstraction. There should be a mechanism that determines which `Factory` class needs to be called. This means that object `A` is not dependent on any particular factory of another object.

# The builder pattern

Separating the plan of a complicated object from its imitation is the main idea of the builder pattern. In object-oriented software development, we sometimes need to create objects that are quite complex. For example, we might create an object that uses other objects, which in turn use other objects. Creating or instantiating this kind of object could be difficult when you just need that object to carry out another kind of work. It might also make the code more complex and reduce its readability.

Let's think about an example. Imagine that you are making some burgers, some of which are chicken burgers and some of which are beef burgers. When creating the chicken burger objects, you have to create a chicken burger patty object, a tomato ketchup object, a cheese object, and a bread object every time you create a chicken burger object, which leads to messy code. You also have to follow the same process when creating a beef burger object. This is a really complex way of handling and creating these objects.

*Understanding Design Patterns and Principles*

The builder pattern provides a nice way to solve this complexity. Using this pattern, we create a class called `Builder` whose main task is to create complex objects and return the newly-created object. With the builder pattern, we use another type of class, which is normally called the `director` class. The task of this class is to call the `Builder` class and get the object from it.

Let's return to our burger example. We can have a `ChickenBurgerBuilder` class and a `BeefBurgerBuilder` class. These will set the items, the burger patty, the bread, the ketchup, and the cheese, in the class. When the `BurgerDirector` class wants to create a `chicken burger`, it will call `ChickenBurgerBuilder`. To create a `beef burger`, it will call `BeefBurgerBuilder`. The complexity of creating the `burger patty` and the other ingredients will be handled by the `Builder` class.

## The factory method pattern

The factory method pattern is very similar to the abstract factory pattern. The difference is that, in the factory method pattern, the factory layer is not abstracted. Using this pattern means that you will create a factory class that will handle the creation of classes that implement the same abstraction. This means that, if there is an interface that is defined by many subclasses, a `Factory` class can create any of those subclasses depending on the logic passed to `Factory`.

Let's think about an example. We will use the Factory method pattern to solve our burger-creating problem from the Builder pattern example we mentioned in the section, *The builder Pattern*. We will create a `Factory`, called `BurgerFactory`, that will take an input, such as `typeOfBurger` (Chicken or Beef). Then, `BurgerFactory` will decide which `Burger` type of object should be created. Let's suppose we have an Interface called `Burger` that both `ChickenBurger` and `BeefBurger` implement. This means that `BurgerFactory` will return an object of the `Burger` type. The client will not be aware which `Burger` Object will be created and returned. By using this pattern, we are isolating the client from a specific object, which increases the flexibility of the code.

## The prototype pattern

This design pattern is used when you want to avoid creating new classes of the same type or sub-type using traditional object-creation mechanisms, such as new keywords. Put simply, this pattern states that we should clone an object and then work with the cloned object as another newly-created object. This way, the traditional method of object creation is avoided.

[ 222 ]

# The singleton pattern

The singleton pattern is a very simple design pattern. It involves creating only one object of a class in the whole application. A **singleton object** is an object that can't have multiple instances. Whenever a piece of code needs to use this singleton object, it won't create a new object; instead, it will use the old object that is already available.

This design pattern is applicable when you want to handle some information from one source only. The best example of when we might use a singleton pattern is in a database connection string. In an application, if there are multiple database connections used, the database might get corrupted and cause exceptions in the application. Here, it's better to make the connection string a singleton object, meaning that only one instance is used for all communication. This reduces the chance of discrepancy.

# Structural design patterns

Some of the design patterns that are available in software development are related to the code structure. These patterns help you to design your code in such a way that you will be able to avoid common structural problems. In the *Design Patterns: Elements of Reusable Object-Oriented Software* book by the Gang of Four, there are seven structural design patterns. In this section, we are just going to discuss four of these, which are as follows:

- The adapter pattern
- The decorator pattern
- The facade pattern
- The proxy pattern

If you want to find out more about the other three, take a look at the book *Design Patterns: Elements of Reusable Object-Oriented Software* by the Gang of Four. At first, it might be a little confusing to start using these patterns, but, as you get more experienced, it will become easier to identify which pattern is appropriate for which situation.

## The adapter pattern

Normally, when we think of the word adapter, we think about a small device that helps us plug our electronic devices into a power socket with a different kind of interface on the plug. The adapter design pattern actually does the same thing in software code. This design pattern states that, if two modules of a software want to communicate with each other, but the interface that one module expects is different from the interface that the other module has, instead of changing one interface to match the other interface, an adapter should be used. The benefit of doing this is that, in the future, if you want your code to talk to another interface, you won't have to change your code, but just use another adapter.

For example, imagine you have an Interface, A, but the code that you want to talk to wants another Interface, B. Instead of changing Interface A to Interface B, you use an adapter that converts interface A to interface B. This way, the code that uses interface A will not break, and you will be able to communicate with the code that asks for interface B.

## The decorator pattern

The decorator pattern allows us to add new behaviors to objects dynamically. When this new behavior is added to an object, it shouldn't affect any other behavior that already exists on that object. This pattern provides a solution when you have to add new behaviors to an object at runtime. It also removes the need to create subclasses just to add a behavior to a task.

## The facade pattern

Sometimes, if you have complex object relationships, it is hard to map them all and use them in your code. The facade pattern states that you should use a middle object to deal with the object-relational issues and give the client an easy point of contact. Let's think about an example: when you go to a restaurant and order some food, you actually don't go to each chef or person in the kitchen and collect food portions and make your own food; you tell the waiter what food you want. You don't know how the item will be prepared or who will prepare it. You have no control over the making of the food, you just know that you will get the item that you have asked for. Here, the person taking the order is working as a facade. They take your order and ask different people to prepare the item you asked for.

Let's say that you ordered a beef burger. You call a `GetBeefBurger()` method and the facade will actually call the following:

```
Bread.GetBread()
Sauce.PutSauceOnBread(Bread)
SliceTomato()
PutTomatoOnBread()
Beef.FryBeefPatty()
PutBeefPattyOnBread()
WrapTheBurger()
ServeTheBurger()
```

The preceding methods are not real methods. I just want to give you an idea that the work of a facade is actually to hide the complexity from the client.

## The proxy pattern

This pattern is very similar to the other structural design patterns that we have discussed. If there is a situation in which a piece of code should not call another piece of code directly for whatever reason, the proxy pattern can be used. The proxy pattern is especially useful when a piece of code doesn't have access rights to call another piece of code or when calling a piece of code directly is expensive in terms of resources. An example of when we might want to use a proxy pattern would be if we wanted to use a third-party library in our application, but we don't want our code to call the library directly for security reasons. In this case, we can create a proxy and let it communicate with the third-party code.

## Behavioral design patterns

Behavioral design patterns are design patterns that deal with communication between objects. These design patterns allow your objects to communicate in a way that avoids the common issues that developers face related to object behavior. There are many patterns in this category:

- The chain-of-responsibility pattern
- The command pattern
- The interpreter pattern
- The iterator pattern
- The mediator pattern
- The memento pattern

- The observer pattern
- The state pattern
- The strategy pattern
- The template-method pattern
- The visitor pattern

In this book, however, we are only going to talk about the following behavioral design patterns:

- The command pattern
- The observer pattern
- The strategy pattern

If you want to find out more, refer to the *Design Patterns: Elements of Reusable Object-Oriented Software* book by the Gang of Four that we mentioned earlier.

# The command pattern

This pattern states that, when an object wants to notify another object or call a method of another object, it should use another object instead of doing so directly. The object that will establish the communication is known as the command object. The command will encapsulate the object that holds the method to be called, the method name to be called, and the parameters that are to be passed, if there are any. The command pattern helps to decouple the relationship between the invoker and the receiver.

# The observer pattern

The **observer pattern** is a solution to a problem in which many objects need to know when a particular object changes because they might have to update the data on their end. One way to do this is that all the objects, or observers, should ask the object, or the observable, whether the data has changed. If the data has changed in the observable, the observer will do its work. However, if we do this, the observers have to ask the observable about data changes very frequently to avoid slowing down your application. This requires a lot of resources.

The observer pattern says that the observable should know the list of the observers that want to know about the data changes in the subject and notify each observer when the data in the subject is changed. This could be done by calling a method of the observers. A good use of this pattern is event and delegate in C#.

# The strategy pattern

Let's take a look at a definition of the strategy pattern from the *Design Patterns: Elements of Reusable Object-Oriented Software* book by the Gang of Four:

For example, a method could have different types of implementations depending on which class is using it. The definition, therefore, means that we need to make these different algorithms implement a base class or interface so that they belong to the same family and can be used interchangeably by the clients. The last part of the definition means that this pattern will allow clients to use different algorithms without affecting other clients.

Let's imagine that we have a class, called `Animal`, that has a few common properties, such as `eat`, `walk`, and `noise`. Now, let's say you want to add another property, such as `fly`. Most of the animals in your class can fly, but a few can't. You could break the `Animal` class into two different classes, such as `AnimalWhichCanFly` and `AnimalWhichCantFly`. However, splitting this `Animal` class into two could over-complicate things as these animals could have other different attributes as well. Instead of using inheritance, therefore, you could use composition, which means you can add a property called `fly` in the `Animal` class and use it to indicate this behavior.

The strategy pattern states that instead of using a fixed type, `fly`, as the property type, we should use an interface, such as `IFly`, and then create `subclasses` that implement `IFly` and have different algorithms. Then, we can take advantage of polymorphism and assign the specific subclass at runtime when the subclasses of the `Animal` class are created.

Let's try to apply this on the preceding example. In the `Animal` class, instead of using the `Fly` property, we will use `IFly` and then implement different classes that implement `IFly`. For example, we create the `CanFly : IFly` and `CannotFly : IFly` classes. `CanFly` and `CannotFly` will have different implementations of the `Fly` method. If we create a `Dog` class that implements the `Animal` class, we will set the `Fly` property as the `CannotFly` class. If we create a `Bird` class, we will create an instance of `CanFly` and assign it to the `Fly` property. By applying this pattern, we have achieved a less-complicated object structure and easily-changeable algorithms.

# The MVC pattern

The MVC pattern is one of the most popular design patterns in the industry. You might have heard about it already, even if you are very new to the industry. This pattern is heavily used in web development. Many popular web-development frameworks use this design pattern. Some popular frameworks that use the MVC pattern are given here:

- **C#:** ASP.NET MVC Web Framework
- **Java:** Spring framework
- **PHP:** Laravel framework, Codeigniter framework
- **Ruby:** Rails framework

The MVC design pattern states that we should divide a web application into three parts:

- Model
- View
- Controller

The **model** is the part that will hold the data models or objects and will be used in database transactions. **View** refers to the frontend of the application, which the users or customers look at. Finally, the **controller** is the part that handles all the business logic of the application. All the logic and decision-making parts will be in the controller.

The benefit of the MVC pattern is that your application is decoupled. Your view is independent from your business logic and your business logic is independent of your data source. This way, you can easily change one part of your application without affecting other parts of the application.

# Summary

Software development is interesting because it changes all the time. There are many ways in which you can develop, design, or code something. None of these can be classified as the best way, because your code might need to change depending on the situation. However, because software development is a type of engineering, there are various rules that will make your software stronger and more reliable. Software design principles and design patterns are examples of these kinds of rules. Knowing these concepts and applying them to your own situation will make your life as a developer much easier.

This chapter has hopefully given you an idea of the basics of design patterns and shown you where you can look for more information. In the next chapter, we will get to know a very powerful and interesting software called Git. Git is a version-control system that helps to keep track of software code.

# 13
# Git - The Version Control System

Nowadays, software development has reached a new level. It no longer only involves writing code—a software developer now also has to be familiar with a range of important tools. Without these tools, it becomes very difficult to work in a team or to work efficiently. Version control is one of these tools. Of the various version control systems available, Git is the most popular and powerful. Git version control has been in the industry for quite a long time, but has recently become a part of almost all software companies. Knowing Git is now essential for developers. In this chapter, we will learn about Git version control systems. Let's take a look at the topics we are going to cover:

- What is a version control system?
- How Git works
- Installing Git in Windows
- The basics of Git
- Branches in Git

## What is version control?

A version control system is a system or application that keeps track of software code changes during development. Software developers used to keep backups of their code by copying the code into another folder or machine. If the developer or production machine crashed, they could take the code from the backup and run it. However, manually keeping and maintaining backups is troublesome and prone to error, and backup systems are vulnerable to corruption. For this reason, developers began looking for a system or application that could keep their code safe.

Version control is also useful in situations where more than one programmer is working on a project. In the past, programmers had to either work on different files to avoid conflicts or carefully merge the code after some time. Manually merging code is very risky and time-consuming.

In a version control system, every change in a code file is actually a new version of the code. In the software industry, there are many version control systems available, including Git, Subversion, Mercurial, and Perforce. Git, the most popular version control system, was developed by the software developer Linus Torvalds. It is a remarkable application that is now used in almost every software company in the world.

## How Git works

The main task of Git is to keep track of code versions and allow developers to go back to any previous state if necessary. This is done by taking a snapshot of every version and maintaining it in a local file storage system. Unlike other systems, Git uses local file storage to store snapshots, which means that Git can be used locally—even without an internet connection. With the local version of Git, you can do almost everything that you can do with an internet-connected version of Git.

After you install Git in your project, you can choose which directory of your filesystem you want to keep under Git version control. Normally, a project or directory—which is one entity in Git—is called a **repository**. A repository might contain different projects, one project, or just some of the project files, depending on what you want to keep in Git version control. There are two ways that you can have a Git repository on your local machine. Either you can initialize a Git repository by yourself, or you can clone a repository from a remote server. Either way, you will create a folder called `.git` in the same folder in which the repository was created or cloned. This `.git` file is the local storage file, and all the information related to that repository will be stored there. Git stores data in a very efficient manner, so the file won't get very big, even if you have tons of snapshots.

There are three main states in Git, which we will explore in the following sections:

- Modified
- Staged
- Committed

## Modified

When you have a Git repository initialized and then add a new file or edit an existing file, that particular file will be marked as **Modified** in Git. This means that the file contains some changes from the already stored snapshot that Git has in its local storage/database. For example, if you create a C# console app project in a Git repository, then all the files of that solution will be marked as **Modified**, as none of them are available in the Git repository history.

## Staged

In Git, **Staged** refers to files that are ready to be committed. To prevent accidental commits of unwanted files to the Git repository, Git introduced this step between **Modified** and **Committed**. When you mark files as **Staged**, this means that you want those files to be committed in the next commit. This also gives you the option to edit files and not make them **Staged** so that the changes won't be saved in the repository. This feature is very handy if you want to apply some configurations in your local machine, but don't want those changes in the repository.

## Committed

The **Committed** state is when a version of a file is saved in the local database. It means that a snapshot is taken and stored in the Git history for future reference. When working with the repository remotely, the code that you will push is actually only the committed code.

Let's take a look at the following diagram to understand the flow between these states:

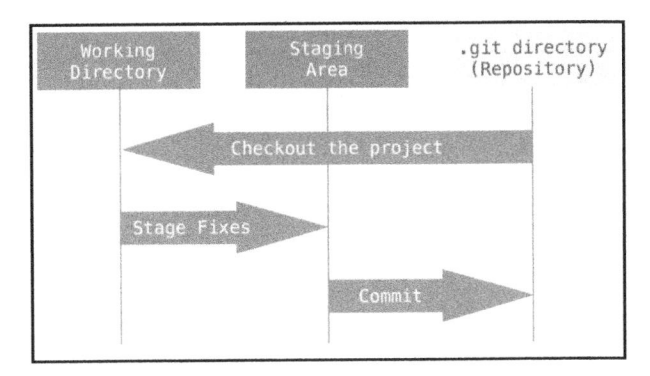

# Installing Git on Windows

Git was primarily developed for Linux- or Unix-based operating systems. When it grew in popularity and Windows users started to demand Git, Git for Windows was launched. Installing Git on Windows is now a very easy process. To install Git, go to `https://git-scm.com/download/win`.

You will be taken to the page shown in the following screenshot:

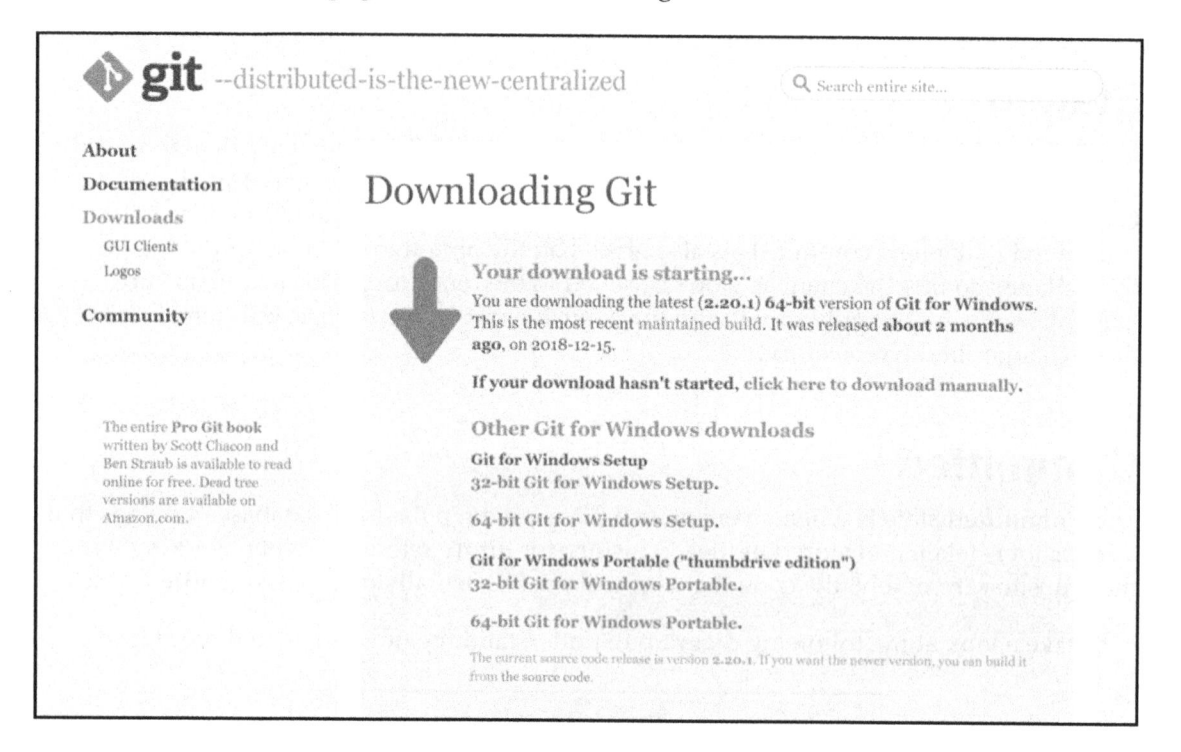

Git for Windows should start downloading automatically. If it doesn't start, you can click on the links given on the website. The download file will be an executable file, so to start installation, execute the executable file. During installation, if you are not sure what to choose, the best option here is to keep everything as default.

The following screenshot shows which components you can install:

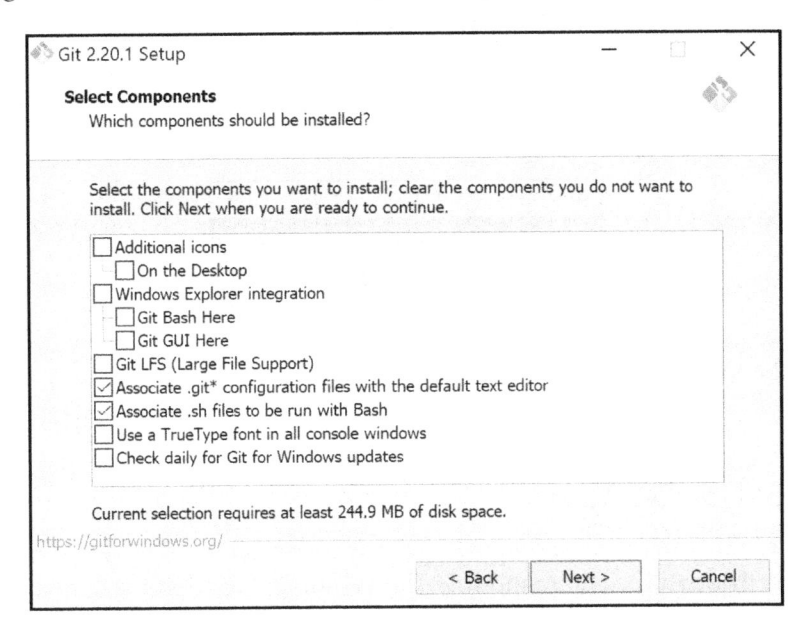

There is a section in which you can choose the default editor to be used for Git. The default editor that is chosen is **Vim**, as shown in the following screenshot. If you are not used to using Vim, you can change it to your preferred one:

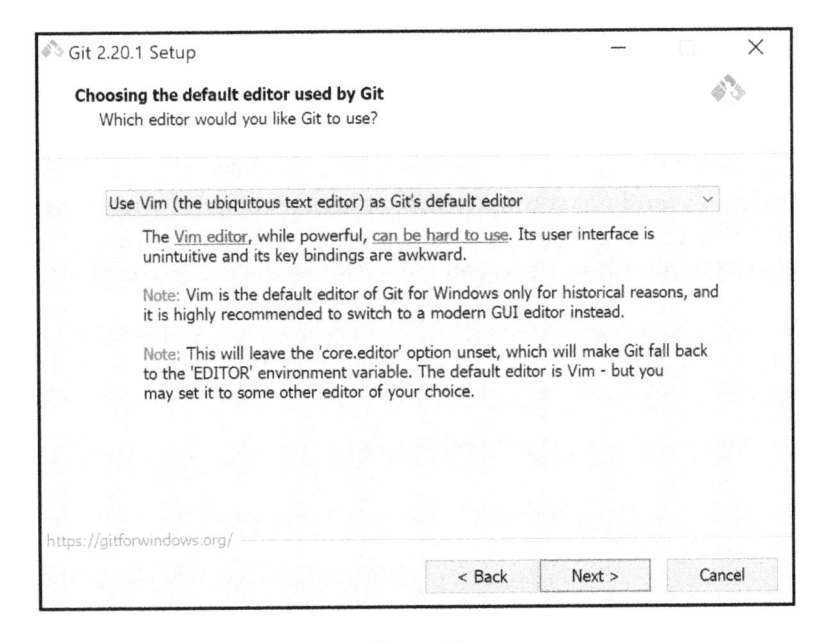

Follow the steps. After Git is installed, to test whether the installation was successful, go to the command line or PowerShell and type the following:

```
git --version
```

You should see an output similar to the following:

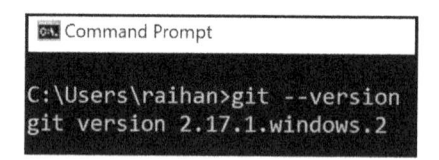

```
C:\Users\raihan>git --version
git version 2.17.1.windows.2
```

If you can see the version number, this means that the installation was successful.

# The basics of Git

As mentioned, Git was first developed for Linux systems, which is why the main way of using this tool is through the command line. On Windows, we don't use the command line as much as a Linux or Unix user, but using it gives you access to all the features of Git. For Windows, there are some GUI tools that can be used for Git actions, but they often have some limitations. As the command line is the preferred method for Git, we will cover only the command-line commands in this book.

# Git config

The `git config` command is a command that is used to configure your Git settings. The minimum setting for Git is to set a username and email address. You can either configure each Git repository differently or configure the settings globally. If you set the configuration globally, you don't have to configure the email address and username every time you initialize a Git repository. You can always override these in each repository if necessary.

To configure your email address and username, run the following command:

```
git config user.name = "john"
git config user.email = "john@example.com"
```

If you want to set the configuration globally, you need to add the `--global` keyword, as follows:

```
git config --global user.name = "john"
git config --global user.email = "john@example.com"
```

If you want to see what other global configuration settings are available, you can use the following command:

```
git config --list
```

You can then change the settings that you want to change.

## Git init

If you have a project that is not currently using Git version control, you can use the following command to initialize the project:

```
git init
```

When you run the preceding command, the Git program that you have installed in your machine creates a `.git` directory in the project directory and starts tracking the source code of that project. After you initialize Git in a new project, all the files are displayed as **Modified** and you have to stage those files to commit those changes.

## Git clone

If you want to use a project that is on a remote server, you have to clone the project. To clone a project, you have to use the following command:

```
git clone [repo-url]
```

For example, if you want to clone the Angular project, you have to type the following:

```
git clone https://github.com/angular/angular.git
```

When you clone a repository to your local environment, the `.git` folder is downloaded. This includes the history of commits, branches, tags, and all other information contained in the remote server. It is basically a copy of a version of the remote server. If you commit a change in your local copy and then push it to the remote repository, then your local copy will sync with the remote copy.

## Git status

While working, you will want to check the status of your current code. This means finding out which files are **Modified** and which files are **Staged**. You can get all of this information by using the following command:

```
git status
```

Let's take a look at an example. If we add a new file called `hello.txt` to our project, which is tracked by Git, and check its status, we will see something like the following:

```
raihan@raios MINGW64 ~/work/code/BookApp (master)
$ git status
On branch master

No commits yet

Untracked files:
  (use "git add <file>..." to include in what will be committed)

        hello.txt

nothing added to commit but untracked files present (use "git add" to track)

raihan@raios MINGW64 ~/work/code/BookApp (master)
$
```

Here, we can see a file called `hello.txt` under `Untracked` files, which means that this file is not yet tracked by Git. The `git status` command also tells you which branch you are currently in. In this case, we are in the `master` branch.

## Git add

The `git add` command is a command that will add **Modified** files/folders to the Git tracking system. This means that the files and folders will be staged. The command looks as follows:

```
git add <file-name/folder-name>
```

Let's continue with our example to see what happens when we add the `hello.txt` file in Git. To do this, we will execute the following command:

```
git add hello.txt
```

The output is as follows:

```
raihan@raios MINGW64 ~/work/code/BookApp (master)
$ git add hello.txt
warning: LF will be replaced by CRLF in hello.txt.
The file will have its original line endings in your working directory.

raihan@raios MINGW64 ~/work/code/BookApp (master)
$
```

Here, we see a warning about **line feed (LF)** and **Carriage Return, Line Feed (CR+LF)**, which refer to some kind of formatting. The reason for the replacement is that we are using the Windows operating system here, but we don't need to worry about that for the time being. The main point here is that the file has been staged properly. Now, if we check the status, we will see the following:

```
raihan@raios MINGW64 ~/work/code/BookApp (master)
$ git add hello.txt
warning: LF will be replaced by CRLF in hello.txt.
The file will have its original line endings in your working directory.

raihan@raios MINGW64 ~/work/code/BookApp (master)
$ git status
On branch master

No commits yet

Changes to be committed:
  (use "git rm --cached <file>..." to unstage)

        new file:   hello.txt


raihan@raios MINGW64 ~/work/code/BookApp (master)
$
```

Here, we can see that the `hello.txt` file is placed in the `Changes to be committed` section. This means that the file has been staged.

[ 239 ]

*Git - The Version Control System*

In a real project, you might work on several different files at a time before you stage the files. It could be very tedious to add the files one by one, or even to write the file names separated by commas. If you want all your modified files to be staged, you can use the following command to add all files in the staged area:

`git add *`

## Git commit

The `git commit` command is used when you want to commit your code to the Git history. This means taking a snapshot of your code base and storing it in the Git database for future reference. To commit files/folders, you have to use the following command:

`git commit`

If you execute the preceding code, the default editor that was set for Git will open up and ask you to enter a message for the commit. There is also a shorter way of doing this. If you want to enter a message directly with the commit, you can run the following command:

`git commit -m "your message"`

Let's now commit our `hello.txt` file in our Git repository. To do this, we'll run the following command:

`git commit -m "committing the hello.txt file with hello message"`

The output should look like the following screenshot:

```
raihan@raios MINGW64 ~/work/code/BookApp (master)
$ git commit -m "committing the hello.txt file with hello message"
[master (root-commit) 9879aa3] committing the hello.txt file whith hello message
 1 file changed, 1 insertion(+)
 create mode 100644 hello.txt

raihan@raios MINGW64 ~/work/code/BookApp (master)
$
```

After the successful commit, we will see the line `1 file changed, 1 insertion(+)`. If you check the status again, you will see that there is nothing to commit, as shown in the following screenshot:

Let's continue with our example to see what happens when we add the `hello.txt` file in Git. To do this, we will execute the following command:

```
git add hello.txt
```

The output is as follows:

```
raihan@raios MINGW64 ~/work/code/BookApp (master)
$ git add hello.txt
warning: LF will be replaced by CRLF in hello.txt.
The file will have its original line endings in your working directory.

raihan@raios MINGW64 ~/work/code/BookApp (master)
$
```

Here, we see a warning about **line feed (LF)** and **Carriage Return, Line Feed (CR+LF)**, which refer to some kind of formatting. The reason for the replacement is that we are using the Windows operating system here, but we don't need to worry about that for the time being. The main point here is that the file has been staged properly. Now, if we check the status, we will see the following:

```
raihan@raios MINGW64 ~/work/code/BookApp (master)
$ git add hello.txt
warning: LF will be replaced by CRLF in hello.txt.
The file will have its original line endings in your working directory.

raihan@raios MINGW64 ~/work/code/BookApp (master)
$ git status
On branch master

No commits yet

Changes to be committed:
  (use "git rm --cached <file>..." to unstage)

        new file:   hello.txt

raihan@raios MINGW64 ~/work/code/BookApp (master)
$
```

Here, we can see that the `hello.txt` file is placed in the `Changes to be committed` section. This means that the file has been staged.

In a real project, you might work on several different files at a time before you stage the files. It could be very tedious to add the files one by one, or even to write the file names separated by commas. If you want all your modified files to be staged, you can use the following command to add all files in the staged area:

```
git add *
```

## Git commit

The `git commit` command is used when you want to commit your code to the Git history. This means taking a snapshot of your code base and storing it in the Git database for future reference. To commit files/folders, you have to use the following command:

```
git commit
```

If you execute the preceding code, the default editor that was set for Git will open up and ask you to enter a message for the commit. There is also a shorter way of doing this. If you want to enter a message directly with the commit, you can run the following command:

```
git commit -m "your message"
```

Let's now commit our `hello.txt` file in our Git repository. To do this, we'll run the following command:

```
git commit -m "committing the hello.txt file with hello message"
```

The output should look like the following screenshot:

```
raihan@raios MINGW64 ~/work/code/BookApp (master)
$ git commit -m "committing the hello.txt file with  hello message"
[master (root-commit) 9879aa3] committing the hello.txt file whith hello message
 1 file changed, 1 insertion(+)
 create mode 100644 hello.txt

raihan@raios MINGW64 ~/work/code/BookApp (master)
$
```

After the successful commit, we will see the line `1 file changed, 1 insertion(+)`. If you check the status again, you will see that there is nothing to commit, as shown in the following screenshot:

```
raihan@raios MINGW64 ~/work/code/BookApp (master)
$ git commit -m "committing the hello.txt file with hello message"
[master (root-commit) 9879aa3] committing the hello.txt file whith hello message
 1 file changed, 1 insertion(+)
 create mode 100644 hello.txt

raihan@raios MINGW64 ~/work/code/BookApp (master)
$ git status
On branch master
nothing to commit, working tree clean

raihan@raios MINGW64 ~/work/code/BookApp (master)
$
```

# Git log

To check which commits have been made in the repository, you can use the following command:

`git log`

The output will look as follows:

```
raihan@raios MINGW64 ~/work/code/BookApp (master)
$ git log
commit 9879aa3534b7037eb8237b95ead25d60c3b50888 (HEAD -> master)
Author: Raihan Taher <raihan.taher@gmail.com>
Date:   Tue Feb 5 16:41:12 2019 +0800

    committing the hello.txt file whith hello message

raihan@raios MINGW64 ~/work/code/BookApp (master)
$
```

From the log, we can see that only one commit has been made so far. We can see the hash of the commit, which is the number next to the word `commit`. We can see that the `commit` was made on the `master` branch by `Raihan Taher`. We can also see the `commit` message in the log. This is a very helpful command to check what has been committed.

## Git remote

The `git remote` command is used to see whether you have any connections with a remote repository. If you run the following command, it will show you the name of the remote repository. Normally, the remote name is set as `Origin`. You can have multiple remote repositories. Let's take a look at the command:

```
git remote
```

If we execute this command, we won't see anything as there is no remote repository yet, as shown in the following screenshot:

```
raihan@raios MINGW64 ~/work/code/BookApp (master)
$ git remote

raihan@raios MINGW64 ~/work/code/BookApp (master)
$
```

Let's add a remote repository. We will use GitHub as our remote server. After creating a repository in GitHub, I have copied the URL of that repository. We will add it to our local repository. To do this, we use the following command:

```
git remote add <remote-name> <repository-link-remote>
```

In our example, the command is as follows:

```
git remote add origin https://github.com/raihantaher/bookgitexample.git
```

After we add our remote repository, if we execute `git remote`, we will see that the `origin` is listed as a remote repository, as shown in the following screenshot:

```
raihan@raios MINGW64 ~/work/code/BookApp (master)
$ git remote add origin https://github.com/raihantaher/bookgitexample.git

raihan@raios MINGW64 ~/work/code/BookApp (master)
$ git remote
origin

raihan@raios MINGW64 ~/work/code/BookApp (master)
$
```

If you want to see a little more detail about the remote repository, you can execute the following command:

```
git remote -v
```

This will display the URLs of the remote repositories that you have added, as shown in the following screenshot:

```
raihan@raios MINGW64 ~/work/code/BookApp (master)
$ git remote -v
origin  https://github.com/raihantaher/bookgitexample.git (fetch)
origin  https://github.com/raihantaher/bookgitexample.git (push)

raihan@raios MINGW64 ~/work/code/BookApp (master)
$
```

# Git push

When you want to upload or push your local commits to the remote server, you can use the following command:

```
git push <remote-repo-name> <local-branch-name>
```

The following is an example of how to use this command:

```
git push origin master
```

After you execute this command, should the push be successful, you will see a message that looks as follows:

```
raihan@raios MINGW64 ~/work/code/BookApp (master)
$ git push origin master
Counting objects: 3, done.
Delta compression using up to 4 threads.
Compressing objects: 100% (2/2), done.
Writing objects: 100% (3/3), 289 bytes | 144.00 KiB/s, done.
Total 3 (delta 0), reused 0 (delta 0)
To https://github.com/raihantaher/bookgitexample.git
 * [new branch]      master -> master

raihan@raios MINGW64 ~/work/code/BookApp (master)
$
```

## Git pull

The `git pull` command is used when you want to get the latest code from the remote repository. As Git is a distributed version control system and multiple people can work on a project, there is the possibility that someone else has updated the remote server with the latest code. To access the latest code, run the following command:

```
git pull <remote-repo-name> <local-branch-name>
```

The following is an example of how to use this code:

```
git pull origin master
```

If we run this code, the message that pops up is as follows:

```
raihan@raios MINGW64 ~/work/code/BookApp (master)
$ git pull origin master
From https://github.com/raihantaher/bookgitexample
 * branch            master     -> FETCH_HEAD
Already up to date.

raihan@raios MINGW64 ~/work/code/BookApp (master)
$
```

This means that our local repository is up to date with the remote repository. If there were new commits in the remote repository, the `git pull` command would pull those changes to our local repository and indicate that changes have been pulled.

## Git fetch

The `git fetch` command is a very similar command to `git pull`, but, when you use `git fetch`, the code will be fetched from the remote repository to the local repository, but it won't be merged with your code. After checking the remote code, if you feel like you want to merge it with your local code, you have to explicitly run a `git merge` command. The command to do this is as follows:

```
git fetch <remote-repo>
```

If you run the preceding command, all the branches from the remote repository will be updated. If you specify a local branch, only that branch will be updated:

```
git fetch <remote-repo> <local-branch>
```

Let's try to execute a `git fetch` command in our example code:

```
git fetch origin master
```

You will see the following output:

```
raihan@raios MINGW64 ~/work/code/BookApp (master)
$ git fetch origin master
From https://github.com/raihantaher/bookgitexample
 * branch            master     -> FETCH_HEAD

raihan@raios MINGW64 ~/work/code/BookApp (master)
$
```

# Branching in Git

Branching is often thought of as one of the best features of Git. Branching has made Git distinct from all other version control systems. It is very powerful and easy to use. Before we learn about the different branching commands, let me explain briefly how Git deals with commits, because that will help you understand Git branches. In Git, we already know that every commit has a unique hash, and that that hash is stored in the Git database. With the hash, every commit stores the hash of the earlier commit, which is known as the parent of that commit. As well as this, another hash that stores the files that were staged on that commit is also stored, along with the commit message and information about the committer and the author. For the first ever commit of a repository, the parent commit is empty.

# Git - The Version Control System

The following diagram shows an example of hashing in Git:

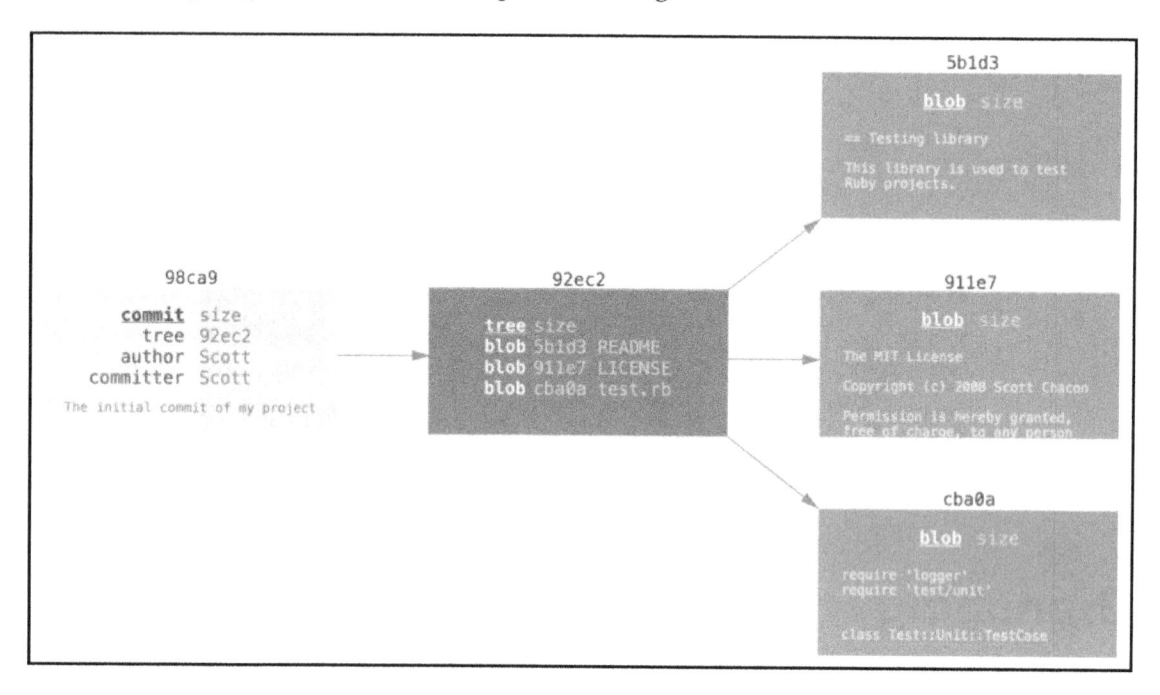

We call all the information in a commit a snapshot. If we have made three commits, we can say that we have **Snapshot A**, **Snapshot B**, and **Snapshot C**, one after another, as shown in the following diagram:

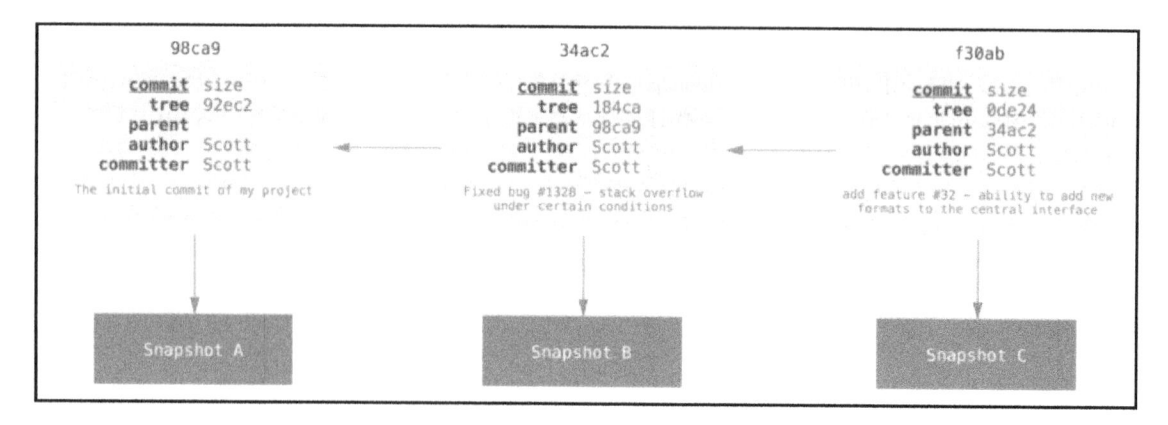

By default, when you initialize a local Git repository, a branch called `master` is created. This is the branch that most developers treat as the main branch in a Git tree. This is optional; you can treat any branch as your main branch or production branch, as all branches have the same capacity and power. If you create a branch from **Snapshot C** (**Commit 3**, or **C3** for short) and name it `feature`, a branch will start from C3 (**Commit 3**) and the next commit on the testing branch will treat C3 as the parent commit.

The following diagram shows the branching:

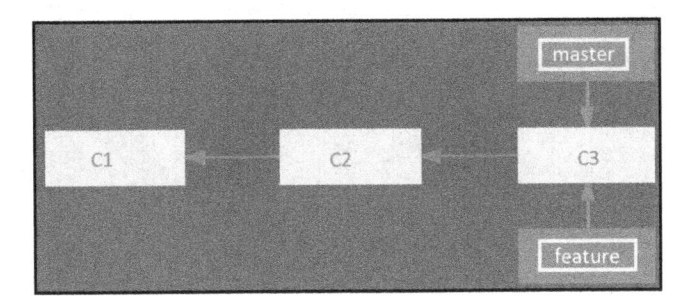

**HEAD** is a pointer that points to the active commit or branch. This is an indicator for the developer, as well as for Git version control. When you make a new commit, the HEAD moves to the latest commit, as that is the snapshot that will be created as a parent for the next commit.

# Creating a branch

Let's now take a look at the command to create a branch in Git. Creating a branch is very easy, because it doesn't copy the whole code base to a new place, but only keeps a relationship with the Git tree. There are a few ways to create a branch, but the most general way is as follows:

```
git branch feature
```

This should look as follows on the command line:

```
raihan@raios MINGW64 ~/work/code/BookApp (master)
$ git branch feature
```

## Viewing available branches

To view which branches are available in the local Git repository, you can write the following command:

`git branch`

After executing the preceding code, you should see the following output:

```
raihan@raios MINGW64 ~/work/code/BookApp (master)
$ git branch
  feature
* master

raihan@raios MINGW64 ~/work/code/BookApp (master)
$
```

We can see that we have two branches in our local repository. One is the `master` branch and the other is the `feature` branch. The `*` character indicates where the HEAD is pointing.

## Changing branches

In the previous example, we saw that, even after creating the feature branch, the HEAD is still pointing to the master. The command to switch to another branch is as follows:

`git checkout <branch-name>`

In our example, if we want to change from the `master` to the `feature` branch, we have to write the following command:

`git checkout feature`

The output is as follows:

```
raihan@raios MINGW64 ~/work/code/BookApp (master)
$ git checkout feature
Switched to branch 'feature'
```

After running the command, we can see that Git has switched to the `feature` branch. Now we can run the `git branch` command again to see where the HEAD is pointing, as shown in the following screenshot:

```
raihan@raios MINGW64 ~/work/code/BookApp (feature)
$ git branch
* feature
  master
```

The likelihood is that, when you create a branch, you will want to work on that branch straight away, so there is a shortcut to create a branch and then switch to it, as shown in the following code:

```
git checkout -b newFeature
```

## Deleting a branch

To delete a branch, you have to execute the following command:

```
git branch -d feature
```

If the branch is deleted successfully, you should see a message similar to the one shown in the following screenshot:

```
raihan@raios MINGW64 ~/work/code/BookApp (newFeature)
$ git branch -d feature
Deleted branch feature (was 9879aa3).
```

## Merging in Git

To merge one branch with another, you have to use the `merge` command. Remember that you need to be on the branch that you are going to merge the code with, not the branch that is going to be merged, or any other branch. The command is as follows:

```
git merge newFeature
```

[ 249 ]

The output should be as follows:

```
raihan@raios MINGW64 ~/work/code/BookApp (master)
$ git merge newFeature
Updating 9879aa3..7a6b0e5
Fast-forward
 discuss.html | 1 +
 1 file changed, 1 insertion(+)
 create mode 100644 discuss.html
```

# Summary

In this chapter, we have learned about a concept that is not directly related to the C# programming language, but which is nonetheless an essential tool for C# developers. Microsoft has recently purchased GitHub, the biggest remote code repository website based on Git, and integrated most of the Microsoft IDEs/editors with it, including the newest code editor, Visual Code. This shows just how important Git has become to our industry. I believe that every developer, new or senior, should use version control for their code. If you don't use Git, you can use any other version control system on the market. Git, however, is the best, even if you are not using Git in your workplace, I would recommend that you use it in your personal projects. Git commands are very simple, so you'll only need to practice with it a few times before you understand it completely.

The next chapter is a little different. We will look at some questions that are commonly asked in job interviews.

# 14
# Prepare Yourself - Interviews and the Future

This is an unusual chapter in an **Object-oriented programming** (**OOP**) book. Job interviews are an important part of a software developer's career. An interview is like a test of your knowledge. It gives you an idea of how much you know and what you should learn more about. It's also a way to learn from experienced developers in other companies.

The main purpose of this chapter is to give you a glimpse into the types of question that are asked in a job interview and how you can prepare yourself for them. Bear in mind that job interview questions depend on the position you have applied for, the company, the interviewer's knowledge, and the technology stacks the company is using. While not all of these questions will be asked, there is a high possibility that some might be, as these determine your basic OOP and C# knowledge.

Let's review the topics we will be covering in this chapter:

- Interview questions
- Interview and career tips
- Things to learn next
- Importance of reading

# Interview questions

In this section, we are going to discuss some of the most common interview questions for a beginner to mid-level developer. As this book is about C#, we will also have questions that directly relate to the C# programming language.

## What are the fundamental principles of object-oriented programming?

Object-oriented programming has four fundamental principles:

- Inheritance
- Encapsulation
- Abstraction
- Polymorphism

## What is inheritance?

**Inheritance** means that a class can inherit the attributes and methods of another class. For example, `Dog` is a class, but it is also a subclass of `Animal`. An `Animal` class is a more general class that has the basic attributes and methods that all animals have. As a dog is also an animal, a `Dog` class can inherit the `Animal` class, so that all the attributes and methods of the `Animal` class also become available in the `Dog` class.

## What is encapsulation?

**Encapsulation** means hiding the data of a class. Access modifiers in C# are mainly used for the purpose of encapsulation. If we make a method or field private, that method or field is not accessible outside the class. This means we are hiding that data from the outside world. The main reason for having encapsulation is that we want to hide more complicated implementations and only show simple interfaces to the outside world for easy usage.

## What is abstraction?

**Abstraction** is an idea, something that is not real. **Abstraction** means providing the idea of a certain object to the outside world but not it's implementation. Interfaces and abstract classes are examples of abstraction. When we create an interface, we don't implement the methods in it, but when a class implements the interface, it has to implement the method as well. This means the interface is actually giving an abstract impression of the class.

## What is polymorphism?

**Polymorphism** means many forms. In OOP, we should have the option of creating one thing in many forms. For example, you can have an `addition` method that might have different implementations, depending on the input it receives. An `addition` method that receives two integers and returns the sum of those integers could be one implementation. There could be another form of `addition` method, which might take two double values and return the sum of those double values.

## What is an interface?

An **interface** is an entity or feature of the C# programming language that is used to apply abstraction in a program. It's like a contract between a class and the interface itself. The contract is that the class that will inherit the interface must implement the method signatures that the interface has within itself. An interface can't be instantiated, it can only be implemented by a class or struct.

## What is an abstract class?

An **abstract class** is a special kind of class that can't be initialized. No object can be created from an abstract class. Abstract classes can have concrete methods as well as non-concrete methods. If a class implements an abstract class, the class must implement the abstract methods. It can override non-abstract methods if necessary.

## What is a sealed class?

A **sealed class** is a class that can't be inherited. It is mainly used to stop the inheritance feature in C#.

## What is a partial class?

A **partial class** is a class that has its source in separate files. Normally, one class has all its fields and methods in the same file. In a partial class, you can separate the class code in different files. When compiled, all the code from the separate files is treated as a single class.

## What are the differences between interfaces and abstract classes?

The following are the major differences between an interface and an abstract class:

- A class can implement any number of interfaces but can only implement one abstract class.
- An abstract class can have abstract methods as well as non-abstract methods, whereas an interface can't have non-abstract methods.
- In an abstract class, data members are private by default, whereas, in an interface, all data members are public and this can't be changed.
- In an abstract class, we need to use the `abstract` keyword to make a method abstract, whereas this is not needed in an interface.

## What is the difference between method-overloading and method-overriding?

**Method-overloading** is when a method with the same name has different input parameters. For example, let's say we have a method called `Sum` that takes two integer type input and returns an integer type output. An overloaded method of `Sum` could take two double type input and return a double output.

**Method-overriding** is when a method with the same name, the same parameters, and the same return type is implemented in a subclass for a different kind of implementation. For example, imagine we have a method called `Discount` in a class called `Sales`, where the discount is calculated as 2% of the total purchase. If we have another subclass of `Sales` called `NewYearSales`, in which the discount is calculated as 5%, using method-overriding, the `NewYearSales` class can easily apply the new implementation.

# What are access modifiers?

**Access modifiers** are used to set the security levels of different entities in a programming language. By setting access modifiers, we can hide data for classes of different levels.

In C#, there are six types of access modifier:

- Public
- Private
- Protected
- Internal
- Protected Internal
- Private Protected

# What is boxing and unboxing?

**Boxing** is the process of converting a value type to an object. **Unboxing** is when the value type is extracted from an object. Boxing may be done implicitly, but unboxing has to be explicit in the code.

# What are the differences between a struct and a class?

Structs and classes are very similar concepts with some differences:

- Structs are of the value type and classes are of the reference type.
- Structs are usually used for small amounts of data, whereas classes are used for large amounts of data.
- Structs can't be inherited by other types, whereas classes can be inherited by other classes.
- A struct can't be abstract, whereas a class can be abstract.

## What is an extension method in C# and how do we use it?

An **extension method** is a method that is added to an existing type without creating a new derived type or compiling or changing the existing type. It works like an extension. For example, by default, we get the string type from .NET frameworks. If we want to add another method to this string type, either we have to create a derived type that will extend this string type and place the method there, or we add the code in the .NET framework and compile and rebuild the library. However, with extension methods, we can easily extend a method in the existing type. To do that, we have to create a static class and then create an extension method that is static as well. This method should take the type as a parameter, but the `this` keyword should be placed before the string. Now this method will work as an extension method for that type.

## What is managed and unmanaged code?

Code that is developed in the .NET framework is called managed code. **Common Language Runtime (CLR)** can directly execute this code. Unmanaged code is not developed in the .NET framework.

## What is a virtual method in C#?

A **virtual method** is a method that is implemented in a base class, but that also can be overridden in child classes. Virtual methods cannot be abstract, static, private, or overridden.

## What do you understand by value types and reference types in C#.NET?

In C#, there are two types of data. One is called value type and another is called reference type. **Value types** are types that hold the value directly in the memory location. If the value is copied, a new memory location holds the same value, and both are independent of each other. A **reference type** is when the value is not directly placed in the memory location but a reference to the value is set instead. Another major difference between value types and reference types is that value types are located in stacks and reference types are located in heaps. An example of a value type is `int`, whereas an example of a reference type is `string`.

# What are design principles?

There are five design principles that make up the acronym **SOLID**:

- The single responsibility principle
- The Open/Closed Principle
- The Liskov substitution principle
- The interface segregation principle
- The dependency inversion principle

# What is the single responsibility principle?

*"A class should have one, only one reason to change."*

– Robert C. Martin

This means that one class should have only one responsibility. If a class is doing multiple things, this is a violation of the **Single Responsibility Principle (SRP)**. For example, if we have a class named Student, it should only be responsible for student-related data. If the Student class needs to be modified when changing anything in the Teacher class, the Student class is violating the SRP.

# What is the Open/Closed principle?

Software components should be open for extensions but closed for modifications. This means that a component should be designed in such a way that, if you need to add a new rule or functionality, you shouldn't have to modify the existing code. If you have to modify the existing code to add new functionality, this means the component is violating the **Open/Closed principle**.

# What is the Liskov substitution principle?

Derived types must be completely substitutable for their base types. This means that if you have an instance of a base class used somewhere, you should be able to replace the base class instances with the child class instances of that base class. For example, if you have a base class called Animal and a child class called Dog, you should be able to replace your Animal class instances with Dog class instances without breaking any functionality.

## What is the interface segregation principle?

Clients should not be forced to depend upon interfaces that they don't use. Sometimes, interfaces contain a lot of information that might not be used by the classes that implement them. The **interface segregation principle** suggests that you keep the interfaces small. Instead of classes implementing one big interface, they should implement multiple small interfaces, where all the methods in the class are needed.

## What is the dependency inversion principle?

High-level modules should not depend on low-level modules; both should depend on abstraction. This means that, when you develop modular software code, high-level modules should not directly depend on low-level modules, but should depend on an interface or abstract class that the low-level module has implemented. By doing this, the modules in the system are independent and, in the future, if you replace your low-level module with another module, the high-level module isn't affected.

There is another part of this principle, which is *abstraction should not depend on details, details should depend on abstractions*. This means that interfaces or abstract classes should not depend on classes, but the classes that implement interfaces and abstract classes should depend on the interface or abstract class.

## Interview and career tips

Now that we have covered some of the most common questions that you can be asked in an interview, I also have a couple of tips to help you to perform better in the interview and in your career.

## Improving your communication skills

It is commonly believed that software developers are unsociable and not good at communication. The reality, however, is very different. All successful developers *have* to be good at communication.

As a software developer, there will be times when you have to explain technical ideas or situations to non-technical people. To be able to do so, you have to communicate in such a way that makes the information accessible and understandable to everyone. This may include both verbal (meetings or discussions) and written communication (documentation or emails).

At the beginning of your career, you might not necessarily understand the importance of communication as you will simply be given tasks to complete. However, as you gain experience and get ahead in your career, you will appreciate the importance of communicating effectively.

As a senior developer, you might have to communicate with your junior developers to explain problems or solutions, or with the business team to ensure that you fully understand the business requirements. You might also have to conduct technical sessions for knowledge-sharing purposes.

Therefore, ensure that you keep interacting with people and read up on resources that will help you to communicate effectively and teach you how to address your audience. Good communication skills will not only help you to ace that interview but will also be valuable to you throughout your career.

## Keep practicing

While no software developer is perfect, by practicing regularly, you can become a knowledgeable and experienced software developer.

Computer programming is an art. By making mistakes, you will develop a sense of what is wrong and what is right. The more you code, the more you will experience different situations. These situations will help you gain experience as you will likely encounter them again in future projects.

And the best way to learn or master programming is to *practice it*.

Try to apply the concepts you have learned in this book in your real-life projects. If this is not possible in your current projects, create demonstration projects and apply them there. Technical concepts are very practical; if you're doing practical implementations, the concepts will become crystal clear to you.

## Things to learn next

After reading this book, you should have a better understanding of OOP and the C# programming language. However, this isn't enough. You must push yourself to learn more about software development. You should learn the other language features of C# and how to use them to get your job done. You should also learn data structures and algorithms for your professional work. In the following list, I have suggested a number of topics and technologies to look into next:

- C# programming language features such as operators, control statements, arrays, lists, operator overloading, Lambda expressions, LINQ, string formatting, and threading
- Data structures and algorithms such as linked lists, binary trees, sorting, and searching algorithms.
- Web/desktop frameworks such as ASP.NET MVC, ASP.NET Web API, WPF, and WCF
- Frontend technologies such as HTML, CSS, and JavaScript, as well as Javascript frameworks such as reactjs/angular
- Database technologies such as MS SQL Server, Oracle, and MySQL
- Design patterns and their implications
- Software architecture and design
- Clean code, code refactoring, and code optimization

There are many other things to learn, but I have covered the topics I believe every software developer should know. This list is quite long and the topics are quite technical, so plan your learning carefully.

## Building the habit of reading

My last tip is to become an avid reader. Reading is super important for software developers. Information is normally distributed to people by text or speech. While video tutorials are a good way to learn, reading gives you time to think and provides you with access to millions of resources.

The following are a few of my must-read books:

- *The Pragmatic Programmer: From Journeyman to Master* by Andrew Hunt and David Thomas
- *Clean Code* by Robert Cecil Martin
- *Code Complete 2* by Steve McConnell
- *Refactoring* by Martin Fowler and Kent Beck
- *Introduction to Algorithms* by Charles E. Leiserson, Clifford Stein, Ronald Rivest, and Thomas H. Cormen
- *Design Patterns: Elements of Reusable Object-Oriented Software* by the Gang of Four
- *C# 7.0 in a Nutshell: The Definitive Reference* by Joseph Albahari
- *C# in Depth* by Jon Skeet

# Summary

Software development is a very interesting field. You can develop amazing applications that can change the world. Apps such as Facebook and Maps, and the myriad products of digital giants, such as Google and Windows, have had a significant impact on our lives. Programs can make people's lives easier by increasing productivity.

My request to you as a software developer is to write good code and develop amazing apps. If you have the right intentions, a passion for software development, and a strong work ethic, you will surely become successful in your career.

Let's make this world a great place by creating amazing software that can aid the progress of human civilization.

# Other Books You May Enjoy

If you enjoyed this book, you may be interested in these other books by Packt:

**The Modern C# Challenge**
Rod Stephens

ISBN: 9781789535426

- Perform statistical calculations such as finding the standard deviation
- Find combinations and permutations
- Search directories for files matching patterns using LINQ and PLINQ
- Find areas of polygons using geometric operations
- Randomize arrays and lists with extension methods
- Explore the filesystem to find duplicate files
- Simulate complex systems and implement equality in a class
- Use cryptographic techniques to encrypt and decrypt strings and files

*Other Books You May Enjoy*

## C# Data Structures and Algorithms
Marcin Jamro

ISBN: 9781788833738

- How to use arrays and lists to get better results in complex scenarios
- Implement algorithms like the Tower of Hanoi on stacks of C# objects
- Build enhanced applications by using hashtables, dictionaries and sets
- Make a positive impact on efficiency of applications with tree traversal
- Effectively find the shortest path in the graph

# Other Books You May Enjoy

If you enjoyed this book, you may be interested in these other books by Packt:

**The Modern C# Challenge**
Rod Stephens

ISBN: 9781789535426

- Perform statistical calculations such as finding the standard deviation
- Find combinations and permutations
- Search directories for files matching patterns using LINQ and PLINQ
- Find areas of polygons using geometric operations
- Randomize arrays and lists with extension methods
- Explore the filesystem to find duplicate files
- Simulate complex systems and implement equality in a class
- Use cryptographic techniques to encrypt and decrypt strings and files

Other Books You May Enjoy

## C# Data Structures and Algorithms
Marcin Jamro

ISBN: 9781788833738

- How to use arrays and lists to get better results in complex scenarios
- Implement algorithms like the Tower of Hanoi on stacks of C# objects
- Build enhanced applications by using hashtables, dictionaries and sets
- Make a positive impact on efficiency of applications with tree traversal
- Effectively find the shortest path in the graph

# Leave a review - let other readers know what you think

Please share your thoughts on this book with others by leaving a review on the site that you bought it from. If you purchased the book from Amazon, please leave us an honest review on this book's Amazon page. This is vital so that other potential readers can see and use your unbiased opinion to make purchasing decisions, we can understand what our customers think about our products, and our authors can see your feedback on the title that they have worked with Packt to create. It will only take a few minutes of your time, but is valuable to other potential customers, our authors, and Packt. Thank you!

# Index

.NET framework
  class libraries 12
  Common Language Runtime (CLR) 12
  Common Type System 12
  just-in-time compiler 12

.NET
  architecture 11
  event guidelines 114, 116

## A

abstract classes
  about 49, 55, 253
  versus interfaces 254
abstract factory pattern 221
abstract methods 55
abstraction 49, 253
access modifiers
  about 255
  types 255
access specifiers, for classes
  about 60
  internal access specifier 61
  private access specifier 61
  protected access specifier 62
  protected internal 63
  public access specifier 60
accessors 59
adapter pattern 224
ADO.NET
  fundamentals 184
aggregation relationship 73, 74, 137
association relationship 72, 137
async streams 208, 210
Async/Await 10
Atomic, Consistent, Isolated, and Durable (ACID) 202

## B

base class constraints 124
behavioral design patterns
  about 225, 226
  command pattern 226
  observer pattern 226
  strategy pattern 227
boxing 255
branches
  changing 248, 249
  creating 247
  deleting 249
  merging 249
  viewing 248
branching 245, 247
breakpoint 172, 173
breakpoints window 167, 168
builder pattern 221, 222

## C

C# 8 10
C# program
  writing, in console application 20, 22
C#.NET
  reference types 256
  value types 256
C#
  Async/Await 10
  conditions 16
  data types 13
  dynamics 9
  evolution 8
  exception filters 10
  exception handling 83
  fundamentals 13

generics 9
Language Integrated Query (LINQ) 9
literals 14
loops 17
managed code 9
nullable types 13
syntax 13
variables 42, 43
virtual method 256
Call Stack Trace 171, 173
Carriage Return, Line Feed (CR+LF) 239
catch keyword 84
characteristics, object-oriented programming
  abstraction 49
  encapsulation 48, 49
  inheritance 47
  polymorphism 50, 51
child classes 47
class diagrams
  about 135, 136
  aggregation relationship 137
  association relationship 137
  composition relationship 137
  dependency relationship 138
  example 138, 140
  inheritance relationship 136
class libraries 12
class-creational patterns 220
classes, object-oriented programming
  about 39
  general form 39, 40
  writing 40, 41
classes
  access specifiers 60
  constructor 45, 46
  methods 44
code-first approach 199
code-optimization techniques 177
command pattern 226
Common Language Runtime (CLR) 12, 256
Common Type System 12
communication link 142
compiler
  using, as service 10
components, data providers

command object 185, 187, 189
connection object 184
DataAdapter 191
DataReader object 190, 191
composition relationship 75, 77, 137
conditions, C#
  goto statements 17
  if-else construct 16
  switch-case construct 16
console application
  C# program, writing 20, 22
constraints types, generics
  about 124
  base class constraints 124
  interface constraints 125
  multiple constraints 126
  reference type constraints 126
  value type constraints 126
constructor 45, 46
contravariance 107, 108, 109
covariance 107, 109
create, read, update, and delete (CRUD) 217
creational design patterns
  about 220
  abstract factory pattern 221
  builder pattern 221, 222
  factory method pattern 222
  prototype pattern 222
  singleton pattern 223

# D

data providers 184
DataAdapters
  about 191, 195
  working with 193
database-first approach 199, 200
databases
  connecting to 192
  Oracle database, connecting to 193
  SQL Server, connecting to 192
DataReader object 190, 191
DataReaders
  about 194
  working with 193
debugging windows

about  166
breakpoints window  167, 168
Diagnostic Tools window  170
Exception Settings window  168
Immediate window  171
Output window  169
Python debugger window  171
decorator pattern  224
delegates
  about  99, 100
  creating  100, 102
  using  100, 102
Dependency Inversion Principle  220, 258
dependency relationship  69, 70, 72, 138
design diagrams
  significance  134
  UML diagrams  134
Design Principles
  about  218, 257
  Dependency Inversion Principle  220, 258
  Interface Segregation Principle  219, 258
  Liskov Substitution Principle  257
  Open Close Principle  219, 257
  Single Responsibility Principle (SRP)  218, 257
Diagnostic Tools window  170
dynamic link library (dll)  22
dynamic polymorphism  50, 51
dynamics  9

## E

Editor window  158, 160, 161, 163
encapsulation  48, 49, 252
Entity Framework (EF)
  entity  197
  used, for code-first approach  199
  used, for database-first approach  200
  using  200, 202
  working with  197
Entity Framework Core  201
Entity properties
  types  198
European Computer Manufactures Association (ECMA)  7
event guidelines
  from .NET  114, 116

events
  about  110, 111
  multicast event  112, 114
exception class  92, 93
exception filters  10, 96, 97
exception handling
  about  81, 83
  best practices  97
  in C#  83
  need for  82, 84, 85
Exception Settings window  168
extension method
  about  256
  using  256

## F

facade pattern  224, 225
factory method pattern  222
features, delegate
  contravariance  107, 110
  covariance  107, 110
features, refactoring
  Encapsulate Field  179
  Extract Method  180
  method signature, changing  178
  Rename  177
finally block
  working  89, 91
fundamental principles, OOP
  abstraction  253
  encapsulation  252
  inheritance  252
  polymorphism  253
fundamentals, ADO.NET
  data providers  184

## G

generic methods
  about  126, 127
  type-inferencing  128, 129
generics
  about  9, 117, 119, 120, 122
  constraints  123
  contravariance  129, 130, 132
  covariance  129

need for 122
git add command 238, 239, 240
git clone command 237
git commit command 240
git config command 236, 237
git fetch command 244, 245
git init command 237
git log command 241
git pull command 244
git push command 243
git remote command 242
git status command 238
Git
  about 236
  branching 245, 247
  in Visual Studio 175, 176
  installing, on Windows 234, 235, 236
  working 232

# I

Immediate window 171
indices 210, 211, 212
inheritance 47, 252
inheritance relationship 77, 78
instance methods
  using, as delegates 103
Integrated Development Environment (IDE) 153
interface 253
interface constraints 125
interface members
  implementation 212, 213
Interface Segregation Principle 219, 258
interfaces
  about 53, 54
  versus abstract classes 254
internal access specifier 61
International Standards Organization (ISO) 7, 134
interview
  tips 258, 259

# J

Java Database Connectivity (JDBC) 184
just-in-time compiler 12

# L

Language Integrated Query (LINQ) 9, 201
line feed (LF) 239
Liskov Substitution Principle 257
literals, C#
  Boolean 14
  character 15
  Integer 14
  real values 15
  string 15
loops, C#
  break statements 19
  continue statements 19, 20
  do-while construct 18
  for construct 18
  foreach construct 19
  while construct 18

# M

managed code 9, 256
method group conversion
  about 102
  instance methods, using as delegates 103
  static methods, using as delegates 103
method-overloading
  about 254
  versus method-overriding 254
method-overriding 254
methods
  about 44
  creating 44
Microsoft Intermediate Language (MSIL) 12
Model-View-Controller (MVC) pattern
  about 154, 217, 228
  Controller 228
  Model 228
  View 228
multicast event 112, 114
multicasting 104, 107
multiple catch blocks 85, 88
multiple constraints 126

# N

nullable reference types 206, 207

# O

object collaboration
  about 65
  case study 67, 68
  examples 65, 66
  types 66, 67
Object Linking and Embedding, Database (OLE DB) 184
Object Management Group (OMG) 134
Object Relational Mapper (ORM) 197
object-creational patterns 220
object-oriented programming (OOP)
  about 37, 251
  characteristics 47
  classes 38, 39
  fundamental principles 252
  objects 41
objects, OOP
  about 42
  creating 42
observer pattern 226
Open Close Principle 219, 257
Open Database Connectivity (ODBC) 184
Output window 165, 169

# P

parent class 47
partial class 56, 57, 254
parts, use case diagrams
  about 141
  actor 141
  communication link 142
  system boundaries 143
  use case 142
Plain Old CLR Object (POCO) class 201
polymorphism
  about 50, 51, 253
  dynamic polymorphism 50
  static polymorphism 50
private access specifier 61
properties 59, 60

properties, transactions in SQL
  about 202
  atomic 203
  consistent 203
  durable 203
  isolated 203
protected access specifier 62
protected internal 63
prototype pattern 222
proxy pattern 225
public access specifier 60
Python debugger window 171

# R

ranges 210, 211, 212
refactoring 177
reference type constraints 126
reference types data 207
repository 232

# S

sealed class 57, 253
sequence diagram
  about 145
  activation 146
  actor 145
  call message 147
  create message 149
  destroy message 149
  duration message 150
  example 150, 151
  lifeline 145
  note 150
  recursive message 148
  return message 147
  self message 148
Single Responsibility Principle (SRP) 218, 257
singleton pattern 223
SOLID 257
Solution Explorer 163, 164
SQL
  transactions 202
states, Git
  about 232
  committed 233

modified 233
  staged 233
static methods
  using, as delegates 103
static polymorphism
  about 50
  method overloading 50
  operator overloading 50
stored procedures
  about 196, 197
  working with 196, 197
strategy pattern 227
structs
  versus classes 255
structural design patterns
  about 223
  adapter pattern 224
  decorator pattern 224
  facade pattern 224, 225
  proxy pattern 225
switch expressions 213, 214
system boundaries 143

# T

target-typed new expressions 215
templates, Visual Studio 2017
  about 157
  ASP.NET Core Web Application 157
  ASP.NET Web Application 158
  Class Library 157
  Console App 157
  Unit Test Project 158
  WCF Server Application 158
  WPF App 158
throw keyword
  using 88, 89
try keyword 84
tuples 58
type-inferencing 128, 129
type-safety 122
types, association relationship
  about 73
  aggregation relationship 73, 74
  composition relationship 75, 77
types, collaboration types

  about 67
  association relationship 72
  dependency relationship 68, 70, 72
  inheritance relationship 77, 78
types, Entity properties
  navigation properties 199
  scalar properties 198

# U

unboxing 255
Unified Modeling Language (UML) diagram
  about 72, 133, 134
  types 134
unmanaged code 256
use case 142
use case diagrams
  about 141
  example 144
user-defined exceptions 94, 95

# V

value type constraints 126
value types data 207
version control 231, 232
Visual Studio 2019
  setting up 206
Visual Studio Code 24
Visual Studio Community 23
Visual Studio Editor 158
Visual Studio Enterprise 24
Visual Studio IDE project
  about 24, 26
  Command window 30
  Immediate windows 30
  main workspace area 28
  output window 30
  search option 31
  Solution Explorer window 26, 28
Visual Studio Professional 23
Visual Studio program
  debugging 34
  debugging, through code 35, 36
  writing 32, 34
Visual Studio project
  templates 154, 155, 156

types  154, 155, 156
Visual Studio windows
  about  158
  Editor window  158, 160, 161, 163
  Output window  165
  Solution Explorer  163, 164
Visual Studio
  evolution  23
  Git  175, 176
  types  23

using, as editor  22
versions, comparing  23

# W

Watch  171
Watch window  174
Windows Communication Foundation (WCF)  158
Windows Presentation Foundation (WPF)  158
Windows
  Git, installing  234, 235, 236

Made in the USA
Middletown, DE
03 June 2019